D1737226

Combating Corruption
in Latin America

COMBATING CORRUPTION
IN LATIN AMERICA

Edited by Joseph S. Tulchin
and Ralph H. Espach

Published by the Woodrow Wilson Center Press
Distributed by the Johns Hopkins University Press

EDITORIAL OFFICES

The Woodrow Wilson Center Press
One Woodrow Wilson Plaza
1300 Pennsylvania Avenue, N.W.
Washington, D.C. 20004-3027
Telephone 202-691-4010
www.wilsoncenter.org

ORDER FROM

The Johns Hopkins University Press
P.O. Box 50370
Baltimore, Maryland 21211
Telephone 1-800-537-5487
www.press.jhu.edu

2 4 6 8 9 7 5 3 1

Library of Congress Cataloging-in-Publication Data

Combating corruption in Latin America / edited by Joseph S. Tulchin and
   Ralph H. Espach.
      p.   cm.
Includes index.
   ISBN 1-930365-00-4 (hard : alk. paper)—ISBN 1-930365-01-2 (pbk. :
alk. paper)
      1. Political corruption—Latin America.   2. Political corruption—Latin America—
Prevention.   I. Tulchin, Joseph S., 1939–   .   II. Espach, Ralph.   III. Title.
JL959.5.C6 C66 2000
320.98—dc21   00-008545

ABOUT THE CENTER

The Center is the living memorial of the United States of America to the nation's twenty-eighth president, Woodrow Wilson. Congress established the Woodrow Wilson Center in 1968 as an international institute for advanced study, "symbolizing and strengthening the fruitful relationship between the world of learning and the world of public affairs." The Center opened in 1970 under its own board of trustees.

In all its activities the Woodrow Wilson Center is a nonprofit, nonpartisan organization, supported financially by annual appropriations from the Congress, and by the contributions of foundations, corporations, and individuals. Conclusions or opinions expressed in Center publications and programs are those of the authors and speakers and do not necessarily reflect the views of the Center staff, fellows, trustees, advisory groups, or any individuals or organizations that provide financial support to the Center.

Contents

Part 3: Views from Three Major Organizations

Preface

This book is the product of a roundtable held at the Woodrow Wilson International Center for Scholars on September 25–26, 1996. The purpose of the roundtable was to provide a multidisciplinary approach to the problem of corruption in Latin America and to probe its various aspects and forms, with the goal of assessing the effectiveness and long-term viability of various anticorruption measures. Of particular interest was the prospective role of the multinational lending agencies and other international institutions in supporting and influencing these reforms. The roundtable was held at a propitious time, just six months after the Organization of American States presented its Inter-American Convention Against Corruption in Caracas, and within days of the annual meeting of the World Bank, at which the executive office announced fighting corruption as the centerpiece of the bank's new agenda.

The activities of the Woodrow Wilson Center in this regard are part of its ongoing interest in examining issues of governance and democratic development across the world. In addition to the activities of the various other programs at the Woodrow Wilson Center, the Latin American Program is presently engaged in producing a series of meetings and publications that examine a variety of issues related to the consolidation of democracy in that region.

Neither the roundtable on anticorruption measures nor this resulting volume would have been possible if not for the generous support of the Inter-American Development Bank and the Bureau for Latin American and Caribbean Affairs at the U.S. Agency for International Development.

The editors would also like to extend our special appreciation to the staff of the Latin American Program, Cynthia Arnson, Allison Garland, Javier Icaza, Katherine Morse, and Heather Golding, and to interns Jacqueline S. Lynch and Adriana Quiñones for their invaluable help in the coordination of the conference and the preparation of the volume.

The papers and presentations assembled in this volume have been re-vised and updated since their presentation at the roundtable. The only paper included that was not originally presented on that occasion is that of Alberto Ades and Rafael Di Tella.

Combating Corruption
in Latin America

Introduction

JOSEPH S. TULCHIN AND RALPH H. ESPACH

Latin America today is going through as profound a period of political change as it has seen since the era of independence. Over the last decade, a consensus has formed that the future growth and security of the region depends on the expansion of democratic governance and free-market economic policies. Democracy is now the norm in every country except Cuba, and with each passing year it is strengthened by the increasing activities and expectations of the citizenry. Liberal economic reforms for more open markets, less government interference, and regional integration are moving forward and promise positive results in increased economic growth. Latin American leaders, joined by the United States and other industrial powers, and the chief multilateral institutions, have forecast a new age of prosperity to follow this double transition of political and economic liberalism. After decades of authoritarian rule, protectionist economies, political instability, and economic stagflation, Latin Americans are eager to share in the fruits of the modern world.

One of the many expectations that accompanied these political and economic reforms was that democratic governments with reduced economic roles would work more cleanly and efficiently. On this score most observers profess to be disillusioned. Corruption scandals have brought down popularly elected administrations in Venezuela and Brazil. Mexico's ex-president Carlos Salinas, a champion of neoliberal reforms, has been forced to flee the country by allegations of corruption and criminality among his closest associates. Money from drug trafficking has purportedly corrupted Colombian presidential elections, and even the privatization of state enterprises designed to eliminate government mismanagement—most famously the sale of Aerolineas Argentinas to the Spanish carrier

Iberia—have proven lucrative opportunities for government officials to line their own pockets. Such scandals fuel public suspicions about the methods and true intentions of neoliberal reformers and can undermine citizens' confidence in the democratic system altogether. Although unsupported by the historical record, a troublesome perception persists throughout the region that authoritarian leaders of the past were more honest and more committed to serving the nation's interest than are today's democratic politicians. The fragility of Latin American citizens' trust in and support for their democratic leaders has both political and economic costs. Potential investors can be put off by the risks of political instability. Less obvious than public scandals, but potentially a greater drag on the region's economic growth, is the issue of judicial probity. In a competitive global market, if investors are deterred either by demands for bribes or by the perception that transaction conflicts will not be adjudicated in a timely and equitable manner, the results will be disastrous for economic reforms and growth. In the elegant formulation of the economists, corruption increases the transaction costs, sometimes to unacceptable levels.

The threats corruption poses to regional economic growth and democratic consolidation have generated a sense of urgency to confront the problem. Policymakers throughout the region and in the multilateral institutions now view corruption as a principal obstacle to further growth and modernization. National governments, citizens' groups, business associations, and international lending agencies have begun to formulate policies and push for action. This synthesis of effort is most evident in the Inter-American Convention Against Corruption, signed by the member states of the Organization of American States (OAS) in Caracas, Venezuela, in March of 1996.[1] By this convention, the OAS has made fighting corruption central to its efforts to reinforce democratic governance throughout the region. Since then, the Inter-American Development Bank (IDB) and the World Bank have both declared the reduction of corruption to be a top priority in their agendas over the next decade. Most recently, the International Monetary Fund (IMF) has negotiated a new standby agreement with Argentina in which, for the first time, conditionalities such as judicial reform and the reduction of corruption are made requirements to qualify for currency support. In this manner, the banks have begun to make the reduction of corruption one of their requirements in offering loans to developing countries. In response to this pressure, governments universally have denounced corruption and have declared campaigns for better, cleaner governance. In some countries this rhetoric has been accompanied by the passage of new anticorruption measures. These measures have varied widely, from the strengthening of police forces or the judicial system to encouraging citizen action or cutting specific problematic government departments, and have met with greater or lesser success at national and local levels. In many cases, local governments have proven to be more innovative and aggressive in their reforms than their national counterparts. Efforts are even being made to bring these measures in some form into international trade accords. As the dramatic political and economic costs of corruption become more apparent, efforts have intensified at all levels to come up with appropriate, effective measures for their reduction.

As part of its ongoing interest in issues of governance and the consolidation of democracy in the region, the Latin American Program at the Woodrow Wilson International Center for Scholars organized a roundtable, *After Caracas: Strategies for Combatting Corruption in Latin America*, on September 25–26, 1996. Participants from a range of countries and institutions, including government officials, academic experts, officials of multinational institutions, and businesspeople, were invited to contribute their expertise and experience with the purpose of examining regional corruption and national policies for its control. The roundtable was cosponsored by the Inter-American Development Bank and the Bureau for Latin American and Caribbean Affairs at the U.S. Agency for International Development. Transparency International, a private international organization promoting anticorruption reforms, also participated in the planning of the event.

Most of the papers collected in this volume were presented in draft form at the roundtable. In response to various issues raised at the meeting, authors revised their papers for the volume. The pieces by Steven Quick of the Inter-American Development Bank, Mark Schneider of the U.S. Agency for International Development, and Ibrahim Shihata of the World Bank are revised transcriptions of their actual remarks. These presentations represent the perspectives of multinational institutions and donor agencies. They explain how fighting corruption has risen to the top of the regional agenda and what these agencies perceive to be their appropriate roles and strategies in the struggle. These documents are of special value because of the importance of the international community's role in initiating anticorruption reform. Recently, pressure from the international community in the form of government reports, focused activities of nongovernmental organizations, or, more often, embarrassing headlines in the *Wall Street Journal* or other international media, has provided the greatest impetus for Latin American governments to address the issue. The other papers, which come from experts both within and without the region and include both practitioners and scholars, seek to illuminate the nature of corruption in the region—at times by comparing it to corruption in other parts of the world—and offer a variety of approaches to anticorruption reform. In their contrasts and complementarities they touch upon the most significant points of contention in current thinking on the issue.

The first challenge in examining political corruption is to establish a working definition. Although it appears easy to identify certain specific actions as corrupt—such as bribing a policeman to avoid a traffic ticket—in reality, the motives and purposes behind corrupt acts, as well as their results, can bear differing degrees of legitimacy. Most analysts today use some form of the basic definition that corruption is the application of public property or license for private gain. Although simple and succinct, this definition covers an enormous range of activities. Also, its effectiveness depends upon a clear division between public and private domains, a distinction that varies among cultures and is better established in some societies and political systems than in others.[2] In this volume, this issue is examined in detail by Luis Moreno Ocampo (Chapter 2), who notes that in addition to the differences among national legal norms, in today's global economy there exist significant and often contrasting differences among the behaviors and ethical standards within various types of systems, such as those of countries, private corporations, and international organizations. Corruption is also difficult to define because it assumes a variety of forms, each with different functions and effects within a society and government. Anyone from the president to mid-level bureaucrats, policemen, or tax collectors can be corrupt, often in ways many citizens do not object to because they can seem to be of benefit to them as well. Different institutions are corrupt in different ways, and groups, companies, or individuals can show incredible ingenuity in creating new methods for venality or for covering up their past misdeeds. Another important consideration in defining the issue is that corruption is in large part a sociocultural phenomenon, a result of deeply seated patterns in a community's social and economic history. Because of its relationship to fundamental aspects of political and social culture, the exact parameters of what governments should identify as corrupt activity, along with policies for its detection and control, must be sensitive to the peculiarities of specific countries and regions. Policies that work well in England, Italy, or the United States may not be equally applicable or effective in Mexico or Brazil.

Economists and political scientists have led the way in analyzing political corruption, as well as in delineating anticorruption measures.[3] Some argued that political corruption improves efficiency in cases of large, rigid state administrations and serves to facilitate political transition.[4] Others stressed differences among cultures and societal norms, and questioned the usefulness of overarching international standards as laid out by Western theoreticians. But since the end of the cold war, as belief in the efficacy of democracy and free-market economics has spread around the world, a general consensus has developed that (1) in all systems corruption has an overall negative effect on economic growth and stability and on democratic consolidation; and (2) the reduction of state bureaucracies and the encouragement of more transparent, free-market operations, along with improving the government's capacity to regulate these processes and to enforce the law, are the most effective methods of controlling corruption.

Many economists view corruption less as an issue of ethics than as a source of gross inefficiency. They urge market-based reforms that would increase transparency and competition in government services, thereby limiting opportunities for the growth of monopolies. Alberto Ades and Rafael Di Tella (Chapter 1) argue that this strategy is of optimal value to governments with limited resources and public support for reforms, and use quantitative analysis to support the assertion that corruption has significant negative economic effects. In a series of econometric models, they attempt to define and quantify the various factors behind the decision to engage in graft. Susan Rose-Ackerman (Chapter 4), one of the earliest champions of the economist's approach to anticorruption policies, argues that fighting corruption requires limiting the incentives of potential actors, increasing the disincentives by raising the costs of engaging in corruption, and shrinking the bureaucratic space in which nontransparent activity can take place. Competitive and, in some cases, overlapping systems of government services, which encourage efficiency and transparency, must be coupled with tougher laws, better detection systems, improved enforcement in the courts, and higher penalties in order to persuade vulnerable officials that their potential gain is not worth the risks.

Luigi Manzetti (Chapter 6) presents a sophisticated form of this analysis, focusing on the incentives, risks, and rewards for each actor involved in the transaction, and applies it to case studies in Brazil and Argentina. The analytical thoroughness and depth of these papers, as well as their clear assessment of policy options, effectively demonstrate why this approach enjoys such currency in policy formulation throughout the hemisphere.

This correlation, however, between economic and political liberalization and reduced corruption is far from proven, either through empirical
experience or theoretical argument. The modern histories of Latin America and Europe suggest, in fact, that corruption tends to increase in periods of democratization and economic opening.[5] Peru's economic liberalization in the late 1800s, the documented bribery and strong-arming of
regional governments at the hands of multinational corporations throughout the twentieth century, recent scandals involving Presidents Fernando
Collor de Mello in Brazil and Carlos Andrés Perez in Venezuela, and the
still unfolding legacy of corruption within Mexican President Salinas' neoliberal ranks are some of the foremost examples of this disturbing pattern.
Laurence Whitehead (Chapter 5) points to this historical record and cau-
tions against undue enthusiasm that vibrant capitalism will lead to better,
fairer governance. He stresses the dangers of any broad, sweeping anticorruption strategy, such as that urged by the most ardent supporters of
neoliberal style reforms. Due to the complicated, ambiguous nature of
corruption and its variety of forms, policies that are aggressive and easy to
enact are not likely to address the central issues of the problem and instead
may simply lead to other forms of corruption. To be effective, anticorruption measures must be specific, well defined, and directed against a
particular type of illicit activity. In his examination of recent incidents in
Argentina and Brazil, Luigi Manzetti (Chapter 6) stresses that economic
liberalization alone is not enough. Economic reforms must be coupled
with improved transparency and regulatory procedures. Reducing corruption requires stronger democratic institutions, especially an active and independent judiciary and media, free and responsible enough to act as a
watchdog over government operations. A stronger, more independent
media is a central recommendation in many of the papers. The courage
and tenacity of reporters and publishers is credited with having a principal
role in spurring the anticorruption scandals and public support for reforms
in Brazil, Venezuela, and Argentina. However, Carlos Eduardo Lins da
Silva (Chapter 7), himself a journalist, warns that the media needs to examine its own practices and standards as well. In his analysis of the media's
role in the Collar scandal in Brazil, he paints a picture of a communica-
tions industry as engrossed in self-interest and clientalism as the officials
they pretend to uncover. In many Latin American societies corruption is
systemic and must not be perceived as having either its beginnings or ends
only in the conduct of government officials. Reform and vigilance are
needed in all sectors of the society, and the media in particular must promote the highest standards of professionalism if they are to serve the pub-

lic effectively. Over the long term, reducing corruption demands that policymakers be innovative and resolute, but the success of any political strategy ultimately will depend on receiving sustained support from the public. Individuals must not only be wary and unaccepting of government scoundrels, but also must seek to change their own behaviors and attitudes in their dealings with the government and to accept their responsibilities as democratic citizens.

Another danger in relying on the apparent linkage between anticorruption reform and economic liberalization is that the long-term success and popularity of current economic policies is far from certain. Anticorruption reforms should be publicly communicated as a step toward better, more modernized governance, regardless of the current fashion in economic policies. If citizens perceive the reform of government systems is tied to the program of a particular administration, then public support for these measures could drop if the popularity of the president were to decline. Similarly, if these measures are perceived to be in response to pressures from international institutions or foreign governments, then their public support would be vulnerable to nationalist criticism. Policymakers must design reforms so that they do not appear to be politically motivated against an opposition party or group. In order to be successful, an anticorruption program must enjoy a broad base of support in the civil society and must be seen as a national project of benefit to all.

Accountability has two mutually dependent aspects in a democratic system. First, elected officials are accountable to the electorate. This accountability is properly enforced through the institutions of an independent judiciary, an effective police force, and an autonomous press. Second, the probity and effectiveness of the government is also the responsibility of the citizenry. Without the institutions of an active, informed democratic society, government itself can do little against corruption within. The expression of this accountability is not limited to participating in elections. Citizens must be active in and supportive of their own democratic institutions, such as community groups, nongovernmental organizations (NGOs), and unions, and must use these institutions as leverage in demanding superior performance from their elected representatives. Eventually, success at fighting corruption regionwide or on a global scale will depend on the strengthening of an international democratic society. A prominent example of the type of organized civil society activity required to serve as the arbiter of good government is Transparency International, an international nongovernmental organization that promotes anticorruption reforms and greater public awareness of the issue. As described by

Luis Moreno Ocampo (Chapter 2), Transparency International is a successful network of private citizens and business leaders working with governments and citizen groups worldwide to encourage increased transparency and accountability.

The problem of political corruption is not limited to democracies or authoritarian states, to socialist or capitalist systems, or to large, bureaucratic states or small ones. Democratic states, or those with open, free-market economies, are neither better nor worse environments for its proliferation. In the final analysis, corruption thrives in the gaps between an institution's aims and the management of its operations. As Susan Rose-Ackerman (Chapter 4) points out, no institution will ever be totally free of corruption. There will always exist some discrepancy between an institution's general goals and the execution of its practices, even if only in the minds and practices of a few individuals. Within those gaps lie opportunities for practice contrary to the mission of the institution. Corruption increases in times of political transition because it is at those times, when power relations are being renegotiated and ideological direction is uncertain, that these gaps between intention and practice are at their widest.[6] At least theoretically, these gaps will tend to be wider in a more fluid democratic system than in one of strict authoritarian control. While corruption certainly has existed under rigid hierarchical systems, in those cases a control mechanism exists in that the prices of the illicit transactions tend to be limited to what those at the top deem to be a tolerable level. In a weakly regulated democracy, however, and especially in times of significant change or turmoil, the dimensions and prices of corruption can expand to fit the political market. Demand for the funding of political campaigns, for favors distributed by incumbents, for political appointments of key supporters, and for personal gain in an industry where one's job is determined by the electoral cycle, can be limitless. In a similar way, economic liberalization without effective regulatory and adjudication systems in place leaves ample room for graft. It is in the periods between the delegitimizing of old sets of rules or systems and the formulation of new ones that corruption is most likely to expand.

In an era of rapid democratic transition and increasing openness, it is not surprising that political corruption seems to have increased in Latin America. This development should not, however, constitute an argument against the further spread of democracy. Instead it underlines the need for the strengthening of democratic institutions. The administrative systems of political parties, judicial systems, congressional bodies, electoral boards, police forces, local governments, and other components of the democratic system must be better regulated and made more transparent. Procedures for the procurement and distribution of government services, including those related to privatization, downsizing, and reform, must be better defined to ensure fairness and transparency. Government financial operations must meet the standards of modern international accounting systems. Perhaps most important of all, judicial systems must be strengthened and given more independence so that cases of corruption are dealt with fairly but effectively, no matter the wealth or political status of the perpetrator. This demand for the improvement of democratic institutions is common to all the papers in this volume. The aim of such reforms is twofold: to close the gaps between institutional objectives and operations, thus reducing the space within which illicit behavior can prosper, and to raise the accountability, the risks, and potential costs to government officials tempted to engage in graft. The challenge for policymakers is especially difficult, because success in fighting corruption requires a comprehensive, integrative approach. Reforms must be carried out in a variety of areas and at different levels simultaneously. Otherwise, instead of being reduced, corruption will simply be transferred from one form to another. If, for example, a congress enacts tighter regulations and penalties but the judicial system remains weak, then bureaucrats will likely continue their practices but with more bribery of regulators, prosecutors, and judges. Since corruption thrives due to structural problems in government bureaucracies and transactions with the public, Susan Rose-Ackerman (Chapter 4) warns that without real reform of these bureaucracies and operations, initiatives like privatizations and downsizing are not likely to reduce corruption but only to shift it to different actors and into different forms. To increase the potential costs of corruption, more stringent regulations aimed at catching corrupt officials should be imposed simultaneously with stronger penalties and better prosecution techniques, along with incentives for probity, such as wage increases or rewards for good performance. Only such an integrative set of reforms implemented in many areas at once to provide both incentives for professional honesty and disincentives for impropriety can be successful in attacking systemic corruption.

It is sometimes suggested that corruption is inevitable in Latin American politics; that Latin Americans, as a result of their culture, are naturally corrupt. Such fatalism is both unjustified and untrue. Of course the countries of Latin America share a history and political culture distinct from those of Europe, Asia, or the United States. If we set aside the wide variety of political traditions in the region and instead focus on the similarities among the countries of Iberian heritage, patterns of political behavior do emerge. Clientelist political systems, tight familial and communal bonds, and rigid social hierarchies are a legacy of the region's history of conquest, colonialism, and racial division. The region's social and economic development, the prominence of government and church hierarchies, the patrimonialist style of the Spanish and Portuguese monarchies, and other factors created an environment favorable to clientelism and the use of public office for private enrichment or protection. Also the influence of Enlightenment philosophy, which had such dramatic effect in England and much of Europe, spread more slowly through Spain, Portugal, and their colonies and was obstructed there by entrenched political and economic interests. As a result of these legacies, political systems in Latin America have tended to exhibit an exorbitant mixing of the public and private spheres and a tradition of clientalist governance.[7] The same can be said, however, for Spain, Portugal, and Italy, the region's cultural progenitors in southern Europe. Japanese and other Asian societies receive similar criticism, and Africa is reputed to be worse than Latin America.

This determinist argument ignores the fact, however, that all systems have suffered from extensive corruption at one time or another, including that of Britain and—rather often, it seems—the United States. While cultural attitudes do play a major part in either accepting or rejecting corrupt behavior, these attitudes are far from fixed. In fact, one of the principal puzzles to anticorruption reform is in understanding at which point exactly, and owing to what factors, does a public finally reach a breaking point in its acceptance of malfeasance—that is, what are the limits of "cultural acceptance"? In recent years societies reputed to be relatively indifferent to corruption, including the Italians, Brazilians, Japanese, and Spanish, have shown the power of their collective disgust by backing dramatic government shakeups. Luca Meldolesi (Chapter 3) compares the connection between Italy's history and its political system, and the elements behind its tendency for political graft as well as its recent progress in passing radical reforms. He sees many similarities between the experiences of Latin America and Italy, but challenges the assessment that changes in current political culture are restrained by a region's democratic history.[8] The increased activities of civil society in response to the prevalence of scandals in recent years indicate that profound changes are underway not only in government structures, but also in political attitudes worldwide. If it is true that Latin American governments have always struggled against innate propensities for corruption, it is also true that most countries have never before seen so much open support from such a range of actors for increased democracy. Individual people and societies by themselves are not corrupt; political systems are. Anticorruption reformers in Latin America must take heart in the fact that the rapid and dramatic changes underway in their political systems are motivated largely by the evolving political attitudes of the public.

Today's policymakers enjoy an unprecedented degree of support from a spectrum of actors, both domestic and abroad, for anticorruption initiatives. A consensus exists that the costs of corruption to Latin America's long-term political and economic growth are too high to sustain and any delay to action is costly. In the long run, however, sheer enthusiasm may prove less valuable than vigilance and perspicacity. Corruption's relation to the specific culture of the people and to the economics of Latin America's historically divided populations and unequal allocations of resources lends to the issue an added dimension of complexity. While specific policies to strengthen judicial systems and increase transparency in financial management are necessary steps to improved government performance, corruption must ultimately be seen as an issue of citizenship. Citizens of Latin American countries must find the means to communicate and participate within the democratic system and to demand from their governments an acceptable level of integrity and effectiveness. In a democratic government, no matter how resolute the efforts of a legislature, an attorney general's office, or an international bank, the limits of corruption ultimately will be defined by the expectations and demands of the people. As with so many issues concerned with democratic governance, we must stimulate a strong, articulate, and involved citizenry. In a democracy, only citizens can effectively demand transparency and accountability from elected leaders.

The declaration of Caracas represents an heroic and perhaps quixotic mission. By striving to reach the prescribed standards and principles, the countries of the region are engaged in an effort to boost the current quality of their democratic governance to a higher level. Its objectives are clear but extremely demanding. So demanding, indeed, that considering the weakness and precarious circumstances of many of the region's democracies, the declaration's comprehensiveness and loftiness of spirit can make it seem rhetorical and empty. It need not be. Fighting corruption is a solid, achievable, fundamental step toward improved democratic governance. To be successful, the mission will require coordination and determination across national and bureaucratic boundaries and support from both public and private actors. Policymakers and officials at all levels must be resolute, and violators must be publicly identified and punished. Above all, the success of the mission will rest on the political will and vigilance of the citizenry.

Notes

1. Organization of American States, Inter-American Convention Against Corruption (Caracas, Venezuela: March 29, 1996). For a more recent formulation of the OAS anticorruption agenda, please see the *Program for Inter-American Cooperation in the Fight Against Corruption*, OEA/Ser.P AG/doc.3571/97 (Lima, Peru: June 5, 1997).

2. Another popular, more precise definition is that of Joseph S. Nye: corruption is "behavior which deviates from the formal duties of a public role (elective or appointive) because of private-regarding (personal, close family, private clique) wealth or status gains." See "Corruption and Political Development: A Cost-Benefit Analysis," *American Political Science Review* 61 (June): 417–427.

3. An excellent survey of this scholarship is Arnold J. Heidenheimer, Michael Johnston, and Victor T. LeVine, eds., *Political Corruption: A Handbook* (New Brunswick, N.J.: Transaction Publishers, 1989).

4. See Samuel P. Huntington, "Modernization and Corruption," in *Political Order in Changing Societies* (New Haven, Conn.: Yale University Press, 1968): 59–71.

5. See Walter Little and Eduardo Posada-Carbó, eds., *Political Corruption in Latin America* (New York, N.Y.: St. Martin's Press, 1996).

6. See S. P. Huntington, "Modernization and Corruption." On the role of privatization and regulatory reform, see Moisés Naim and Joseph S. Tulchin, eds., *Competition Policy, Deregulation, and Modernization in Latin America* (Boulder, Colo.: Lynne Rienner Publishers, 1999).

7. For more on corruption as a consistent element of the development of democracy in Latin America, see Little and Posada-Carbó, eds., op cit.

8. Meldolesi argues in particular against some of the conclusions of the influential book by Robert D. Putnam, *Making Democracy Work: Civic Traditions in Modern Italy* (Princeton, N.J.: Princeton University Press, 1993).

Part I

Theoretical Approaches to Corruption and Anticorruption Policies

1

The New Economics of Corruption: A Survey and Some New Results

ALBERTO ADES AND RAFAEL DI TELLA

I. Introduction

Governments of all political colors in countries of all levels of wealth are affected by corruption scandals with a frequency and intensity that seem to be always on the increase. Corruption has become a "hot issue" and a subject of significant political attention, even in the industrialized democracies. Yet to a large extent, economists have remained vague about what can be done to reduce it. A main concern is the lack of evidence in support of the main policy alternatives. This chapter reviews the state of economic knowledge on the phenomenon of corruption, with special emphasis on the theories behind the most common policy proposals and the evidence that supports them.

During the last thirty years or so, economists from different fields have made scattered contributions to the analysis of corruption, resulting in a diverse body of literature. The first published piece on corruption by an economist that received wide attention was a political economic approach by Rose-Ackerman (1975), although the topic was also on the minds of people doing research in the economics of crime (Becker and Stigler 1974), agency theory (Harris and Raviv 1978), and rent seeking (Tullock 1967). The lack of data on corruption to test the theoretical contributions allowed conflicting theories on the causes and consequences of corruption

15

to coexist. As a result, the field has been unable to provide coherent policy guidelines to curb corruption and has remained somewhat disconnected from the discussion arena, a place mainly dominated by lawyers, businesspeople, and judges.

More recently, an emerging body of empirical research has appeared employing subjective indices on corruption produced for business-related purposes. We organize the literature into two broad categories: theories about the causes of corruption and theories about its effects. Regarding the latter, we show how the new data has shed light on a controversy that originated in the 1960s about the theoretical possibility that corruption may be beneficial to investment and growth in countries with particularly obtrusive bureaucracies. Regarding theories on the causes of corruption, we present the theoretical background and empirical performance of some of the most often voiced policy proposals. Broadly speaking, there are three types of policy proposals aimed at curbing corruption, which we call the lawyer's approach, the businessperson's approach, and the economist's approach. These approaches result, respectively, in producing tougher new laws and tougher enforcement of existing laws;[1] in paying higher wages to bureaucrats;[2] and in increasing the level of competition in the economy, both among firms and bureaucrats.[3]

Two of the least corrupt countries in the world, Singapore and Hong Kong, have draconian laws on corruption and so are usually set forth as examples of successful applications of the lawyer's approach. They are also examples of countries that pay their bureaucrats exceptionally well (especially Singapore), so they are examples of the businessperson's approach as well. However, there is little political competition and few civil liberties in these countries, which has led to exceptional levels of pay in the bureaucracy without much political opposition, and has also allowed the anticorruption agencies to enjoy sweeping powers that amount to a "guilty until proven innocent" principle and the right to violate the privacy of individual citizens. Since these experiences do not seem to be easily adapted to other countries, it becomes necessary to distinguish how much of these countries' clean records should be attributed to their policy of high wages in the bureaucracy and how much to their tough approach to law enforcement. The third proposal, the economist's approach of unleashing the forces of competition against corruption, has the least cost in terms of civil liberties. As it happens, Singapore and Hong Kong are also examples of this approach, as these countries are models of laissez-faire societies with dynamic market forces that effectively complete away rents. Thus, what is required is an assessment of the relative impact of each policy proposal based on wider empirical evidence.

The purpose of this chapter is, therefore, twofold: first, to describe the main topics in the economics of corruption, including the present directions of research; and second, to place special emphasis on the theory and evidence behind the policy proposals in combating corruption. The structure of the chapter is as follows: in section II, we provide a brief description of the sources of data on corruption that have become available to economists in recent years. In section III we review the literature on the costs of corruption, while in section IV, we analyze the causes of corruption. Section IV also contains most of the policy implications. In section V we give a brief evaluation of the relative merits of the lawyer's and economist's approaches to controlling corruption. In section VI we conclude. In appendix I we explore the ambiguities in the definition of corruption with reference to the British privatization experience. In appendix II we present further readings to complement the literature review.

There are no general surveys of the corruption literature available yet. A possible exception is a survey by Andvig (1991), which focused on the literature of multiple equilibrium in corruption.

II. The New Data on Corruption

In general, recent empirical studies of corruption have used data from three different sources. All three data sets have been created for business-related purposes, to be consumed by banks, institutional investors, or multinational firms. The first two data sets are bought at high prices.

The first data set comes from the journal *Business International* (BI), a division of *The Economist Intelligence Unit*. The data are produced using the reports of BI's correspondents based in each of the countries covered. Data is available for the period 1980–83 and covers sixty-eight countries. The corruption measure in this data set is quite general and is provided by BI's network of correspondents who must grade on a scale from one to ten "the degree to which business transactions involve corrupt payments" in each of the countries covered (for a statistical breakdown of these numbers, see Appendix IV). All correspondents use the same methodology and their reports are further checked for comparability at the regional level and at BI's headquarters.

A second data set comes from the *World Competitiveness Report* (WCR), a business publication produced by the World Economic Forum in Switzerland, and consists of a survey of top and middle managers in the most dynamic firms in each of the countries covered. The surveys have included a question on corruption since 1989 (published in 1990) and include a minimum of thirty-two countries and over one thousand executives. The question asked is "the degree to which improper practices (like corruption) prevail in the public sphere." An advantage of the WCR over the BI data is that it covers people with an intimate knowledge of business practices in each of the countries covered. But the apparent lack of a centralized WCR office to consolidate the answers of those surveyed could be a disadvantage of the WCR data in a cross-section study, as it calls into question the comparability of the answers between countries. The fact that the companies to which the survey respondents belong are successful and internationally oriented is only a partial answer to that concern.

The third data set was gathered by Peter Neuman and his collaborators at *Impulse,* a German business publication, and published in 1994. It also consists of a survey, this time of German businesspeople (typically exporters) who normally conduct business with each of the 103 countries covered. On average, ten people were interviewed for each country, and an effort to have a minimum of three respondents per country was made. An important advantage of this data set is that there is less subjectivity involved as respondents must simply provide an estimate of the kickback per deal (as a percentage of the deal's value) that would have to be paid in order to conduct business in each country. Another advantage is that it was gathered from a very homogeneous group of people (German exporters) with practical business experience in each country covered and who each answered a quantitative question.

Traditionally, empirical economists expect to use hard data in their research. For the case of corruption, attempts have been made to use data on the number of convictions on corruption charges, but this type of legal data is extremely difficult to compare between countries. It also fails to capture undiscovered corruption cases, so that it is more a measure more of the effectiveness of enforcement policy than of the level of corruption. In addition, these indexes can be defended using an argument of revealed preference: they are the market's choice for a corruption indicator.

The degree of correlation between the three corruption measures is quite high, as shown in Table 1.1.

The raw data shows that corruption is strongly negatively correlated with the level of development of the country, as measured by the level of income per capita or the average years of schooling in the population over twenty-five. The lack of political competition (as measured by the Gastil Index of political rights) is positively associated with the level of corruption. The weakest relationship is shown for the WCR data set and is due to the inclusion of two very "clean" countries, similar to Hong Kong and

Table 1.1
Simple Correlations

	BI	WCR	GERMAN
WCR	0.84		
	(0.00)		
GERMAN	0.81	0.84	
	(0.00)	(0.00)	
GDP	−0.74	−0.74	−0.61
	(0.00)	(0.00)	(0.00)
Political Rights	0.50	0.23	0.35
	(0.00)	(0.20)	(0.00)
Schooling	−0.70	−0.59	−0.56
	(0.00)	(0.00)	(0.00)
Openness	−0.21	−0.41	−0.21
	(0.11)	(0.02)	(0.04)

NOTE: The correlation between BI and WCR is based on 39 observations, the one for WCR and GERMAN is based on 39 and that for BI and GERMAN is based on 62 observations. The rest of the correlations for BI are based on 55 observations, those for WCR on 32 while those for GERMAN are based on 92 observations. The significance probability of the correlation under the null hypothesis that the statistic is zero is shown in parenthesis.

Singapore, that also have limited political rights in a relatively small data set.[4] The raw data also show that the degree of openness is negatively correlated with the three corruption indicators.

Table 1.2 presents a frequency histogram for the BI data.

III. The Costs of Corruption

One of the reasons often cited for the relative neglect of corruption as a research topic in economics is that a bribe is simply a transfer and therefore entails no serious welfare losses. Myrdal (1968) seriously questioned this view arguing that if corruption is allowed, government officials will have an interest in generating bureaucratic hurdles to demand bribes.[5] Thus, rather than supporting production, the bureaucracy becomes a burden obstructing efficiency.[6]

If, instead, delays are the product of preexisting rules devised by overzealous social planners, then corruption may serve a useful purpose. This is the approach taken by Leff (1964) and others, who argue that corruption improves social welfare, both because it is a way to avoid cumbersome regulations and because it is a system of building in rewards for badly paid bureaucrats.

Table 1.2

Frequency Histogram for the Business International *Corruption Index (BI)*

BI=O	O<BI<l	l<BI<2	2<BI<4	4<BI<6	6<BI<9
Australia	Belgium	Angola	Argentina	Algeria	Egypt
Canada	Chile	Austria	Cameroon	Bangladesh	Ghana
France	Denmark	Hong Kong	Dominican	Brazil	Haiti
Iraq	Finland	Japan	Greece	Colombia	Indonesia
Netherlands	Germany	Jordan	Italy	Ecuador	Iran
New Zealand	Ireland	Nicaragua	Ivory Coast	India	Liberia
Norway	Israel	South Africa	Kuwait	Jamaica	Mexico
Singapore	U.K.	Uruguay	Malaysia	Kenya	Nigeria
Switzerland	Sweden	Zimbabwe	Peru	Korea	Thailand
United States			Portugal	Morocco	Zaire
			Spain	Pakistan	
			Sri Lanka	Panama	
			Taiwan	Philippines	
			T&Tobago	Saudi Arabia	
			Turkey	Venezuela	

NOTE: The BI corruption index covers sixty-eight countries.

These two approaches, corruption as "sand" and corruption as "oil" in the machine, coexisted with ingenious rationales behind each approach constantly being added to the list.[7] But the lack of data prevented these competing hypotheses from being tested directly against one another.

Mauro (1995) presents the first systematic empirical analysis of the effects of corruption by focusing on the relationship between investment and corruption. Mauro uses the BI index of corruption to estimate the effects of corruption on the average ratio of total and private investment to gross domestic product (GDP) for a cross-section of sixty-seven countries during the period 1960–85. Mauro finds that corruption lowers investment, thereby reducing growth. The negative association between corruption and investment, as well as growth, is significant in both a statistical and an economic sense. For example, he finds that if Bangladesh were to improve the integrity and efficiency of its bureaucracy to the level of that of Uruguay (this corresponds to a one standard deviation improvement in the index), its investment rate should rise by almost 5 percent and its yearly GDP growth rate would rise by over .5 percent. The magnitude of the estimated effects is even larger when instrumental variables are used.

Mauro also constructs a "bureaucratic efficiency index" as the arithmetic average of the BI indexes of "efficiency of the legal system and the judiciary," "bureaucracy and red tape," and "corruption." The constructed index is again negatively and significantly associated with invest-ment. Furthermore, the effects are quite strong. A one standard deviation improvement in bureaucratic efficiency is associated with an increase in the investment rate by 4.75 percent of the GDP. The estimated magni-tude of the effects are higher and remain significant when controlling for possible endogeneity using two-stage least squares techniques.

Similar results are obtained in the context of a more general investment regression as in Barro (1991), where several other additional determinants of investment are included in the regression. In this more general setup, Mauro adds the bureaucratic efficiency index to the standard set of con-trols from Barro (1991). These include the level of income per capita in 1960, primary and secondary school enrollment in 1960, the average share of government consumption expenditure to GDP from 1960 to 1985, the number of revolutions and coups per year from 1960 to 1985 in each country, the 1960 PPP value of the investment deflator (U.S.=1.O) and the absolute value of its deviation from 100, and average per capita polit-ical assassinations. In this regression, the magnitude of the effect of bu-reaucratic efficiency on investment is halved, though it remains significant at the 5 percent level.

The results from Mauro are supportive, therefore, of the claim that cor-ruption has a negative impact on investment, and through that channel it negatively affects growth. It is still worth considering whether the effects of corruption are different depending on the level of red tape in the econ-omy, as argued by Leff and his followers. Mauro provides some evidence against Leff's argument by dividing his sample into high red-tape and low red-tape subsamples, and finds a negative and significant association between investment and corruption regardless of the level of red tape. However, he finds that the negative impact is smaller in the high red-tape sample, though he makes no attempt to test whether this difference is significant.

To examine this proposition more closely, we regress the level of in-vestment in country i on the BI corruption index, a dummy variable that takes a value of I if the BI index for bureaucracy and red tape exceeds the median, and an interaction term between the two. Essentially, this is just testing whether the negative effect of corruption on investment is signifi-cantly lower in countries with high levels of red tape. The regression below shows our results, with standard errors in parentheses.

$$INV_i = 0.270 - 0.019 \ CORR_i - 0.087 \ BUREAU_i + 0.014 \ INTERACT_i$$
$$\quad\ (0.012)\ (0.008) \qquad\quad (0.027) \qquad\qquad\ (0.009)$$

As shown, the negative and significant coefficients of the corruption and bureaucracy indexes indicate that both have a negative impact on investment. Interestingly enough, the coefficient on the interaction term, while statistically weak, has the sign predicted by Leff and his followers, indicating that in countries with high levels of red tape, corruption has less damaging effects on investment.

Corruption may, however, affect growth through channels other than investment. Mauro (1994) estimates the effects of corruption on the composition of government expenditure. This approach consists of examining in more detail some of the possible channels through which corruption affects economic performance, such as the allocation of government spending. For a cross-section of countries, Mauro finds that corruption and political instability are negatively and significantly correlated with the share of government expenditure on education in total spending and in the GDP. As a possible explanation, he conjectures that it may be more difficult to collect bribes on education projects than on other components of government expenditure. These are preliminary efforts, however, as one would want to make sure that this is not merely capturing the effect of the level of development in the composition of government expenditure.

The results obtained so far on the effects of corruption on investment and the allocation of government spending should be treated with caution given the narrowness of the data sets used. However, there is already suggestive evidence to indicate that corruption is mostly "sand in the machine," and any positive effect in countries with high levels of red tape does not receive strong support from the data.

IV. The Causes of Corruption

In order to analyze the causes of corruption and compare the three approaches to anticorruption policies, namely tighter enforcement of laws, higher wages in the bureaucracy, and more competition in the product market, we find it convenient to focus on a stylized case of corruption. As a heuristic device, we can think of most cases of corruption as occurring in a structure similar to this:

THE PUBLIC
Objective: maximize social welfare
Actions: chooses rules and regulations
                 sets market structure of firms and bureaucrats

designs formal and informal incentives

carries out monitoring of activities and outcomes

Constraints: resources

participation

information

BUREAUCRATS

Objective: maximize utility

Actions: decides to participate

apply regulations to please voters and receive wages

not apply regulations to please Firms and demand bribes

invent regulations to later relax in exchange for bribes

Influences: monitoring by The Public

formal and informal incentives specified by The Public (influenced by the market structure in which Firms operate)

the market structure in which Bureaucrats operate

FIRMS

Objective: maximize profits net of bribes

Actions: decides to participate

obeys rules invented by The Public and by the Bureaucrat

disobeys rules and offers bribes

denounces bribe demands to The Public

Influences: regulations imposed by bureaucrats (influenced by the
market structure which Bureaucrats operate)

monitoring by The Public

the market structure in which Firms operate

The public wishes to maximize social welfare. For this it uses a variety of instruments such as pollution regulation (to keep the air clean), or export subsidies (to promote "national champions" that are technological leaders) to name just two. To pursue its objectives, the public can do one of two things: it can either set up a bureaucracy or it can periodically elect politicians. Each alternative has its advantages as bureaucrats usually have longer tenure but politicians are more accountable for their actions. Typically the public will want to employ both types, and we will stress some of the differences below, but for now we shall call them bureaucrats.

The public's choice of policies to maximize social welfare typically entail the transfer of rents in favor of some groups at the expense of others, as when import duties or quotas are imposed. This implies that the bureaucrat's action has a value for the private agents involved. Ideally, bureaucrats should have a high degree of social conscience, so that their objectives would be perfectly matched with those of society, acting only as a "veil" and perfectly translating those objectives into policies. In practice, however, the public's objectives are less clear cut than implied above. Furthermore, bureaucrats have, like most other economic actors, an agenda of their own, and monetary income is certainly one of the arguments of their objective function. Corruption can take place if the bureaucrat decides to cash-in the value of his control right by taking bribes.

Therefore, the public must provide the bureaucrat with the appropriate incentives if its goals are to be achieved. Broadly speaking, there are three types of constraints that affect the eliciting of desired behavior from the bureaucrat. The first limitation is a constraint on the amount of resources and technological possibilities that are available at any one time. Examples are the limitations in the monitoring technology, and the characteristics of the population of potential bureaucrats such as history, risk aversion, or moral scruples. A second limitation is the possibility that bureaucrats and firms have in free societies of refusing to participate in the contract with the public. Regulated firms may decide to close their operations and relocate elsewhere, or simply switch to other activities. Bureaucrats may seek employment in the private sector. The third limitation is the amount of information that the public has. As stressed by Laffont and Tirole (1993) among others, informational asymmetries are important in understanding why voters have incomplete control over the agencies they set up. Even in this highly stylized representation we can guess that the design of an optimal program to achieve the public's objective can be an extremely demanding task. In a more realistic setting, where the bureaucracy is divided into many agencies, the constraints are interdependent as they must take into account both the natural uncertainty in the environment and the effects of other regulatory agencies.[8] Thus, for example, if restrictions on imports are increased, the value of the control rights of the bureaucrats in the pollution regulation department are increased, so the optimal contract of the bureaucrats implementing commercial policy and of the pollution regulators must change.

Bureaucratic performance will also depend on the bureaucratic market structure in which they operate. As shown by Rose-Ackerman (1978) and Shleifer and Vishny (1993) and discussed below, the equilibrium amount of corruption will critically depend on whether bureaucrats collude, acting as joint monopolists in the process of maximizing bribes, whether they act independently of each other, or whether overlapping jurisdictions induces some competition between them.

In our example, firms are the third and final party to the corrupt relationship. Their objective is to maximize profits. Their behavior is affected by the amount of rules and regulations the public decides to impose on the private sector. A second influence on the behavior of firms results from direct monitoring by the public to ensure compliance with its regulations. Lastly, there is the market structure in which firms operate, something that is the outcome both of natural technological possibilities and of intentional policy choices of the public, such as the level of the tariff rates on foreign trade. The market structure in which firms operate will affect the value of the control right owned by the bureaucrat. Typically, the ability of bureaucrats to extract bribes in exchange for softer regulations will be higher in environments in which firms enjoy monopoly rents. Thus, bribe determination between bureaucrats and firms is akin to the rent-sharing models of wage determination, where the exchange of control rights takes the place of labor.

To summarize, the public can influence the level of corruption in this very general setting by acting on two broad fronts: providing the right incentives to bureaucrats and designing competitive market structures for both bureaucrats and firms. The businessperson's and the lawyer's approach to curbing corruption are both part of the former, while the economist's approach is an example of the latter.

A. Incentives

Traditionally there are three ways in which incentives are provided: through formal incentives, such as wages or bonus schemes; through informal incentives, such as career concerns and reputations; and, finally, by directly monitoring inputs through periodic inspections or by employing supervisors.[9] Businesspeople usually argue that there is a very simple way to curb corruption: do what a private firm would. This implies that the public should provide formal incentives, usually in the form of very high wages, according to the importance of the bureaucrat's position. The lawyer's approach is to increase monitoring of inputs and performance and to improve the enforcement of laws.

Formal Incentives

Formal incentives, such as wages and bonus schemes, usually play a minor role in controlling corruption, basically because measurable performance indicators are not always easy to construct. In some areas of government, where performance is clearly defined, some attempts have been made to tie pay to performance. For example, in 1989 employees at the Bolivian customs service were promised part of the agency's revenues, which led to a 60 percent increase in customs revenues.[10] In Italy, the inspectors working at the Instituto Nazionale della Providenza Sociale (the national social security body) have significantly improved the collection of social security contributions motivated by performance-related bonuses, which in 1993 added $8,000 a head in salaries.[11]

In general, however, multiplicity of objectives characterizes government activities.[12] At the defense ministry, for example, procurement officers are supposed to be discreet when advertising their operations so as not to circulate sensitive information to the country's enemies, while at the same time obtaining goods of a certain quality/price ratio. A complete formal contract directed at providing incentives for such a multiplicity of objectives can at times be difficult, if not prohibitively costly, to write. As a result of this, defense procurement is one of the areas most prone to corruption. One extreme example of this is the procurement procedures of the U.S. Defense Department, where pursuance of the secrecy objective led to buying ordinary screws at one hundred times the price at which common citizens buy them (Stiglitz 1986).

The most common proposal to control corruption involves using formal incentives by simply paying a very high fixed wage to bureaucrats who might possibly commit corrupt acts. The logic of paying a high wage in every state of the world to prevent corruption stems from the fact that if there is probability of malfeasance detection and an associated penalty, say a fine or employment at a lower wage, then honest actions are incentive compatible for the government bureaucrat. This proposal, originally credited to Becker and Stigler (1974), has rarely been observed in practice although one of the most honest countries in the world, Singapore, pays exceptionally high wages to government officials.[13]

To provide some empirical content to this hypothesis, we collected data on the relative remunerations of comparable bureaucrats across countries. Table 1.3 provides some interesting comparisons.

Though no definite conclusions should be drawn on such a narrow set of countries, we note that the correlation coefficient between column (1) and the level of corruption in 1990 (with US=100) is close to zero, although excluding Japan brings it close to –0.5.

In a sense, pension privileges to elected officials perform a similar role as high wages during their time in office. Pensions are particularly important for elected politicians who may have a short employment horizon and

Table 1.3

Relative Salaries of Bureaucrats by Nation

	Top Bureaucrat (1)	Chief Executive Officer (2)
Australia	82	35
Canada	149	56
France	78	45
Germany	116	47
Ireland	87	20
Japan	160	31
Netherlands	97	35
Sweden	63	27
U.K.	155	43
U.S.	100	100

Note: (1) Relative to the U.S., based on OECD figures for 1990. Source: Michael Dynes, *The Times,* December 29, 1994. Figures correspond to the maximum salary and may differ slightly due to rounding. (2) Purchasing power U.S. CEO=100, data for 1989. Source: World Total Remuneration, World Competitiveness Report.

hence may give too little weight to the transitory wage income and too much weight to corrupt income.

The idea of paying very high wages or pensions to prevent corruption is attractive, although not always feasible. For example, some trade unions limit the wage that can be paid to the trade union leader to the wage earned by the highest paid member of the union.[14] Politicians are seldom paid relative to the importance of their post as they are subject to severe public scrutiny.[15] It is perhaps not unrelated that public opinion polls systematically rank politicians and trade union officers as more corrupt than other professions, particularly businesspeople. It surely comes as an irony that those who are supposed to be more socially motivated are perceived to be more corrupt than those who are supposed to be purely profit motivated.

Another social constraint that may increase the level of corruption is the ability to use the statement of wealth as a corruption-controlling device. In many countries politicians are obliged to sign a sworn declaration of their wealth when they start office. This can be of great help in controlling corruption.[16] Some countries, such as the United Kingdom, do not enforce this type of regulation as it is judged to invade the privacy of the politicians.[17] As a policy matter, it is difficult to promote changes in habits that are considered essential to a way of life, like the right to privacy of British politicians; but in countries where these social norms do not have such a strong grip, policies directed at raising the level of pay earned by public-sector employees and directed at making extensive the use of the statement of wealth would be a positive influence on that country's general level of honesty.

Informal Incentives

Informal incentives usually take the form of career concerns in agents whose future jobs and income depend on the reputation they develop while they are in office. Holmstrom (1982), formalizing an argument made by Fama (1980), showed under which circumstances the labor market for managers provided incentives for incumbent managers to exert effort. By working hard, the manager in Holmstrom's model attempts to fool observers in the labor market about his ability to perform his task. In the final equilibrium, managers end up working hard just to prevent an adverse evaluation.

The implications of such an argument for corruption control, especially for elected officials such as trade union officers and politicians, have not been explored but one could conjecture that a related mechanism may prevent corruption when political competition is intense.[18] Based on this basic model one could conjecture that informal incentives work well only if voters observe the performance of the official, if the official's performance in the present task is informative about his ability for future tasks, and if the government official is not too impatient. This last condition can be stated somewhat differently. Assume there is an agent with some amount of discretion to commit a corrupt act. If the act is observable but unverifiable (in court), or if the only fine that can be imposed is dismissal from the agent's job, then corruption is highly likely, especially if the official is near the end of an unrenewable term in office. Deterrence can only be exercised if the agent has something to look forward to, like a pension or the reputation of having been a (not-dismissed-in-the-last-period) politician. Thus reputations can act like a bond posted by cash-constrained politicians with their employers (the public) that can be confiscated in the event of any wrongdoing during their time in office.[19]

This can be seen as a rationalization for the public's preference for politicians with a prestigious or valuable background.[20] If this interpretation of the politician's reputation as a bond is taken seriously, then libel laws when viewed as anticorruption instruments have at least two conflicting objectives to achieve: they are supposed to be lax to encourage the cheap production of information, and they are supposed to be strict to protect the reputations of politicians from short-term electoral attacks.[21]

The literature on tournaments (e.g., Lazear and Rosen 1981; Green and Stokey 1983; Mookherjee 1984) uses the information produced when comparing the performance of agents operating under similar circumstances for monitoring purposes. The electoral process could be interpreted as a way of comparing (and thus inducing competition between) political candidates in a tournament-like fashion.[22] For example, in a presidential race, governors from a political party compete for the party's nomination based on their performance as governors. Their efficiency in governing their states, including the amount of corruption, can be compared. It should be pointed out that the evidence, though as yet very preliminary, suggests that the effect of electoral competition (measured by the Gastil Index of political rights) on a country's level of corruption is negligible. In small samples, however, the inclusion of Hong Kong and Singapore, two of the least corrupt countries with very little political competition, skew the results and limit what would intuitively seem to be a correlation.

Monitoring Inputs

The third and final way to provide incentives against corruption is to collect information about the activities of the bureaucrats and then prosecute any dishonest behavior that is detected. The traditional way to do this is by directly monitoring bureaucrats to spot any deviations as they occur or to audit the outcome of their work. However, information obtained in this way is sometimes difficult to use in a court of law.

The lawyer's approach to combat corruption is illustrated by the proposals of Judge Antonio Di Pietro, the judge in charge of Italy's recent corruption investigations, who favors judiciary system reform to allow for plea bargaining and allowing judges to grant immunity from prosecution to those who cooperate with the investigations. Some of the most successful and celebrated anticorruption campaigns have complemented monitoring and auditing efforts with drastic measures on the uses that can be given to the information thus obtained. For example, the Prevention of Bribery ordinance passed by the government of Hong Kong in 1971 (see Klitgaard 1988, 104) allowed the burden of the proof to be shifted so that those accused of corruption should demonstrate their innocence. The agents working for the ICAC (Independent Commission Against Corruption) created in Hong Kong in 1973 had the power of search and seizure without need for a legal warrant. This is not always an acceptable alternative in politically open societies.

One of the conditions for an anticorruption agency of this sort to be effective is its independent nature. The idea behind this requirement of independence is that it is the only way the public will have confidence in such a body and will contribute with information and support to its success. The experience of the Australian state of New South Wales is interesting in this respect. The state governor, who set up one of the first ICACs in the world, was falsely accused by the head of the ICAC of corruption charges (actually quite minor charges). The independence of the ICAC was never questioned and the governor resigned. Again a dilemma arises. For the ICAC to be fully effective it must operate independently from other government agencies. However, the ICAC has to be set up by a branch of government, typically the executive, who will be reluctant to do so if they themselves could be investigated.

B. The Market Structure

While bureaucrats may receive incentives to carry out the public's objectives, they do not operate in a vacuum. Indeed, some recent research has emphasized that both the decision to give bribes and the amount of the bribe depend on the market structure in which both bribers and bribee's operate.

Bureaucratic Market Structures

The first to emphasize the effect of bureaucratic market structure on corruption was Rose-Ackerman (1978) when she introduced what is sometimes called the "principle of overlapping jurisdictions" (or Gresham's law in reverse). Rose-Ackerman analyzed the effects of competitive pressures on a corrupt bureaucracy dispensing a scarce benefit. In this case, competition can be introduced by allowing benefit applicants to reapply in other departments if they are asked for bribes. If the cost of reapplication is low enough, the existence of some honest officials could drive bribes to zero.[23]

In a similar vein, Shleifer and Vishny (1993) present a simple model to examine how the structures of government institutions and the political process determine the level of corruption. They consider the case in which the state has the monopoly on the provision of a government-produced good, such as a passport, or an import license. The good is sold for the government by an official who has the opportunity to restrict the quantity of the good that is sold.

Specifically, the official can deny a private agent the passport or the import license. For simplicity, it is assumed that the official can restrict supply without any risk of detection or punishment from above. Also, it is assumed that provision of the good costs nothing to the official, except for the official price of the good p that must be turned in to the government.

If the official cannot discriminate between buyers of the public good, he will simply set the marginal revenue equal to the marginal cost p of providing the good. For a downward sloping demand for the public good, the total price with the bribe always exceed the official price.

Shleifer and Vishny also examine the case in which the state acts as a joint monopolist agency that sets the bribe prices p, and p, for the two complementary government goods. The extension is interesting because, in many cases, a private agent might need several complementary government permits to conduct business. For example, an importer might need permits to unload, transport, and sell a government good obtainable from different agencies. The different agencies that supply the complementary good might collude, sell the different goods independently, or even compete in the provision of the public goods. It turns out that these different bureaucratic market structures have important implications for the extent of corruption.

Let $x1$ and $x2$ be the quantities of these goods sold. Let the official prices, equal to the monopolist's marginal costs, be denoted MC, and $MC2$. The per unit bribes are then $p1-MC1$ and $p2-MC2$. If agencies *collude* (acting as a joint monopolist), the joint monopolist will set $p1$ at which

$$MR1 + MR2 \ dx2/dx1 = MC1$$

where $MR1$ and $MR2$ denote marginal revenues for the sale of goods 1 and 2, respectively. When the two goods are complements, at the optimum $MR1 < MC1$. In other words, the joint monopolist keeps the bribe on good 1 down to expand the demand for the complementary good 2 and thus raise profits from bribes on good 2. For the same reason, the agency keeps down the price of good 2.

This contrasts sharply with the case in which agencies act independently. Each agency then takes the other's output as given, and in particular, $dx1/dx2$ is set to zero. At the independent agency's optimum, $MR1 = MC1$. Hence, the per unit bribe is higher and the output is lower.

The final case is that in which each agency is allowed to provide either good. In this case, both agencies will effectively compete for the provision of the good, as when different agencies or cities in the United States can provide a passport. It is a straightforward conclusion that competition between the providers will drive the bribes to zero.

Thus the level of bribes is lowest in the case in which agents are induced to compete for the provision of a public good, intermediate in the case the official acts as a joint monopolist agency (collusion), and highest when the briber acts independently. This is formally close to the analysis of the extraction of renewable resources by competing players in the classical fishing game (see Lancaster 1973 and Fudenberg and Tirole 1991 for an exposition).

The Briber's Market Structure

Bureaucrats' actions are valuable to firms. For example, the decision by a bureaucrat to apply a regulation aimed at providing pollution control can be very costly for the firms affected. These actions will affect the firm's marginal or average costs and therefore impact its profits. In general, the value of the bureaucrat's action will depend on the market structure of the industry to be regulated.

Consider, for example, a standard Cournot equilibrium with linear demand (with intercept A and unit slope) constant marginal cost c and n firms. At the margin, the benefit of having lower marginal costs is given by $2(A-c)/(n + 1)^2$, which is decreasing in n. If firms could pay regulators a bribe in exchange for a more lenient application of regulations to reduce their MC, the incentive to do so would be decreasing in n.

In general, the lack of product market competition can benefit not only the firms in the industry, but can potentially also benefit tax inspectors, regulators, suppliers, and other agents with some control rights over those firms. The reason is that as competition decreases, the value of their control rights increase so they are more likely to exchange them for bribes.[24]

To fix ideas we develop a simple model that focuses on the regulatory power as the type of political control right enjoyed by the bureaucrat. There are three players in this model: the public, the bureaucrat, and the firm. The public has discretion over a policy instrument k, that controls the degree of product market competition in the economy. The use of k may respond to public concerns over too little employment under free trade, so that k would be the amount of protection imposed through tariff or non-tariff barriers. Alternatively, k may reflect the public's concern over too little investment in research and development when there is too much entry into a certain industry, so that k would reflect restrictions on the number of firms allowed to operate based on these "Schumpeterian" considerations.[25] In general, we do not require these policy choices to lead to efficient outcomes.

The bureaucrat who has no power to affect k directly has certain control rights over a firm that operates within his area of political influence. For example, he might have discretion over the application of certain regulatory controls on the firm (such as those that apply to fire safety or pollution), resulting in a reduction of the firm's profits. There is a continuum of firms in the unit interval. Before regulation, aggregate and average rents in the economy are given by $\pi(k)$, with $\pi_k(.)>0$. After the bureaucrat exercises his control right and a tough regulation is enforced, profits are zero. Thus, the value of the politician's discretion is equal to $\pi(k)$, and this value is increasing in k.

We assume that the bureaucrat is not under any sort of optimal contract that prevents him from pursuing his own interests.[26] We simply assume that the bureaucrat is paid the ongoing wage in the economy w, regardless of whether he enforces a tough or a soft regulation.

Since the politician cares about bribes, regulating the firm is not efficient (for the bureaucrat/firm coalition). In a Coasian spirit, we allow the bureaucrat and the firm to bargain over bribes to avoid regulation and, thus, restore efficiency. With probability 0, corrupt deals become public (as when opposition parties or the press uncover them) and the bureaucrat is fired under corruption accusations.

The corrupt politician's income is given by his wage w plus the bribes b that he takes. When a corrupt politician is fired, he immediately obtains employment in the private sector at the ongoing wage w, but suffers a utility loss with monetary value of m.[27] Thus, his utility is given by

$$U_b = (1 - 0)(w + b) + O(w - m) \qquad (3)$$

If the manager is caught offering bribes, his firm leaves the industry to earn normal returns (zero profits with certainty). The manager's utility is given by

$$U_m = (1 - 0)(\pi - b) \qquad (4)$$

The bureaucrat and the firm bargain over bribes. The disagreement point for the bureaucrat is simply his wage w and the disagreement point for the firm is zero profits. The Nash bargaining solution maximizes

$$\text{Max}_b \left[((1 - 0)(w + b) + O(w - m)) - w \right] \left[(1 - O)(\pi - b) \right] \qquad (5)$$

which solves for

$$b^* = \frac{1}{2} \left[\pi + m0/1 - 0 \right] \qquad (6)$$

Then the condition for observing corruption in the economy is equivalent to the condition that the bureaucrat wishes to exercise his control rights over the firm. This amounts to

$$m \leq ((1-0)/0)\pi \tag{7}$$

Call m_i^* the value of m that obtains equation (5) above with equality in country i. Assume that m is distributed according to the cumulative function $F(.)$. Then, the fraction of bureaucrats in country i that are corrupt is given by

$$p(m < m_i^*) = F[m^*(0_i, \pi(k_i))] \tag{8}$$

Equation (6) shows the level of corruption in country i as a function of the exogenous probability 0_i and of π. It is quite straightforward to see that $p(.)$ is decreasing in 0 and increasing in π (or k). The expression can be interpreted as the fraction of politicians or transactions with public employees in country i that involve corruption or questionable payments. This interpretation closely matches the definition of the corruption indices used in this chapter. The model thus provides a very direct theoretical framework to examine the effects of monopoly power on the incentives faced by politicians to engage in corrupt activities.

In Ades and Di Tella (1995), we examine the role of product market competition in determining corruption. Using corruption indexes from *Business International* and the *World Competitiveness Report*, we find that controlling the level of development and the degree of political competition, corruption is higher in countries with economies dominated by a few firms or where domestic firms are sheltered from foreign competition by high tariffs. The effect holds after controlling for year and country fixed effects. We also correct for the possible endogeneity of market structure, as it might be that bureaucrats influence market structures or erect barriers to trade in order to later extract bribes, as in the rent-seeking literature. Using a series of instruments, we identify strong effects on corruption of exogenous changes in product market competition. Policy conclusions follow directly from the finding that protectionist or other policies directed at restricting the competitive pressures faced by domestic firms have the effect of fostering corruption. Rather than investing in mechanism design and auditing procedures, governments interested in curbing corruption should perhaps first consider opening up their economy to trade and making domestic markets more competitive.

In a similar spirit, Ades and Di Tella (1994a) find strong positive effects of active industrial policy on corruption. This result is especially relevant as many countries have developed a domestic demand for industrial policy, supposedly on the grounds that they can lead to faster capital accumulation and technological growth. Using corruption data from the WCR, we decompose the effect of industrial policy on investment and research and development spending into a direct positive effect, and an indirect, negative, corruption-induced effect. The data shows that the total effect of industrial policy on investment is only 56 percent of the direct effect, with the remainder being dissipated by an indirect negative impact of the induced corruption on investment. A similar decomposition on the effects of industrial policy on research and development spending yields a total effect that is only 59 percent of the direct effect.

The data suggests that policy initiatives aimed at fostering the competitiveness of domestic industries through active industrial policies are doomed to yield only partial success. The magnitude of the negative effects found suggests that the consideration of corruption should not be absent from cost-benefit analyses of industrial policies.

V. Controlling Corruption

The evidence of the effect of market structure on corruption is suggestive, although ideally we would like to know how it interacts with more traditional corruption controlling activities. In this final section we attempt to provide an empirical assessment of the relative merits of two approaches to controlling corruption, namely the lawyer's emphasis on law enforcement vis-à-vis the economist's emphasis on control through product market competition. Indeed, most noneconomists may claim that more traditional methods of crime prevention should be emphasized, such as increasing the autonomy and resources of judges undertaking corruption investigations or following Judge Di Pietro's proposals regarding the possibility of introducing judiciary reforms such as plea bargaining.

We explore this possibility by analyzing the interaction of openness (OPEN), measured by the share of imports in the GDP, and the independence of the judiciary system (JUD) that is measured by a dummy variable that takes the value I when the independence of the judiciary system in the country is above the mean of the sample. We use data from BI to measure both the degree of independence of the judiciary system and the level of corruption (CORR).

We regress corruption on these two variables and their interaction, and on a standard set of controls for the level of development of the country (income per capita (GDP) and schooling (SCHOOL)) and political competition (the Gastil Index of political rights (POL)).[28] The focus of the test is the coefficient on the interaction term in the following equation:

$$CORR_i = 8.442 + 0.317 \; GDPI - 0.196 \; SCHOOL_i - 0.113 \; POL_i$$
$$\quad (1.23) \quad (0.10) \quad \quad (0.15) \quad \quad \quad (0.17)$$

$$- 8.708 \; OPEN_i - 1.87 \; JUD_i + 7.104 \; OPENJUD_i$$
$$\quad (3.73) \quad \quad (0.91) \quad \quad (3.85)$$

We find that corruption is high in economies that are closed to foreign competition as proxied by a low share of imports in the GDP. We also find that corruption is higher in countries where judiciary institutions are not well developed, or are not independent of political influence.

But even more importantly, the positive sign on the interaction term indicates that opening up an economy to foreign trade is particularly important in countries where institutions are not yet fully developed. In a country where the judiciary system is relatively independent (above the mean), a one standard deviation increase in openness reduces corruption by 0.15 of a standard deviation. In countries with judiciary systems below the mean, a one standard deviation increase in openness reduces corruption by 2.09 points, some 0.81 standard deviations in the corruption index. Thus, competition is much more effective in controlling corruption in countries where the judiciary system is not well developed.

VI. Conclusion

The availability of subjective data on corruption has finally provided the field of the economics of corruption with the empirical discipline that is essential to turn its fertile theorizing into policy recommendations.

In this survey, we review the literature organized into two broad themes: theories of corruption and theories of the effects of corruption. We show that the new empirical approach has helped to shed light on a controversy regarding the effects of corruption on investment and growth has lasted since the 1960s. We show that the data suggest that there is a negative effect of corruption on investments, and that this effect is less severe in countries with particularly obtrusive bureaucracies, though this difference with low red-tape countries is only mildly significant.

Our main aim is to review theories of the causes of corruption and their policy implications. Broadly speaking, we analyze theories that blame corruption on poorly designed incentive contracts or monitoring devices, and theories that blame corruption on the lack of competition in the bureaucracy and/or the product market. We test the relative merits of two practical policy proposals: controlling corruption through tighter enforcement of laws or through increases in product market competition. The evidence suggests that both have negative and significant effects on a country's level of corruption. But more significantly, the interaction term is positive indicating that opening up the economy to foreign trade is particularly important in countries where institutions are not yet fully developed. In a country where the judiciary system is relatively independent, the effect of competition on corruption is over five times higher than in countries with judiciary systems below the mean.

Though the recent empirical contributions represent a major step forward in establishing the field of corruption as a progressive research program, much work remains to be done. Progress will be constrained by data availability, and our guess is that data improvements will come on two fronts. First, cross-country data from risk analysts is now available for a reasonably long time series (almost sixteen years), though at quite high commercial rates. Second, cross-industry studies of corruption based on the work of large accounting firms would finally allow research into the microfoundations of corruption to begin. With this data at hand, future research could tackle questions such as: What are the effects of corruption? What are the causes of corruption? What is its relationship with variables such as growth, inequality, political competition, inflation, or product market competition? What are the mechanisms involved? Which industries and which professions are more prone to corruption? Does corruption distort specialization in trade? Is corruption procyclical? If corrupt payments are tax deductible, who ends up paying for corruption? What are the true effects of anticorruption laws, such as the American Foreign Corrupt Practices Act of 1977?

Appendix 1: On the Definition of Corruption

One of the problems with "general" theories of corruption is that what is considered corruption in one country constitutes perfectly acceptable behavior in another country. Take a country like England, for example, which is traditionally thought of as not being particularly corrupt. There is a list of activities considered normal practice in England that would be considered illegal in other, perhaps more disreputable, countries. English members of Parliament, for instance, are allowed to receive "renumerated directorships" as long as they declare it in the Register of the Member's Interest. The idea of a member of Parliament who receives a wage (£33,169 in December 1994) from the British public, receiving a second wage, in some cases of up to £60,000, from a private company would certainly look like a conflict of interest to most outside observers. Even a seemingly narrow and uncontroversial definition of corruption like that in the opening sentence of Shleifer and Vishny (1993, 1): "We define government corruption as the sale by government officials of government property for personal gain" could implicate most privatization programs since they are a source of popularity for incumbent governments and thus of personal gain for them. The matter is less innocent than it sounds. Take the British privatization program as an example. The method of sale for most companies involved severe undervaluations. The total undervaluation in the sale of British Telecom alone, measured by the rise in price of BT shares at the end of the first trading day, is calculated at £1295 millions (see table 7.1 in Vickers and Yarrow 1988). The gain for those lucky enough to have applied and been allocated BT shares at the end of the first trading day amounted to a massive 86 percent. The question is why did Mrs. Thatcher's government produce such massive redistribution of wealth? There are two potential answers. The first possibility is that she was spending the British state's money to get the conservative party (led by herself) reelected. The mechanism used is tactfully explained by Vickers and Yarrow (1988, 1801): "An important feature of the process is that the gainers know that they have gained, but the losers are less aware that they have lost. A windfall profit of £200 on BT shares is much more obvious than the effective of £20 to each of ten who failed to apply. John Kenneth Galbraith once remarked that few things enhance the overall feeling of wealth better than undiscovered theft. Without wishing to push the analogy too far, we would suggest that there is a common element in the two cases."

The second possibility, credited to Sir Alan Walters (1988) and more formally to Vickers (1991), is that shares of companies being privatized that are underpriced promote a wider share of ownership. This, in turn, is a "bulwark against socialism" and reduces the probability that a future government nationalizes the company again. Hence the highest obtainable price in a privatization involves underpricing. Crucially, nationalization must occur without full compensation. Since the objective of this process (efficiency through private ownership) is what would be in the best interest of the state, it is exactly not corruption.[29]

To the extent that the first possibility is not in the best interest of the state, but to benefit the political party that is in government and the personal gain of Mrs. Thatcher, it could be called a form of corruption even under Shleifer and Vishny's seemingly narrow definition.[30] It also warns us of the possibility that wealth redistribution through nationalization and privatization could be used by political parties as just another electoral weapon. Thus given some time after this privatization wave, center-left parties may again be fighting elections with nationalization proposals, just as in the 1940s and 1950s, generating a "political ownership cycle." This distinction between corruption for one's own personal pocket and for one's own political party is useful in determining less extreme forms of corruption. Thus economists who investigate the political business cycle (see Nordhaus 1975) that postulate politicians who maximize their chance of reelection are in a way, studying this lesser form of corruption. But evidence from the Italian corruption scandals shows that the two forms of corruption feed on one another. The funding of political parties still varies across countries, with some countries like Argentina providing some of the funding through a subsidy to the political parties (at rate of approximately $2 per vote), with other countries leaving it all to voluntary private contributions. We are unaware of theoretical work analyzing the optimal degree of state funding of political parties when corruption is a possibility (but see Baron 1989). This is a major area for future research on corruption as many questions still remain unanswered: Should we limit campaign spending? Should all spending be publicly funded? In what proportion should parties receive funding?[31]

Appendix II: Further Readings on the Economics of Corruption

II. A. More on the Costs of Corruption

Instead of focusing on the effects of corruption, other authors have analyzed the effects that the laws *against* corruption may have on economic performance. The United States provides an interesting case as, while most countries penalize corruption of national officials, only the United States has a law penalizing the bribing of foreign officials.[32] Some have argued that this regulation has caused U.S. companies to lose export markets and speculated that this could be part of the explanation behind its massive trade deficit. A recent study by Graham and McKean has proved this to be unfounded, however.[33] Using information from fifty-one U.S. embassies in countries that together account for four-fifths of its trade deficit, they divide countries into corrupt and not corrupt. They then show that during the eight years following the passing of the Foreign Corrupt Practices Act (FCPA), the U.S. share of imports in the corrupt countries grew as fast as its share of imports in the noncorrupt countries. Instead, Hines (1995) finds mixed evidence. Using the BI data, Hines shows that the U.S. share of corrupt countries' aircraft imports fell significantly after 1977, controlling for changes in the share of all U.S. exports. The U.S. government estimates the loss to American business of passing the FCPA at around $3 billion annually.

The literature on rent seeking was the first to point out that the possibility of corruption entailed welfare losses.[34] The original emphasis of this literature was on the point that even if a bribe is simply a transfer, some resources are wasted by those who are competing to be in a position of obtaining the bribes (e.g., the government officials granting licenses) and by those paying out the bribes (the firms trying to obtain the licenses). As far as corruption is concerned, its importance lies in having pointed out that even rather harmless bribes, of the kind paid to bypass exchange rate controls for instance, may involve significant welfare costs. As Tullock (1988) puts it, "Traditionally economists have tended to view this kind of bribery as in itself desirable, because it gets around an undesirable regulation. However, it leads to rent seeking."

The lack of data to test the effect of corruption on some measure of welfare allowed theoretical predictions to run amok. An early paper by Leff (1964) argued that corruption may help economic growth by providing a way to bypass welfare-reducing regulations. Lui (1985) presents an elaborate model of queuing where bureaucrats may speed up the administrative process to obtain more bribes. Mookherjee and Png (1991) is an elegant model in a similar spirit, whereby bribes provide an incentive scheme for badly paid bureaucrats. Salant (1991) analyzes a regulator who is in a position to regulate prices so low as to effectively confiscate a firm's investment. He notes that the promise of future employment with the regulated firm might induce the regulator not to maximize welfare at each moment in time. This might be a good thing since an inability to precommit future regulatory policy might lead, in some cases, to a well-known underinvestment problem. In a sense, in Salant's argument corruption acts like a form of vertical integration.[35] The latest version of this benign corruption argument is Basu and Li (1994), who argue that a one-time surge in corruption may be a catalyst for reform by providing an incentive for bureaucrats with the power to allow or block change.

Thus corruption is a way of making privatizations and other institutional changes incentive compatible for bureaucrats or trade union leaders who may otherwise have the power to oppose such change. Those really hurt by corruption in this setting are would-be bureaucrats whose control rights are curtailed by the reforms and who receive no compensation for their loss. This possibility had already been noted by Lui in his 1986 article. Using data from the European Bank for Reconstruction and Development on the speed of reform in Eastern Europe and a new data set on corruption, we obtained preliminary results that indicate that corruption was negatively and significantly associated with the indicators of reform. Thus this hypothesis is not borne out by the limited data available today.[36]

A dissenting voice is Romer (1994) who observes that one of the main welfare losses through high fixed costs, such as taxes or corruption, is the lack of diversity. This is an important point since it switches attention from relatively small welfare losses through price distortions (Harberger triangles) to large losses in consumer surplus (Dupuit triangles) due to lower numbers of products.[37]

II. B. More on the Causes of Corruption

The Economics of Crime

Becker (1968), in the article that started the economics of crime, argued that since fines are transfer payments and enforcement is costly, society should combine infinitely large fines with minimal monitoring. Several solutions to what is sometimes called the monitoring puzzle (Dickens et al 1989) have been proposed. Stigler (1970) suggested that maximum fines lose marginal deterrence, so that in order to have expected fines increasing with the size of the offense society should not set all fines at a maximum. Andreoni (1991) presents a model where law enforcers suffer from mistakenly punishing innocent defendants so they endogenously reduce the probability of conviction as fines go up.

Should we monitor at all times or wait until crimes are reported and then investigate? Mookherjee and Png (1992) find the conditions under which each regime is optimal. Investigation is more cost efficient since the degree of deterrence can be graduated with the severity of the offense, but we need the reporting of crimes to be above a certain threshold. We conjecture that the inclination to spontaneously report corruption offenses depends on the climate for political involvement and on the degree of civil responsibility in society.[38] McCormick and Tollison (1984) estimate the degree to which visible monitoring reduces offenses. Using basketball statistics, they estimate that there is a large reduction in fouls (34 percent) in a game when the number of referees increases from two to three.

Two of the main contributors to the literature that analyzes criminal activities as the outcome of rational choice made an early application to corruption (Becker and Stigler 1974). This article introduced a more general concept for economics, that supervision is necessary for inducing desired behavior. This concept forms the basis for a hierarchical theory of the firm (see Calvo and Wellisz 1978 and 1979) that explains why employees with supervisory functions earn more than production workers, even if both have comparable ability. Moreover, when monetary fines for improper behavior are not allowed, the resulting wage for those under supervision may be above the market clearing wage, so that inefficiencies such as aggregate unemployment may be observed to exert a disciplining effect on those still in employment (see Shapiro and Stiglitz 1984). Apart from providing a rational theory of involuntary unemployment, it also provides a rationale for the often heard idea that high wages for bureaucrats may help deter corruption (see also Palmier 1983). Wages should be raised above the opportunity wage by an amount that varies proportionally with the size of the potential bribe and inversely with the probability of detection. As emphasized by Besley and McLaren (1993), this is not necessarily the optimal wage regime in an economy with monitoring problems. Both paying reservation wages (the economy's opportunity wage) and paying capitulation wages (wages below the reservation wage) to the bureaucrats may be observed in equilibrium.[39] Besley and McLaren's paper point out a problem with these types of hierarchies: unless a rather sophisticated scheme of rewards and fines is used, paying efficiency wages does rely on there being some honest members in the bureaucracy who will do the monitoring. It is relatively easy to construct examples with mechanisms that allow for hierarchies of corrupt agents behaving honestly, a tough formal treatment of what outcomes are actually feasible is the topic of the implementation literature (for a survey see Moore 1992).

In the only empirical paper testing Becker's crime model in the context of corruption, Goel and Rich (1989) show that the probability of being convicted and the severity of punishment both reduced the extent of corruption measured by the proportion of all government employees that were convicted for bribery at the federal, state, and local level for the years 1970–83. They also show that low relative earnings for public officials, high local unemployment, and the amount of advertising expenditure (taken to proxy the degree of impatience through the demonstration effect in consumption) all increased corruption.

Indoctrination

Indoctrination has sometimes been proposed as a low-cost alternative to corruption control (Klitgaard 1988). For example a conscious effort is often made in anticorruption agencies (e.g., Hong Kong's ICAC) to raise the moral costs of being corrupt by emphasizing high ethical standards for recruitment and conduct in the organization.[40] The idea that at least part of the actual preference structure of individuals was subject to choice was explored in Akerlof (1983). He observed that one of the more economically successful groups in the United States, the Quakers, is also quite prone to economic irrationality (as measured by their tendency to cooperate when playing a game of prisoner's dilemma in a series of experiments reported in Amstein and Feigenbaum (1967). Akerlof shows that such apparently irrational behavior may be rooted in a "loyalty change" induced by religious education, and that "honesty may begin as a means of economic betterment, but then there is a displacement of goals so that the person so trained will refrain from embezzlement where there is no penalty."

Collusion

A related literature, started by Tirole (1986), explores the possibility of collusion between the supervisor and the employee in a simple agency setting (Nash and Bayesian implementation are known to be affected by the possibility of collusion). Though still in its infancy, some themes relevant to a theory of bureaucracy are already emerging, like the possibility of collusion leading to low-powered incentive schemes (for a survey see Tirole 1992). Felli (1992) is a paper exploring the benefits of using delegation of authority as a low-cost mechanism for preventing collusion. The basic idea is that parties acquire information in the process of coalition formation, so that if the supervisor has the authority to use his new information against the agent in the future, the agent will be more reluctant to collude with the supervisor today.[41] Koffman and Lawarree (1993) is a paper exploring the interaction between two types of supervisors, an honest-expensive external auditor and a corrupt-cheap internal supervisor, that provides yet another explanation for the monitoring puzzle by emphasizing the increase in the incentive to collude with the enforcer as expected fines increase.

Regulation

Perhaps the most prevalent form of corruption is misrepresentation of costs and revenues in projects where the ultimate cost is borne by the state. Laffont and Tirole (1993, ch. 12) created a model that combines an often-used model of regulation under moral hazard (where there is unobservable cost reducing effort) with the possibility of cost padding. Under no cost padding, the regulator balances the use of fixed-price contracts (that provide perfect incentives for efforts in cost reduction) and contracts that reimburse the cost of service (that allow full rent extraction). They then introduce the possibility of cost padding. The immediate result is that this tilts the balance in favor of the use of fixed-price contracts.[42] The general result is that the possibility of cost padding increases the power of incentive schemes, a result that holds when they introduce the possibility of auditing the costs claimed to have been incurred by the firm, both when the auditor is benevolent and when the auditor can be bribed by the firm.[43]

A somewhat more cryptic point is in order. There are two types of principal-agent models, those where the agent picks his action before observing the state of the world (e.g., see Milgrom and Roberts 1992, ch. 7) and those where the agent picks his action after observing it (e.g., see Laffont and Tirole 1992). The important point is that a priori we do not know what the principal likes best. Allowing the agent to pick his action after observing the state of nature (so that the agent's strategy space is richer) has an indeterminate effect on the principal's revenue. More options for the agent is bad from the point of view that he is more difficult to control, but it is good from the point of view that more information about the technology before an action is taken expands the production possibilities set, so that the net value of information could have either sign. In a simple cost-padding setting, the agent's action (misrepresenting costs) has negative value, hence in most cases there is no expansion of the production set. The point is that the order of moves may be a choice itself, and that in most corruption settings it would pay for the principal to have the agent choose his action first.[44]

Capture

Stigler (1971) noticed that regulation often tended to defend the industry that was supposed to be subject to regulatory controls. The paper's basic contribution was to establish the possibility of there being a market for regulation, where the price of the good exchanged (favorable regulation to the industry) was personal favors to the regulators. These not only included bribes, but also promises for future employment with the industry and campaign contributions to political parties akin to the regulator.[45] Peltzman (1976) and Becker (1983) included consumer groups as another force in the market, so that effectively, the regulators arbitrate between interest groups. As Laffont and Tirole (1993, ch. 2) point out, this approach has two serious limitations. First, they take the control fights of the politicians as given and do not explore the possible sources of these control fights, such as superior information. If there are no informational asymmetries the public could simply instruct the regulators what to do in each instance and punish any deviation. The second shortcoming of this approach is their exclusive focus on the demand for regulation with no attention to the supply of political and regulatory institutions. We mention just three papers that go some way toward redressing the balance. Baron (1989) shows the interaction of politicians who need money to finance political campaigns and their sponsors. He assumes favoring an interest group is costly and that the exact cost is learned by the politician when he reaches office. He then analyses how interest groups use campaign contributions for reelection to obtain information from the candidates. Spiller's (1990) is a paper analyzing the effects of competition between an industry and Congress (who have conflicting preferences) to influence a regulatory agency. Laffont and Tirole (1991 and 1993, ch. 2) offer a model that explains the extent of discretion in the hands of the regulatory agency, where discretion is modeled as the possibility of making monetary transfers to the industry. If capture is not an issue, then the regulator's ability to make transfers can never hurt the public. If capture is a possibility, then under certain conditions, forbidding lump-sum transfers to the industry may increase welfare. The paper explains a stylized fact of regulation, that lump-sum transfers are hardly ever allowed in practice.[46]

Multiple Equilibria

Some authors have described models of corruption with multiple equilibria. This possibility is important since one prediction of these type of models is that apparently similar conditions of deterrence may give rise to different levels of corruption, something that is claimed to have empirical validity. The precise mechanism that gives rise to the multiplicity of equilibria differs between authors. For example, Andvig and Moene (1990) assume that the probability of detection for one corrupt official decreases as the number of colleagues that are corrupt increases. A similar approach is taken by Lui (1986) in the context of an overlapping generations model where it becomes more costly to audit bureaucrats as more of them become corrupt. Tirole (1993) examines a model where the profitability of trading requires trust, something that depends on the interaction of individual and collective reputations. Hence, if an individual belongs to a group that has a reputation for not being corrupt, it pays to take apparently costly actions to maintain this reputation. Once corruption increases within one's group, dishonesty is individually profitable. In this setting corruption ratchets up and not down. This line of research may provide a rationale for large-scale anticorruption campaigns and may be why sometimes governments resort to very severe deterrence policies. Note that these multiple equilibria should be interpreted somewhat loosely to capture the evidence presented in Ades and Di Tella (1994) whereby small increases in the degree of competition do result in lower corruption levels.

Appendix III: Business International's Sample of Fifty-Five Countries

Algeria, Ghana, Kenya, South Africa, Zaire, Zimbabwe, India, Iran, Iraq, Israel, Japan, Jordan, Korea, Malaysia, Pakistan, Philippines, Singapore, Sri Lanka, Thailand, Austria, Belgium, Denmark, Finland, France, Germany, Greece, Ireland, Italy, Netherlands, Norway, Portugal, Spain, Sweden, Switzerland, Turkey, United Kingdom, Canada, Dominican Republic, Jamaica, Mexico, Nicaragua, Panama, Trinidad and Tobago, United States, Argentina, Brazil, Chile, Colombia, Ecuador, Peru, Uruguay, Venezuela, Australia, New Zealand, Indonesia.

Appendix IV

Summary Statistics

Variable	Obs	Mean	Std. Dev	Minimum	Maximum
CORR	55	2.99	2.54	0	9
BURO	55	0.51	0.50	0	1
GDP, U$000	55	6.21	4.38	0.45	15.00
GOV	55	15.30	5.85	7.71	37.04
INV	55	22.93	7.05	4.28	42.00
JUD	55	0.53	0.50	0	1
OPEN	55	0.26	0.24	0.08	1.68
PPI 1980	55	102.6	41.76	24.42	229.9
POL	55	2.88	1.98	1	6
REV	55	0.14	0.18	0	0.73
SCHOOL 1980	55	5.75	2.87	1.74	12.14

NOTE: All variables are averages of their 1981 to 1983 observations, except PPI 1980 and SCHOOL 1980, which correspond to the 1980 observations. The BURO and JUD dummies take a value of 1 in countries with an average value above the sample mean.

Notes

1. One such policy proposal is by Italy's judge Antonio Di Pietro, who argues that a way to curb corruption is to reform the judiciary system to allow for plea bargaining and to give judges the ability to grant immunity from prosecution to those that cooperate with the investigations.

2. See, for example, Becker and Stigler (1974).

3. See Ades and Di Tella (1995).

4. In some regressions that hold constant the level of development, the lack of political rights can even have a significant and positive effect on corruption. Again, this is due to the inclusion of the two extreme countries and only shows if the sample size is small.

5. See also Chapter 5 in Rose-Ackerman (1978).

6. The Santhanam Committee report on corruption in India (cited by Myrdal 1968) notes that "(w)e have no doubt that quite often delay is deliberately contrived so as to obtain some kind of illicit gratification."

7. We review some of these contributions in Appendix II.

8. Though one would like to know why there is such division of labor within government, and why government agencies are sometimes *designed* to have opposing objectives (for example, into a "spending" ministry and a budget control ministry). See, for example, the preliminary work by Dewatripont and Tirole reported in Tirole's Clarendon Lecture (Tirole 1994).

9. This classification is for simplicity, as monitoring inputs can be seen as a way to provide formal incentives. An accessible survey of the literature on incentives applied to government is Tirole (1994), on whom part of this section draws. See also Holmstrom and Tirole (1989).

10. Reported in *Business Week,* December 6, 1993.

11. Reported in *The Economist,* January 28, 1995.

12. See, for example, Laffont and Tirole (1993) and Armstrong et al. (1994).

13. The annual salary of Goh Chok Tong, Singapore's prime minister, is $780,000, almost four times that of Bill Clinton. Starting annual salaries for cabinet ministers are $419,285 (over three times that of John Major), and are to be raised by 25 percent in 1995. Reported in *The Economist,* November 26, 1994.

14. The United Electric Workers (163,000 members) in the United States paid its top official $14,618 in 1972. Compare this with the head of the teamsters (2.5 million members) who earned $125,000, or the head of the National Maritime Union (36,000 members) who was paid $92,200. Reported in *Business Week,* August 18, 1972.

15. Mr. Gordon Foxley, a senior Defense Ministry official in Britain who was convicted for accepting over £2 million in bribes, earned £25,000 per year on a job that involved awarding multimillion-pound contracts for procuring supplies for the armed forces.

16. A large number of solved cases in corruption are related to audits following signs of unexpected wealth by public servants. An extraordinary case is the former police chief of Mexico City, who had a salary of US $1,000 a month had 1,200 servants in his house. As with many examples of Mexican corruption, the numbers sound at least one order of magnitude wrong. Reported in *The Economist,* April 7, 1984.

17. In the United Kingdom, members of Parliament are only required to declare which topics will present them with a conflict of interest. These declarations are included in the Register of the Members' Interest, and it has a very weak effect in preventing ethically dubious votes. Members of the House of Lords are not required to state their interests.

18. Note that when other responsibilities are given to the manager, like an investment decision as in Holmstrom and Ricart i Costa (1986), career concerns may give rise to inefficiencies.

19. The idea of posting a bond to deter malfeasance (which subsequently became known as the bonding critique to efficiency wages) was already noted in Becker and Stigler (1974). Note that firms entering contractual relationships with the state could be asked to post bonds that would be confiscated if the firm engaged in any wrongdoing. In fact, the relatively light punishment for firms found guilty of bribing public officials is one of the puzzles of corruption deterrence.

20. In a sense artists turned politicians, such as Ronald Reagan or Palito Ortega, are posting a bond (their popularity) when entering politics.

21. Exactly this conflict is present in the project for libel law reforms in Argentina known as the "gag law" (or *ley mordaza*).

22. A recent paper by Besley and Case (1995) provides a theoretical framework and empirical evidence in support of the view that vote-seeking and tax-setting are tied in together through the nexus of yardstick competition.

23. Admittedly, this sort of competition involves some duplication of costs.

24. Rose-Ackerman herself stressed the need for further research on this aspect of corruption when she stated that "the role of competitive pressures in preventing corruption may be an important aspect of a strategy to deter bribery of low-level officials, but requires a broad-based exploration of the impact of both organizational and market structure on the incentives for corruption facing both bureaucrats and their clients" (Rose-Ackerman 1988).

25. Notice that k may also lead to inaction, as when society does not build trading infrastructure or does not contribute to the solution of market imperfections that enable some agents to enjoy market power.

26. The effect of product market competition on managerial slack is theoretically ambiguous. Competition may improve incentives by providing comparative performance information, but may also reduce the value to the principal of inducing desired behavior from the agent. But see the varying findings of Hart (1983), Scharfstein (1988), Hermalin (1992), and especially Schmidt (1994).

27. Reputation, retraining, or moral costs can be counted in this category. The model would remain essentially the same if we assumed heterogeneity in terms of different outside options.

28. All variables are averages of their 1981–83 observations, except schooling that is the 1980 observation.

29. Vickers (1991) formalizes Walters argument and shows that the conditions under which a benevolent planner privatizing a state-owned company would choose to build a "bulwark against socialism" through giveaways in the form of underpricing of shares, are unlikely to be met in practice.

30. Thus we can distinguish two levels of corruption: diversion of funds for the benefit of a political group and diversion of funds for the politician himself. The idea of "stealing for the Crown" refers to the first, supposedly ethically less abject form of corruption. But note that because of corruption's secret nature we can't tell if everything goes to the Crown or the intermediary keeps a part.

31. See, for example, Levitt (1995).

32. Under the 1977 Foreign Corrupt Practices Act, American companies found guilty of bribing foreign officials are liable to a fine of US$1 million for each violation, and individuals are made liable to a fine of US$10,000 and five years in jail.

33. Reported in *Business Week,* December 6, 1993.

34. The rent-seeking literature has been surveyed extensively elsewhere (e.g. Tullock 1988 and see also the collection of papers in Buchanan et al. 1980). For an analysis of rent seeking within business firms and the organizational response see Milgrom and Roberts (1988) and Meyer, Milgrom, and Roberts (1992).

35. Integration or long-term contracts are the usual way to overcome the *holdup* problem (the tendency for a downstream firm to reduce asset-specific investments when there are few upstream firms).

36. We thank Amu Singh for referring us to this data.

37. We hasten to add that there is the theoretical possibility that this type of monopolistic competition models produces "too much variety" (e.g., see Dixit and Stiglitz 1977) in the absence of corruption, so that some corruption could, in principle, be welfare enhancing.

38. An indicator of such free riding may be given by voter turnout in national elections.

39. Examples of capitulation wages are sometimes observed in some African countries where tax inspectors, who meet some basic literacy standards, earn less than the minimum wage in the economy (see Besley and McLaren 1993). This passage from Macaulay's "Lord Clive," cited in Klitgaard (1988) is also relevant: "The salaries were too low to afford even those indulgences which are necessary to the health and comfort of Europetitis . . . it could not be suppose that men of even average abilities would consent to pass the best years of their lives in exile, tinder a burning sun, for no other consideration than those stinted wages. It had accordingly been understood, from a very early period, that the Company's agents were at liberty to enrich themselves by their private trade."

40. See Klitgaard (1988).

41. Loosely speaking, it acts like a ratchet effect.

42. If rent extraction where not a problem the regulator could use a pure fixed-price contract, so that there would be no point in misrepresenting costs.

43. Though the possibility of auditor-firm collusion reduces the power of the incentive scheme relative to the benevolent auditor situation.

44. Of course risk sharing is also a concern.

45. The practice of employment of civil servants in the industry they had contact while in office is usually called revolving doors, a practice that in the United States is restricted by the 1978 Ethics in Government Act. However, as Warren (1982) (cited in Laffont and Tirole 1993, ch. II) notes, "Conflict of interest laws are virtually impossible to enforce unless government employees agree not to violate them."

46. Armstrong et al. (1994) cite a study of electricity regulation in the United States by Joskow and Schmalensee (1986) who observe that "to our knowledge no state statute permits commissions directly to fine or subsidize utilities subject to their jurisdiction." They also note that regulators and industry might prefer transfers as an instrument of redistribution since they are less visible than high prices.

References

Ades, Alberto, and Rafael Di Tella. 1994a. National Champions and Corruption: Some Unpleasant Competitiveness Arithmetic. Oxford University. Mimeographed.

———. 1994b. The Determinants of Corruption. Oxford University. Mimeographed.

———. 1995. Competition and Corruption. Applied Economics Discussion Paper Series No 169. Oxford University.

Akerlof, George. 1983. Loyalty Filters. *American Economic Review* 73:54–63.

Amstein, Fred, and Kenneth Feigenbaum. 1967. Relationship of Three Motives to Choice in Prisoner's Dilemma. *Psychological Reports* (June 20), 751–55.

Andreoni, James. 1991. Reasonable Doubt and the Optimal Magnitude of Fines: Should the Penalty Fit the Crime. *Rand Journal of Economics* 22:385–95.

Andvig, Jeans Christopher. 1991. The Economics of Corruption: A Survey. *Studi Economici* 43:57–94.

Andvig, Jeans Chistopher, and Karl Moene. 1990. How Corruption May Corrupt. *Journal of Economic Behavior and Organization* 13:63–76.

Armstrong, Mark, Simon Cowan, and John Vickers. 1994. *Regulatory Reform: Economic Analysis and British Experience.* Cambridge: MIT Press.

Baron, David. 1989. Service Induced Campaign Contributions and the Electoral Equilibrium. *Quarterly Journal of Economics* 104:45–72.

Barro, R. 1991. Economic Growth in a Cross-Section of Countries. *Quarterly Journal of Economics* 106:407–44.

Basu, Susanto, and David Li. 1994. Corruption and Reform. NBER Working Paper.

Becker, Gary. 1968. Crime and Punishment: An Economic Approach. *Journal of Political Economy* 76:169–217.

———. 1983. A Theory of Competition among Pressure Groups for Political Influence. *Quarterly Journal of Economics* 98:371–400.

Becker, Gary, and George Stigler. 1974. Law Enforcement, Malfeasance, and the Compensation of Enforcers. *Journal of Legal Studies* 3(1):1–19.

Besley, Timothy, and John McLaren. 1993. Taxes and Bribery: The Role of Wage Incentives. *The Economic Journal,* forthcoming.

Besley, Timothy, and Anne Case. 1995. Incumbent Behavior: Vote-Seeking, Tax-Setting, and Yardstick Competition. *American Economic Review* 85, no. 1.

Bologna, Jack. 1978. *Corporate Fraud: The Basics of Detection and Prevention.* Buttleworths Publishers.

Braithwaite, John. 1984. *Corporate Crime in the Pharmaceutical Industry.* Routledge & Kegan.

Buchanan, J., R. Tollison, and G. Tullock, eds. 1980. *Toward a Theory of the Rent-Seeking Society.* College Station: Texas A&M University Press.

Calvo, Guillermo, and S. Wellisz. 1978. Supervision, Loss of Control, and the Optimum Size of the Firm. *Journal of Political Economy* 86, no. 5:943–52.

———. 1979. Hierarchy, Ability, and Income Distribution. *Journal of Political Economy* 87, no. 5:991–1010.

Fama, Eugene. 1980. Agency Problems and the Theory of the Firm. *Journal of Political Economy* 88:288–307.

Felli, Leonardo. 1992. Collusion in Incentive Contracts: Does Delegation Help? London School of Economics. Mimeographed.

Gastil, R. 1997. *Freedom in the World.* Westport: Greenwood Press.

Goel, R., and D. Rich. 1989. On the Economic Incentives for Taking Bribes. *Public Choice* 61:269–75.

Green, J., and N. Stokey. 1983. A Comparison of Tournaments and Contracts. *Journal of Political Economy* 91:349–64.

Harris, M., and A. Raviv. 1978. Some Results on Incentive Contracts with Applications to Education and Employment, Health Insurance, and Law Enforcement. *American Economic Review* 68:20–30.

Hart, Oliver. 1983. The Market as an Incentive Scheme. *Bell Journal of Economics* 14, no. 2.

Hart, Oliver, and Bengt Holmstrom. 1987. The Theory of Contracts. In *Advances in Economic Theory,* edited by T. Bewley. Cambridge University Press.

Hermalin, Benjamin E. 1992. The Effects of Competition on Executive Behavior. *Rand Journal of Economics* 23, no. 3.

Hines, James. 1995. Forbidden Payments: Foreign Bribery and American Business after 1977. Harvard. Mimeographed.

Hollinger, R., and J. Clark. 1983. *Employee Theft.* Lexington: University of Kentucky Press.

Holmstrom, Bengt. 1982. Managerial Incentive Problems: A Dynamic Perspective. In *Essays in Economics and Management in Honour of Lars Wahlbeck.* Helsinki: Swedish School of Economics.

Holmstrom, Bengt, and Jean Tirole. 1989. The Theory of the Firm. In *Handbook of Industrial Organization,* edited by R. Schmalensee and R. Willig. Amsterdam: North Holland.

Holmstrom, Bengt, and J. Ricart i Costa. 1986. Managerial Incentives and Capital Management. *Quarterly Journal of Economics* 101:835–60.

Klitgaard, Robert. 1988. *Controlling Corruption.* University of California Press.

Koffman, F., and Lawarree, J. Collusion in Hierarchical Agency. Sloan School of Management, MIT Mimeographed. *Econometrica,* forthcoming.

Laffont, Jean Jacques, and Jean Tirole. 1991. The Politics of Government Decision-Making: A Theory of Regulatory Capture. *Quarterly Journal of Economics* 106:1089–127.

———. 1993. *A Theory of Incentives in Procurement and Regulation.* MIT Press.

Lazear, Edward, and Sherwin Rosen. 1981. Rank Order Tournaments as Optimal Labor Contracts. *Journal of Political Economy* 89:841–64.

Leff, Nathaniel. 1964. Economic Development through Bureaucratic Corruption. *American Behavioral Scientist* 8–14.

Levitt, Steven. 1995. Congressional Campaign Finance Reform. *Journal of Economic Perspectives* 9, no. 1:183–93.

Lui, F.T. 1985. An Equilibrium Queuing Model of Bribery. *Journal of Political Economy* 93:760–81.

———. 1986. A Dynamic Model of Corruption Deterrence. *Journal of Public Economics* 31:215–36.

Mauro, Paolo. 1994. The Composition of Government Expenditure: The Good Guys and the Bad Guys. Harvard University. Mimeographed.

———. 1995. Corruption, Country Risk, and Growth. Harvard. Mimeographed. *Quarterly Journal of Economics.*

McCormick, R., and R. Tollison. 1978. Legislatures as Unions. *Journal of Political Economy* 86, no. 1.

———. 1984. Crime on the Court. *Journal of Political Economy* 92, no. 2.

Milgrom, Paul, and John Roberts. 1988. An Economic Approach to Influence Activities in Organizations. *American Journal of Sociology* 94:S154–S179.

———. 1992. *Economic Organization and Management.* Prentice-Hall.

Mookherjee, Dilip. 1984. Optimal Incentive Schemes with Many Agents. *Review of Economic Studies* 51:433–46.

Mookherjee, Dilip, and Ivan Png. 1987. Optimal Auditing, Insurance, and Redistribution. *Quarterly Journal of Economics* 399–415.

———. 1991. Corruptible Enforcers of Incentives: How Should They be Compensated. UCLA Working Paper 90-23.

———. 1992. Monitoring vis-à-vis Investigation in Enforcement of Law. *American Economic Review* 82, no. 3:556–65.

Moore, John. 1992. Implementation, Contracts, and Renegotiation in Environments with Complete Information. In *Advances in Economic Theory: Sixth World Congress,* edited by Jean-Jacques Laffont, Vol. 1.

Myrdal, Gunnar. 1968. *Asian Drama: An Inquiry into the Poverty of Nations.* Vol. 2. New York: Pantheon.

Nordhaus, W. 1975. The Political Business Cycle. *Review of Economic Studies* 42:169–90.

Palmier, L. 1983. Bureaucratic Corruption and Its Remedies. In *Corruption: Causes, Consequences, and Control,* edited by Michael Clarke. New York: St. Martin's Press.

Peltzman, Sam. 1976. Towards a More General Theory of Regulation. *Journal of Law and Economics* 19:211–40.

Rogerson, William. 1994. Economic Incentives and the Defense Procurement Process. *Journal of Economic Perspectives* 8, no. 4:65–90.

Romer, Paul. 1994. New Goods and New Trade Theory. *Journal of Development Economics* 1–22.

Rose-Ackerman, Susan. 1975. The Economics of Corruption. *Journal of Public Economics* 4, no. 2:187–203.

———. 1978. *Corruption: A Study in Political Economy.* New York: Academic Press.

———. 1988. Bribery. In *The New Palgrave: A Dictionary of Economics,* edited by J. Eatwell, M. Milgate, and P. Newman. Stockton Press (softcover edition).

Salant, D. 1991. Behind the Revolving Door: A New View of Public Utility Regulation. Boston University. Mimeographed.

Scharfstein, D. 1988. Product Market Competition and Managerial Slack. *Rand Journal of Economics* 19:147–55.

Schmidt, Klaus M. 1994. Managerial Incentives and Product Market Competition. University of Bonn Working Paper.

Shapiro, C., and J. Stiglitz. 1984. Involuntary Unemployment as Worker Discipline Device. *American Economic Review* 74, no. 3:433–44.

Shleifer, Andrei, and Robert Vishny. 1993. Corruption. *Quarterly Journal of Economics* 599–617.

Stigler, George. 1970. The Optimum Enforcement of Laws. *Journal of Political Economy* 78:526–36.

———. 1971. The Economic Theory of Regulation. *Bell Journal of Economics* 2:3–21.

Stiglitz, J. 1986. *The Economics of the Public Sector*. Prentice-Hall.

Spiller, Pablo. 1990. Politicians, Interest Groups, and Regulators: A Multiple-Principals Agency Theory of Regulation (or "Let Them Be Bribed"). *Journal of Law and Economics* 33:65–101.

Summers, Robert, and A. Heston. 1991. The Penn World Table (Mark 5): An Expanded Set of International Comparisons, 1950–1988. *Quarterly Journal of Economics* 106: 327–68.

Tirole, Jean. 1986. Hierarchies and Bureaucracies: On the Role of Collusion in Organizations. *Journal of Law, Economics, and Organization* 2:181–214.

———. 1992. Collusion and the Theory of Organizations. In *Advances in Economic Theory: Sixth World Congress*, edited by Jean-Jacques Laffont, Vol. 2.

———. 1993. A Theory of Collective Reputations. Toulouse. Mimeographed.

———. 1994. The Internal Organization of Government. *Oxford Economic Papers*, 1–29.

Tullock, Gordon. 1967. The Welfare Costs of Tariffs, Monopolies, and Theft. *Western Economic Journal* (now *Economic Enquiry*) 5:224–32.

———. 1988. Rent Seeking. In *The New Palgrave: A Dictionary of Economics*, edited by J. Eatwell, M. Milgate, and P. Newman.

Vickers, John. 1991. Privatization and the Risk of Expropriation. Oxford University. Mimeographed.

Vickers, John, and George Yarrow. 1988. *Privatization: An Economic Analysis*. MIT Press.

Walters, Alan. 1988. Arguing with Success, without Success. *Regulation* no. 3:66–68.

2

Structural Corruption and Normative Systems: The Role of Integrity Pacts

LUIS MORENO OCAMPO[1]

Introduction

Corruption is an act in contradiction with the law.[2] Nevertheless, at the turn of the twentieth century, the laws of each nation are not the only rules that govern the behavior of their citizens. In this sense, corruption is a phenomenon licensed, eventually promoted, and stimulated by other normative systems[3] of formal and informal, public and private, domestic and international rules that coexist with prohibitive laws.

Therefore, in certain contexts criminal prosecution is not a sufficient remedy to reestablish the effective enforcement of the law. For example, the investigations promoted by the magistrates in Milan, Italy, since 1992, known as *Mani Pulite* (clean hands), represent the most recent case of successful judicial action against structural corruption. More than two thousand people (including ninety members of Congress, six ex-prime ministers, and the general secretaries of all political parties) were prosecuted and four hundred have already been convicted. However, different observers, even the judges themselves, agree that corruption in Italy has not decreased as expected.[4]

Exclusively focusing on criminal law disregards the fundamental fact that we live and act under manifold complex rules. In light of the objective of restraining the phenomenon of structural corruption, it is more de-

cisive to alter the incentives created by these multiple rules than to punish the offenders through the extant legal institutions.

In this chapter we will address the perspective of multiple standards as
an analytic tool, helpful in understanding structural corruption and in designing policies oriented to restrain corrupt practices. For these purposes,
the case of worldwide operations of multinational companies serves as an
interesting example of how these multiple normative standards operate.
Similarly, the Integrity Pacts, a mechanism promoted by Transparency
International, is explored as an option based on the recognition of such
complexities.

This chapter has been organized as follows: In the first part I consider
what has been the traditional approach to corruption. In the second part
I address the limitations of the traditional analytic approaches and present
the perspective of multiple standards. Along the way, I will use Argentina
to exemplify many of my arguments since it is the country that I know
best. In the third part I explore the option of Integrity Pacts prior to some
concluding remarks.

I. The Traditional Approach to Corruption
Control and Analysis

Traditionally, the legal perspective on corruption has been based on the
consideration of domestic normative systems, comprising both formal rules
and judicial decisions based on specific cases. Under this approach, the objective of controlling corruption is accomplished by sanctioning new and
stricter laws and forcing a greater compliance with the existing ones.[5]

This definition of the problem assumes the existence of institutions
with the capacity to establish legal duties and control mechanisms. This
assumption is based on the erroneous idea that there is a universal legal
duty not to receive bribes. It does not take into account the fact that the
development of communication has allowed businesses to operate in an
international jurisdiction that lacks both norms that prohibit bribery and
an authority to control the honesty of the transactions. As international
laws do not prohibit bribery, the only legal mechanisms left to restrain
corruption are the domestic normative systems of each country. Nevertheless, these norms vary from one nation to another; as we will further
demonstrate, some provide incentives (i.e., through tax exemptions) to
undertake corrupt practices abroad. These differences among normative
systems make it difficult to use domestic laws to fill the absence of international laws in transnational markets.

Moreover, the traditional legal approach is useful as a means of predicting or controlling society's conduct only under the operation of the following assumptions that pertain to the existence and validity of legal norms:

1. The state monopolizes the power to issue binding norms within its jurisdiction.
2. The state's power is legitimate as it is based on democratic institutions.
3. There is a high degree of compliance with these norms.
4. There is a high probability of punishment to the transgressors.

Unfortunately, only in the domestic jurisdictions of most developed countries do these assumptions appear to be realistic. Nevertheless, legal analysis originating in these countries often tends to extrapolate the circumstances in which they live to the rest of the world without acknowledging crucial differences.

In fact, this traditional legal analysis does not consider that a wide majority of the world's population complies with contracts under conditions that are completely different. Divergent normative systems coexist: some issued by dictators, military interventions, and other nondemocratic means; others, based on the custom to respect power without any foundation in the formal normative systems, and so on.

Moreover, these assumptions are often made within contexts of democratic institutions that create legitimate spaces suitable for promoting transparency. In fact, an overview of the way in which power and societies are organized around the world shows that most of them respond to a different reality. According to Freedom House:[6]

Only 19.5 percent of the population lives in a free society and have a wide range of civil and political rights, including a reasonable public administration, representative legislation, and a reasonable level of compliance with the law.

41.5 percent of the population lives in partially free societies in which there are certain restrictions such as "consequences for practicing insurgencies, political terrorism, and rampant corruption."

39 percent of the world's population lives in not-free societies.

As a consequence, 80 percent of the population does not have legitimate authorities to turn to; legitimate laws to respect; or a context of freedom, transparency, and good governance. These facts alter the fundamental assumptions of the legal approach and suggest that corruption is not an exception in an institutional environment.

II. The Traditional Approach Revisited: Multistandard Systems in the Global Economy

A. Definition and Characteristics: What the Traditional Approach Ignores

Multiple standards refers to the various sets of rules and norms that simultaneously govern a specific situation. By acknowledging its inherent complexities, the multistandard approach goes beyond the limitations of the traditional legal perspective and questions the analysis and policy based on the assumption of the existence of a single source that monopolizes the power to establish rules and norms. As we will see, these multiple standards differ not only in kind but also in substance and can even be contradictory. The multiplicity of standards and their contradiction, moreover, makes it difficult for individuals to comply with a single rule or to anticipate a predictable punishment. In the end, all the assumptions that support the traditional approach are questionable. In the following paragraphs I will explore how multiple standards emerge and operate.

1. Mythical Rules and Operational Codes

The actual validity of the assumptions that support the legal approach has been strongly refuted by Michael Reisman. In his book *Folded Lies: Bribery, Crusades, and Reforms*, Reisman holds that every normative system is composed of a formal subsystem of rules, which he calls *mythical norms*, and a number of informal normative subsystems that he calls *operative codes*.

"In any social process," Reisman points out, "the observer can distinguish between a *mythical system*, clearly expressing all the rules and prohibitions ('permitted' and 'prohibited' behavior expressed without shades and ranges), and an *operative code* that indicates to the 'operators' when, how and by whom it is possible to do certain things notwithstanding the fact that they are prohibited by these rules."[7] With this argument he shows that certain acts that violate the law are not transgressions, but responses to other rules. He explains "there are two pertinent normative systems; one that is supposed to be applied and that the elite profess they follow, and the other that they apply in reality. None of them must be confused with actual behavior which can contradict both."[8]

Reisman clarifies how "The mythical system does not express caducous values, it reinforces those values that continue to be personally and socially important." However, "a large segment of the formal law, which the members of the community still regard as law and are not willing to neglect, will not only be enforced vigorously and efficiently, but its violation will be accepted as the way things are done. The cynic who takes pleasure in his nihilist exercises would say that there is no law. But from an observer's point of view, parts of the mythical system and the operational codes make up the law of the community."

An analysis of what happens in Argentine schools demonstrates the particularities of multiple standards. Despite the fact that there is a rule that forbids cheating during exams, there is an operational code between the students that authorizes and even forces students to copy or accept someone copying from them. In different experiments with high school students, it has been proven that the majority of students cheat, those who do not cheat are ridiculed by their classmates, and that they all consider cheating a duty of camaraderie. A group of students were asked what would happen if a student would not let someone copy from them and one of the students responded: "How can he do that? There is a morality, isn't there?"

Although this is informal, the rule that demands the students cheat is so strong that it lets the students claim it as a right as well as an obligation. However, the existence of this operational code does not supersede the mythical prohibition. If a teacher catches one student cheating, the student cannot claim that he has a right to copy; he knows that there is a sanction in the mythical norm. The informal system reverts to the formal system. The student can demand mercy but does not have the right to ask for impunity.

Those who obey the operative code and violate the mythical norm should act discretely. One of the basic operative codes is not to talk about them or about the conduct they authorize. When the facts are disclosed and brought to light, it is the very operative code that establishes that the mythical norm must be applied.

Rules and norms of behavior are not derived exclusively from formal sources (Congress, authority, etc.) but are also generated from the group, for the group. Any organization then faces formal and informal references that are not necessarily consistent.

Argentina is a good example of this because of its characteristics relative to other countries. The size of Argentina's gross domestic product is seventeenth in the world, above Switzerland, Belgium, Austria, Sweden, Denmark, South Africa, Norway, Finland, and Israel.[9] According to Freedom House, Argentina is one of the privileged "free" countries; Argentines belong to that 19 percent of the world's population with the best democratic conditions. Transparency International's Corruption Perceptions Index places Argentina at thirty-five out of fifty-four countries, meaning Argentina is relatively corrupt. In the Western hemisphere, however, only Canada (5th), the United States (15th), and Chile (21st) rank higher or less corrupt. Bolivia (36th), Mexico (38th), Ecuador (39th), Brazil (40th), Colombia (42nd), and Venezuela (48th) rank lower or more corrupt.

We can use the Argentine case to show the pervasiveness of operative codes (under which bribery is the rule) running parallel to legal prohibitive mandates. The following empirical data shows that bribery payments in Argentina are widespread. It supports the idea that such behavior is the result of the enactment of operational codes, rather than the transgression of mythical norms.

According to a Gallup Argentina survey undertaken in September 1996, 97 percent of the public in the capital and in greater Buenos Aires felt that the level of corruption in Argentina is high or very high. Only 2 percent stated low or very low.[10]

In 1992, a Gallup Argentina survey performed in the same regions for the local foundation Citizen Power asked if there was corruption in different groups. The results show that in the public's perception, corruption exists in Argentina—91 percent of those surveyed said that there were many cases of corruption among politicians, 88 percent felt similarly toward public officials, and 79 percent expressed this attitude toward businesspeople.

The accuracy of these perceptions was confirmed by another study performed by Gallup Argentina for Egon Zehnder[11] International, a worldwide headhunting company. A different question was asked this time. The top 111 businesspeople in Argentina, those who best know the dealings of Argentine business, were asked if it was common for companies to bribe members of the government or public managers in exchange for favors. Eighty-seven percent of the people surveyed indicated that some or most companies bribe public officials. This percentage is significantly higher than that obtained in the other survey about the perception of corruption in the group of businesspeople.

Despite the widespread occurrence of bribery, there is no legal precedence of a conviction for such action. This is despite the fact that the criminal code carries a jail sentence of six months to six years for "those who directly or indirectly give or offer gifts to a public official" and a similar consequence to the public official who "directly or indirectly receives money or any other gift or accepts any promise, directly or indirectly, in order to do or avoid doing something proper of his duties."[12] That is to say that the probability of a businessperson being punished for this type of crime is extremely low.

The survey data demonstrates how in Argentina, a country that ranks high in democratic conditions, the assumptions that support the traditional legal approach are unfulfilled: there is not a high degree of compliance with the norms, nor a high probability of punishment for the violators. Moreover, the surveys underscore the pervasiveness of operational codes that consider corruption as a common, widespread practice.

Despite the fact that the formal system provides prohibitions for paying bribes, there is a system of informal rules within society that allows bribery as a way to resolve conflicts with the state. We should not forget that the incidence of bribery in Argentina is equal to or less than that of the large majority of the developing countries according to Transparency International's Corruption Perception's Index and the analysis done by Freedom House.

2. The Absence of International Prohibitions against Bribery

In addition to the implicit existence of multiple standards embedded in mythical and operational codes, there are also multiple standards within formal normative systems. Such is the case with the international normative system, first, because there is no international prohibition for bribery, and second, because the existing normative systems among nations are different and often contradictory regarding foreign corrupt practices.

Legal expert studies of corruption assume the existence of valid norms in which the prohibition to offer, pay, arrange, or receive bribes is established, but do not acknowledge that these norms do not exist in the international arena. Bribery is not punished by international laws. In this way, bribes constitute internal problems outside the scope of international norms despite having international relevance.

However, there have been some steps taken over the past few years to change this situation. The Organization of American States (OAS) is the first regional organization to sign a convention for this purpose. The Inter-American Convention Against Corruption was sanctioned by the general assembly of the OAS in 1996. The convention was signed by twenty-three member countries, but to date has only been ratified by three (Paraguay, Peru, and Bolivia), limiting the magnitude of this first attempt. As of today, there is no binding international norm that prohibits the payment of bribes.

The United Nations has taken into consideration this regional initiative and has recently incorporated this idea into their recommendations. In an expert group meeting on corruption in March of 1997 held in Buenos Aires, they made the following recommendation: "Making corruption and bribery of foreign officials a criminal offense is extremely important in a consolidated international effort against corruption. States are urged to review their legislation and establish that offense or, as appropriate, to pursue effective enforcement of existing laws prohibiting bribery in international commercial transactions."[13]

For economic and efficiency reasons, the authorities from international financial institutions, such as the World Bank, the International Monetary Fund (IMF), and the Inter-American Development Bank (IDB) are demanding changes. The president of the IDB, Enrique Iglesias, stated in an inaugural speech: "There are still obstacles that limit the strategy of development by its potential to impede the consolidation of a political, institutional, and normative environment that promotes savings, investment, and economic growth. . . . Corruption already constitutes one of the largest obstacles to the success of a development strategy."[14]

James Wolfensohn, president of the World Bank, stated the importance of combating: ". . . the cancer of corruption. The abuse of public power through corruption, today, is a serious obstacle for the process of social and economic development in many countries. Corruption weakens the public's confidence in government, producing deep social and political tension. It diverts the resources to the rich, which should go to the poorer and underprivileged groups. It distorts the democratic system based on the rule of law, allowing wretched prevalent individual interests to override the common good."[15]

The need to restrain corruption is acknowledged worldwide, but there has been no decisive international response. It is perhaps a map of differing interests, as we will show below, what explains the difficulties of building consensus on this issue.

3. Domestic Normative Systems

So far we have seen that international businesses operate without an international normative system that condemns bribery. Can we overcome this difficulty through the application of domestic normative systems? In the following paragraphs I will show why the answer to this question, unfortunately, is negative.

Although the normative systems of developed countries work well within their own territory, when dealing with international trade these norms are aggravated. There are contradictions between the formal normative systems of different countries. For example, the act of bribing a public official in Argentina would be considered differently according to the laws of different countries. It could be

1. prohibited by Argentine criminal law
2. prohibited by law in the United States under certain circumstances
3. prohibited in the United Kingdom
4. permitted in Japan, Ireland, Italy and Portugal
5. permitted and tax deductible in:
   a. Finland, Norway, and Sweden if the bribe is deemed a "normal commercial practice" in Argentina. It is similar in Denmark as long as the person who received the bribe is identified;
   b. Canada, subject to the twofold condition that the petition of the bribe does not involve anyone operating in Canadian territory and the person who receives the bribe is identified;
   c. Australia, France, Ireland, Spain, New Zealand, and Switzerland if the person who received the bribe is identified;
   d. Austria, Belgium, Germany, Greece, Luxembourg, and Holland even if the person who received the bribe is not identified.[16]

International business has developed more quickly than international institutions. Each and every nation in the world has its own particular interests, some of which can restrict its activities against corruption. For example, economically developed democratic countries may find their moral goals contradictory with their interest in boosting exports, maximizing profits, and promoting social welfare. As the German minister of economy has put it: "There are fluid definitions between grease payments and well-deserved commissions. If others pay grease money and commission, but the Germans don't, then I have to accept the justified criticism that we jeopardize jobs, that we are preaching morality, while possibly committing a mistake, and others get the contracts."[17]

Many U.S. companies feel that the Foreign Corrupt Practices Act forces them to compete with an inherent disadvantage.[18] On the other hand, the ruling political parties in developing countries receive the benefits of bribery in large public businesses and have no interest in changing the situation. These examples of differing interests can help explain why there is no international legal mandate with a worldwide reach qualifying the payment of bribes as an international crime, in the same fashion as genocide, or other crimes against humanity.

The Organization for Economic Cooperation and Development (OECD) has asked its members to control this situation by reviewing or reforming some domestic norms.[19] Among the areas for suggested revision were: criminal laws and their application; aspects of public management regarding the bribery of foreign public officials; and tax legislation, regulation, and practices. The recommendations also envisage active collaboration between OECD members and nonmember states as a necessary part of the strategy.[20] However, despite these initiatives, this situation shows how limited the influence of the OECD has been over its nation members on this particular point.

It is shown above that the formal normative systems differ among countries. There are also differing interests between the developing and the developed world, especially exporting economies. There are no international laws against bribery; however, we do find private norms existing within organizations, especially multinationals, that have practical priority over the norms of the country in which these organizations operate. These arguments reinforce the existence of multiple standards at different levels: formal and informal, explicit and implicit, public and private.

The reality of multiple standards makes it impossible to think that the application of domestic normative systems will substitute in the absence of international mandates. Within a context of multiple standards, domestic normative systems only enlarge such multiplicity. However, the precarious nature of the majority of the domestic normative systems limit the extent to which they can be effective in the attempt of corruption control.

4. Private Normative Systems

The modern economy is marked by globalization and the operation of multinational corporations all over the world. The existence of companies that simultaneously act in different countries connects the contradictory public normative systems described above. Those countries with systems that allow or give incentives to pay bribes to foreign officials implicitly authorize private-sector managers to validly order their employees to pay bribes abroad even in a country where such behavior is prohibited. This brings into question the legal monopoly of the foreign state when they act in defiance of domestic norms.

The above situation underscores how those who operate within an organization are subject to a web of private rules, both formal and informal, which claim obedience beyond the prescriptions of the law. It is possible to identify a triad of factors that together establish the preeminence of private over public rules. They are a strong commitment to the organization, a dispositional attitude of respect to the immediate authority, and the distortion of the probability of being punished for actions related to the company's businesses. The case presented below will generously illustrate this point.

5. A Case on Multiple Standards

The following imaginary case is based on real norms and is helpful in illustrating the phenomenon of multiple standards to which I am referring.

The president of a German company with headquarters in Munich is interested in winning a contract with the Argentine government to sell fifteen thousand tons of dehydrated milk to feed public school children between the ages of six and twelve. This contract would allow the company to meet the projected sales for the year and maintain its factories at full employment. To assure the company's success, the president sent one of its youngest and brightest executives to manage the project in Argentina.

Worried about some of the stories in the newspapers concerning corruption in Argentina, the young executive visits the headquarters of Transparency International in Berlin before traveling to Buenos Aires. They inform him that in their Corruption Perceptions Index Argentina is measured as relatively corrupt.

In Buenos Aires, the young executive finds the front pages of the newspapers covered with corruption scandals involving very high government officials, police involved in drug trafficking, and federal judges protecting delinquents. He also finds several surveys from Gallup Argentina supporting his findings. In some old files, he finds that a few years before, the Argentine government bought milk not fit for human consumption at a higher price than that of his company, which offers a top quality product. He also finds out that a French company that competes with the firm he represents has submitted a proposal less competitive than his own but has offered to return a bribe to procure the transaction. Moreover, three other competing Argentine firms have offered bribe payments. Worried about the success of his mission and his personal future he sends all of this information to the president of the company in Germany.

Two weeks later, the president presents the report to the board of directors, along with the analysis of the company's legal department. The legal expert explains that there are no international norms that prohibit bribery, that the German laws allow bribery and admit that it can be tax deductible as a "useful expense," and that although Argentine norms prohibit bribery, it is not a valid argument because it has no enforcement. He adds that further analysis shows it is probable that the Argentine companies will offer bribes and that a French competitor, which shares the same legislation as Germany, will bribe if necessary.

In the board meeting, opinions are divided. A majority supports the payment of a bribe, but the president and one of the board members oppose the idea, stating that it is inadmissible and should not even be discussed. However, the majority present five reasons why they feel it is valid to pay the bribe:

1. Their participation in this contract is vital to the company's economic success this year.
2. The contract will allow the company to keep the 200 workers in Munich employed.
3. The company cannot change the situation in Argentina and the only option it perceives is to accept such reality.
4. They cannot compete against other offers supported by bribes.
5. Their top-quality product would build a healthy diet for the Argentine children.

The president calls the young executive and tells him that the board of directors has given the order for him to find the way to pay any bribe necessary to assure the company's success in the deal.

If we analyze the young executive's dilemma, we see that he is submitted to multiple normative systems, which produce different results. These different normative systems vary from the formal and informal public norms to the formal and informal, explicit and implicit company rules. But it seems to be the company rules, which although they have no value to a judge, do have the strongest claim to obedience by the actors.

The orders coming from the company's headquarters connect not only the normative systems of the different countries but also the private company's own norms. The rules established by the company's hierarchy demand the executive in Argentina to obey the president in Germany. Both receive the mandate from the entire organization, with one end: maximize benefits. Certain informal codes, such as loyalty to the group, demand silence by the other members of the group. In turn, this generates a process by which the operative code reinforces itself.

As we have seen, the multiplicity of standards proceeds from a diversity of sources. Among them we can list international and domestic norms, public and private rules, and mythical and operative codes. In the end, the picture is more complex than that described by the traditional legal approach.

B. The Implications of Multiple Standards
and the Role of Normative Systems

It has been shown how the normative systems within certain societies[21] are complex, comprising rules at different levels. These rules coexist with the legal system and often contradict it, for example, authorizing and promoting bribery.

In order to examine the problem of corruption with a view to advance an effective control policy, it is essential to identify and acknowledge the coexistence of the various normative systems, which legal theorists usually take as their baseline, along with other operative codes.

The multistandard approach requires the identification not only of the diverse systems of rules, but also of the different actors. The simple procedure of incarcerating corrupt leaders does not ensure that incentives or the structure previously established by the operative codes will be modified. The imprisonment of a manager who promotes or authorizes corrupt actions within his company may represent nothing more than a measure allowing his successor to benefit from the same profits with no change in the operational codes that allowed such behavior.

The aim of the analysis we have presented is not to disqualify the role of law enforcement and judicial investigations as means to attack the phenomenon of corruption. On the contrary, some criminal law theories reveal the importance of judicial pronouncements as a reaffirmation of the intersubjective values that are recognized within the society in question.[22] In this sense, the judges and magistrates have a role as guardians of the mythical system. Nevertheless, the loss of the ethical guide offered by mythical norms in a world of multiple standards must be recognized as it is highly disturbing. Criminal punishment for proven misconduct does not definitely establish the preeminence of the mythical norm that the criminal law embodies, as such conduct may even be perceived by the violator as a foreseen consequence and allowed by other systems of rules that interact in the case. As Michael Reisman holds,[23] one of the characteristics of operative codes is the self-referential prescription of their own secrecy and of those conducts that they authorize. Eventually, when the secret is broken, the very operative codes remit to the mythical system. Therefore it is essential to understand that the application of a criminal sanction in a case of bribery may confirm the efficacy of either the criminal law or some other operative system.

In this sense, criminal punishment will only represent a vehicle of change if it appears as the necessary correlate of significant preventive machinery. This fundamental fact must lead to a radical turn in the normative analysis customarily applied to the problem. The traditional approach, which uses ex post facto analysis as a method, gets insufficient results. The focus must shift to the prior examination of the various formal and informal norms, mythical and operative codes, which rule the organization. Within this view, the heads of public and private organizations become the principal change agents. Their leadership comprises a process of awareness on the existence of the operative codes. Their challenge, furthermore, involves the creation of learning processes within their organizations that will modify such codes in order to transform the complex behavior of those who use them as a shelter and a reference point.

III. Options for Taking Action: Integrity Pacts

The interaction of multiple standards generates a limited effect of law enforcement on structural corruption. One avenue to restrain corruption effectively lies in narrowing the disparities between mythical norms and operational codes. The option of creating *Integrity Pacts* (also known as *Islands of Integrity*) are targeted at this aim, as will be explained further.

A. What Are Integrity Pacts?

Transparency International[24] has elaborated a strategy to confront the phenomenon of corruption in international business: the Integrity Pacts. They consist of a specific agreement between the government setting up a public contract and the companies participating in the bid. The government assures transparency in designing the list of conditions and in the process of awarding the contract. It also guarantees that none of its public officials will demand an improper advantage. The participating companies promise not to offer bribes and to denounce any employees who attempt to extort them or their competitors.

The intention is to enable companies to stop bribery by providing assurance that their competitors will also refrain from bribing and to enable governments to reduce the high cost and distortionary impact of corruption on public sector procurements. From this perspective, the Integrity Pacts are not based on mere ethical wishes as they attack the structure of incentives that induce competing parties to bribe. Moreover, they create webs that support and spread transparent behavior.

In essence, these commitments are nothing other than a compromise to respect the existing laws of the country. In this sense, they complement legal mandates, introducing some kind of partial redundancy that contributes to the efficiency of both systems. Within a context of multiple standards, this mechanism provides a set of clear, homogeneous, shared rules on the basis that enforcement is guaranteed. The concept is to have a special program where the procedures and accounting are so transparent that they build commercial confidence in the integrity of the process.

B. How Do the Integrity Pacts Work?

When inviting contractors or suppliers of goods to bid for a specific contract, a government or government agency informs the potential bidders that their offer must contain a commitment signed personally by the bidder's chief executive officer not to offer or pay bribes within the context of the contract. The government commits itself to preventing extortion and the acceptance of bribes by its officials.

The companies promise not to offer or pay bribes or any other form of inducement to any public official in connection with their bids; they promise not to permit anyone (whether employee or independent commission agent) to do so on their behalf; in their bids, they promise to make full disclosure of the beneficiaries of payments relating to the bid (both already made and those proposed to be made in the event of the bid being successful) if those payments are directed to any person other than an employee of the corporation but excluding any bonus payments that may be made to employees (such disclosures being made under terms of commercial confidentiality if the corporation so requires); they also promise to formally issue orders and guidelines to all their employees and agents in order for them to comply with the law and the agreement, particularly not offering or paying bribes or other corrupt inducements to officials (whether directly or indirectly).

Through the commitment, the parties involved submit themselves to a set of sanctions in the case of violation. The sanctions may include loss of contract, liability for damages (to the government and the competing bidders), forfeiture of the bid security, and debarment of the offenders by the government for an appropriate period of time.

Supervision and control of the pact is one of the necessary ingredients for its success. While the structure of the pact generates incentives for each party to monitor and control each other, the intervention of a third neutral party is important to ensure the fulfillment of the accord, and especially to monitor the public sector party's compliance. This role could be assigned to an organization with the international support that would assure neutrality.

One desirable effect of these Integrity Pacts would be their widespread use in different countries and the resulting generation of agreements of reciprocity. Sanctions could then be extended to prohibit violators from undertaking business with other governments, thus, increasing the consequences for companies that engage in corrupt practices.

Furthermore, the Integrity Pacts are mechanisms that can also be applied to private bids, thus expanding the scope and range of desirable and transparent market practices.

Through these mechanisms, the Integrity Pact provides a clear normative system determined by a contract that regulates the rights and obligations of the participants and modifies the incentives to act corruptly. Each competitor will be aware that there are clear rules to the game based on clean competition and will be controlled by the other players. In this sense, the operative and mythical codes work together, and the mythical codes are presented as a set of homogeneous mandates.

This model helps break the complex scheme of political and economic interests found in societies where corruption is a structural phenomenon. It also allows for the creation of a new scheme of interests, in this case, in favor of integrity and transparency. The creation of Integrity Pacts, though a normative system established in accordance with the participants, confronts the problem of international businesses that are submitted to multiple normative systems and represents an initial step in designing and implementing realistic solutions.

IV. Concluding Remarks

The design of public policies directed to articulate preventive systems aimed at constraining structural corruption must account for the existence of the diverse normative systems as well as the conflicting sources of motivation that I have explored in this chapter. Beyond awareness, effective control policies pose the challenge of reducing the costs of acting in conformity with the law, as well as increasing the costs of operating outside it.

Clearly, the operative codes are founded on strategic reasons and, because of this, traditional moral disclosure will hardly be an adequate model to account for the effectiveness of such codes.

Finally, in order to deepen the understanding of multistandard normative systems and examine their bearing on other legal areas, it would be necessary to study the implications derived from two approaches not yet satisfactorily comprehended by legal theorists, namely the advances in the theory of communication and the studies on multiple interests devised by the theorists of negotiation, mediation, and group dynamics.

Notes

1. This chapter was translated by Andrea Goldbarg M.A. and Juanita Olaya M.A., who also contributed to the final revisions.

2. There are many definitions and meanings that can be attached to the word "corruption." By and large, it is approached as an act in contradiction with the law. It can also be understood as the set of conducts characterized as such by the criminal codes or as the behavior of some public officers that depart from their legal duties on behalf of their private interest. Aside from the subjects involved, a more general meaning would comprise the behavior that damages the public interest, where the benefit obtained or the conduct leading to it is not legitimate and is guarded by secrecy. For a discussion on the definitions of corruption see: Luis Moreno Ocampo, *En Defensa Propia. Cómo salir de la corrupción,* (Ed. Sudamericana, Buenos Aires, 1993).

3. I use the definition of normative systems introduced by Eugenio Bulgyin and Carlos E. Alchurron: ". . . a normative system is a set of sentences such that among its consequences there are some sentences which correlate cases with solutions. Every normative set which contains all its consequences will accordingly be called a normative system." In *Normative Systems* (New York: Springer-Verlag, 1971).

4. These data emerged as a result of the conversations I maintained with the public prosecutors Grecco and Colombo during their visit to Argentina. Cf. "Editorial del Puerto," *Pena y estado Journal* 1 (1995).

5. For a summary of the traditional perspectives on corruption see, for example, Rafael Di Tella and Alberto Ades, "The New Economics of Corruption: A Survey and Some New Results," *Political Studies* (1997).

6. Freedom House, *Freedom in the World, 1995–1996, The Annual Survey of Political Rights and Civil Liberties.* New York (1996).

7. The following quotations from W. Michael Reisman have been translated by the author from the Spanish edition of his book: *Remedios Contra la Corrupción? Cohecho, cruzadas y reformas,* Fondo de Cultura Económica, México (1981), p. 11

8. Ibid, p. 35.

9. The World Bank, "From Centralized Planning to a Market Economy. 1996 Report on World Development," Washington, D.C. (1996).

10. Similar results were obtained with another poll undertaken in 1991.

11. 1990, 03–05, Argentina.

12. Argentine Criminal Code, Articles 256 and 258.

13. United Nation's Expert Group Meeting on Corruption, Buenos Aires, March 17–21, 1997.

14. Message from the president of the Inter-American Development Bank, Montevideo, Uruguay, November 6, 1995.

15. Speech by James D. Wolfensohn, president of the World Bank, at the Annual Assembly, October 1, 1996. Translated by the author from the Spanish version of "Boletin del Banco Mundial, Mision Residente en Argentina," December (1996).

16. These data—unpublished to date—were discussed within the context of a study submitted by Michael Wiehen for Transparency International. The formal justification for the legislation in these countries was given during an OECD meeting. This organization released on May 27, 1994, a recommendation to member countries to make an effort against

international corruption and to adapt its formal legislation to criminalize bribery abroad and its deductibility from taxes. The formal arguments against this initiative were based on the extraterritoriality of criminal law and the respect for the cultures of different countries. The real justification is their interest in obtaining business and jobs for their companies located in these countries.

17. Günther Rexrodt, German minister of economics in German television ARD, Friday, January 13, 1995, as quoted in Transparency International Report, 1995.

18. Jill D. Rhodes, "The United States Foreign Corrupt Practices Act, The Effectiveness of a Unilateral Act," Operations Policy Department, The World Bank, Washington, D.C., October 1, 1995. The "FCPA" became a law twenty years ago and was ignored for a long time. Its major problems are that it is so broad that it "punishes some conduct that is hard to distinguish from ordinary and legal business transactions," and that, "what is illegal for U.S. companies is often legal or tax deductible if done by foreign companies" (http://www.tht.com/ClientBulletinForeignCorruptPracticesAct.htm).

19. OECD Recommendations on Bribes in International Business Transactions 1994, 1995, 1996.

20. National Integrity Systems, Transparency International Source Book, Berlin (1996), pp. 111–112.

21. Here we use the term societies and organizations interchangeably. By organizations we refer to any group bound together by a common purpose and, without loss of generality, we include societies as wider "organizations."

22. The theories of general positive prevention, or integration, ascribe to criminal punishment the positive function of reinforcing the citizen's allegiance to the established order, that is, the mythical norms. See for example, Luigi Ferrajoli. *Derecho y Razón* (Madrid, Ed. Trotta S.A., 1995).

23. Ibid.

24. Transparency International is an international nonprofit organization formally constituted in May 1993 to build international and national coalitions against corruption. Its purpose, as of its April 1997 mission statement is "To curb corruption by mobilizing a global coalition to promote and strengthen international and national integrity systems."

3

Corruption, Accountability, and Democracy in Italy: An Outline

LUCA MELDOLESI

The deepening interconnectedness of global economics and culture, which brings into contact what used to be relatively isolated regions and communities, suggests that cross-regional comparative studies are increasingly relevant and useful. These comparisons are particularly interesting when the areas in question share a cultural base, as do Latin America and Latin Europe. In the past few years, due to the liberalization of their economies, the evolution of their political systems, and the reshaping of the state and of its moral foundations in the region, many Latin countries have gone through a process of profound restructuring. I was particularly struck by the interest that *Mani Pulite* (clean hands)—the campaign against corruption launched by a part of the Italian judiciary—aroused in Latin America (Meldolesi, 1994a). I decided that a short outline of the political economy of contemporary Italy written from the point of view of corruption, accountability, and democracy may be of use to the Latin American reader and to anyone interested in comparing Italian corruption and anticorruption policies to those of Latin America.

This chapter draws from Anglo-Saxon literature on contemporary Italy to familiarize the reader with some aspects of its political economy. It also sketches a journey across the country to make sense of the Italian economy and politics. The final conclusion, relevant to international compar-

isons, is that corruption-free behavior should be seen as an essential in-
gredient in the reshaping of many societies.

The Rise of Italy's Modern Campaign against Corruption

There are three basic reasons for optimism in Italy's fight against corruption.

1. The disclosure of widespread corruption that arises from the relationship among the political system, the economy, and the administration publicly placed Italy among the world's most corrupt nations.
   Embarrassing as it is for many Italians, this is an encouraging development: It provides impetus—finally—for something to be done.
2. The end of the cold war had important repercussions in a Latin world
   sharply divided between the right wing and left wing. In Italy, it
   helped to produce an institutional transformation that has not yet
   been consolidated. However, with the collapse of traditional political
   parties and the dramatic reformation of pro-fascist and communist
   groups, democracy seems today more solidly in place than in the past.

   This evolution is also the result of an underlying social trend. Italy
   has had a diffused aristocratic tradition for a long time (this being
   the counterpart of the artistic attractions of the country). The
   demise of aristocracy—a gradual process that has come about since
   the Second World War—has affected Italy's social fabric and has
   shaped the development of Italian democracy. This gradual process
   of overcoming social rigidity and divisions and developing new
   forms of participation and deliberation is still under way.
3. Still plagued by an inefficient state; economic depression across the
   south; and by corruption, criminal organizations, and "assistenzialismo"—a euphemism used to describe all sorts of deviations connected to public expenditure—Italy is now looking for a way out.
   The heart of this tentative development is at the local level, located
   in district governments and small firms, which have grown more and
   more important in the past thirty years. The mushrooming of small
   firms in conservative and progressive regions alike, in the northern,
   central, and southern parts of the country (where it is partly underground), is an important industrial and social development and has
   both attracted international attention and awakened some hopes.

During the half a century that has elapsed since the Second World
War, episodes of corruption in the economic, political, and administrative

spheres have been too numerous to be recorded. As a Western country bordering the Eastern block and hosting the biggest Communist party in the European Community, Italy had a political system of "imperfect bipartisanship," meaning a system dominated by the Democrazia Cristiana, without any effective rotation in power. This setting was characterized by government instability and obsessed with a sort of "immortality syndrome." In a cynical, Andreotti style, all means were legitimated, particularly in the 1970s and the 1980s, to protect political power from the left (and also from the Partito Socialista inside the government coalition). Hence, the road was opened to widespread corruption and to an underground "entente cordiale"—or gentleman's understanding—with organized crime.

In the 1980s, working against this trend, Giovanni Falcone and Paolo Borsellino, together with a talented group of judges and policemen, were able to decode the Mafia and to start a welcome resurrection of public authority in Palermo. Also, early in 1992 in Milano, Antonio Di Pietro, Francesco Saverio Borrelli, and others started the anticorruption campaign known as Mani Pulite that shook the First Republic and strongly contributed to its demise.

This turning point in contemporary Italian history was also the result of international and national events. The fall of the Berlin Wall had considerable repercussions in many countries; in Italy more than in others because it dramatically weakened the raison d'etre of the regime, which was the danger of communism. The end of the cold war also had profound social implications. The large-scale awakening of students, workers, and the population as a whole in the 1960s and 1970s was deeper and more prolonged in Italy than elsewhere. Over ten years it was contained, circumscribed, stemmed, and finally suffocated. The people who passed through this experience were later "absorbed" into a society that turned to private concerns and "yuppyism." But, understandably, most of them were ready to approve of Mani Pulite—a campaign that somehow vindicated their previous objections.

Mani Pulite was a divine surprise, an unexpected and welcome process that set in motion a "judiciary revolution" beneficial for the country. Its international impact gave Italians the opportunity to see their problems mirrored in those of other nations. Following a period of economic expansion, the disclosure of the corruption of the Italian system provoked a sudden change in attitudes across Europe, particularly in France. "Un pays formule 1"—as in the title of Jacques Fayette's book—was now condemned, and the devaluation and recession that followed in Italy were felt as a deserved punishment. But the opposite occurred in Brazil and in other countries in Latin America and throughout the world. Mani Pulite was interpreted by these countries as a sign that the state could be run better and that democracy could be consolidated by freeing them from corruption and other illegitimate practices.

Finally, in the United States, Italy's turmoil was halfheartedly, if not suspiciously, acknowledged.[1] "For the Anglo Saxons"—said Professor Giacomo Becattini in his opening speech at the fifth Artimino Conference on local development (September 11–15, 1995)—"we are the country of Machiavelli where 'the ends justify the means,' or the country, of the Borgia family, where at the bottom of a glass of tasty Brunello wine a bitter poison may hide itself."

The truth is, however, that Italy has an intrinsically ambivalent, if not ambiguous texture; a contradictory image—a mixture of positive and negative elements—often pointed out, but insufficiently scrutinized. To make this point, I will draw from two recent books that have attracted much attention: *Making Democracy Work* by Robert Putnam and *Remaking the Italian Economy* by Richard Locke.

Analytical Shortcomings

Putnam's book is the outcome of long and original research on Italian regional governments—a new institution that was inaugurated in 1970. The book focuses on differences in performance and on their explanation in terms of their level of civic activity and culture, a concept Putnam refers to as *civicness*. It contains two threads: one that studies the evolution of Italian regionalism, another that looks for conditions favorable to democracy. My advice is that, in the light of Mani Pulite, the first should be revised, and the second should be reassessed.

The book aptly documents the great differences in performance between southern and northern regional governments. We know, however, that the period considered covers precisely the decline of the First Republic, as it were, marred by a growing influence of gangsterism and corruption. The latter was part of a general illness generated by crime, clientelism, and corporativism that infected Italian society and the state and that grew particularly strong at this period in the South and in the ruling parties.

It follows, therefore, that, though connected to the North-South divide and to the southern deficit of "civismo"—civil society—the differences in local government performance were probably dramatized by the rising diseases of the South[2]—particularly of Calabria, Campania, and Sicilia, the strongholds of organized crime, which, unsurprisingly, come often at the bottom of Putnam ladders.

At the top, on the other hand, one often finds Emilia-Romagna, Umbria, and Toscana, which are "high-civicness" regions but also are traditionally ruled by the opposition. The three highly civilized Veneto regions, which are traditionally pro-government and are now taking the economic lead, do not look particularly well-off as far as the region is concerned.

My conclusion is, therefore, that Italy's ambivalence is more complicated than Putnam would like it to be. Theoretically, his search for a "primum mobile" that rules the roost is not new in social science. Actually, Putnam's civicness and social capital look like the preconditions for development in development economics, the Protestant ethic for capitalism in sociology, or the consensus for Western democracy in political science. The dethroning of the latter (see my *Discovering the Possible*, 1995a, ch. 3, 8) suggests that the former might also have a similar fate.

Given the historical heritage, recent developments, and the North-South cleavage, the social conduct prevalent in the south interacts with regional governments and employees in such a way that it produces a relatively poor performance. But this does not mean that southern psychology is homogeneous or that the results of its interactions are predetermined. Typically, "amoral familism" and other troubling behaviors are mixed with opposite values of hard work, thriftiness, integrity, and so on. The latter have a historical origin as well since they come from peasant and artisan traditions. They were gradually overtaken by illegality, but did not disappear. Indeed, the anticrime and anticorruption waves, which have developed in the South since the mid-1980s, indicate their return.

Conversely, northern regions praised by Putnam were not immune from Italian pathologies. Lombardia, the most important region of the country, did not fare well in the book tests, while, at the time, it was becoming the cradle of Mani Pulite. Tangentopoli, "Bribesville," was indeed Milano. There, big firms, political parties, and local and national administrative bodies were connected by a developed network of complicities that exchanged bribe money for procurements, favorable decisions, and so forth. Even the cooperative movement of Emilia-Romagna received some charges of corruption.

The picture disclosed by the judiciary provoked wide repercussions and opened up a new phase in the country's evolution. One may scrutinize it by keeping in mind the following points (Meldolesi, 1992, 1994a, 1995–96).

First, the North-South divide exists in economic structure as well as in collective psychology. This implies that North-South differences go hand-in-hand with an underlying economic continuum.

Second, the psychological mix is a dynamic phenomenon. Both North and South may improve or worsen over time. The decline phase of the First Republic affected both regions negatively, with the South particularly suffering from this turn of events.

Third, the anticrime and anticorruption campaigns of the Italian judiciary, as symbolized by the solicitor's offices of Palermo and Milano, embody a tentative reversal of that trend.

Addressing Contradictions

Let me turn to *Remaking the Italian Economy*. Locke became interested in Italy because of its many contradictions and anomalies. "On the one hand," he writes in the preface, "Italy is seen as the 'sick man' of Europe, because it suffers from just about every conceivable problem. . . . On the other hand, even a cursory examination of the comparative data reveals that Italy performs well on key political economic dimensions: GDP growth, personal savings rates, labor productivity, and investment in new equipments."

Does the book effectively reconcile "these two apparently contradictory images of the same country"? Only in part. It helps in documenting why Italy performed well on key economic dimensions while suffering from so many problems. But it takes for granted (see pp. 1–2) many things that should be explained—such as the weak Italian state; the unstable governments; the incompetent civil service; the backward, clientelistic features of Italian social life; the irresponsible public spending; the archaic fiscal policies; and so forth—down to the corruption scandal that triggered Mani Pulite.

During the 1980s, a series of reforms comparable to the ones adopted successfully by other countries fell victim to political infighting among Italy's key socioeconomic actors. Despite these failures, "the Italian economy underwent a dramatic restructuring that resulted both in patterns of entrepreneurial vitality and in cases of industrial decline. I seek to explain this paradoxical mixture"—Locke writes (p. x)—"by arguing that the Italian economy should be viewed not as a coherent national system but rather as an incoherent composite of diverse subnational patterns that coexist (often uneasily) within the same national territory."[3]

Locke's analysis flows in a one-way direction—from negative political outcomes to the economy and from the government to local subsystems—not an interactive, or two-way, direction.[4] This demarche is linked to two choices that may go unnoticed. First, by studying policy failures at a national level, the political (or superstructural) history of the country is acknowledged but not discussed. Second, Locke's local case studies are strictly northern.

While Locke is good at connecting social, political, and economic elements at the local level, he is not so good at dealing with the national question. In this respect, he draws from a long-standing tradition—nearly a knee-jerk effect that goes as far back as Saint-Simon (1810–20)—according to which the economy is assumed to be more "determinant" than politics. This economistic bias helps him to overlook the South, which in his book is compressed to one conventional page (p. 176).[5]

While Putnam is not often friendly to the South, Locke seems to believe that the study of the region does not deserve a top priority for "Making Sense of Italy"—the title of his introduction. In his "Selected List of Persons Interviewed," not a single southerner is included.

I cannot but speculate on what additional work should be done to complement otherwise valuable research. Despite the widespread discussion of the last two decades on the so-called Third Italy (Piore and Sable 1984; Porter 1990; Pyke, Becattini, and Sengenberger 1990), Locke's study on small firms and industrial districts belongs to the northwest and not to the central northeast of the country. His work on the automobile industry overlooks a simple—perhaps symbolic—reality: The majority of Italian cars are presently produced in the central south of the country.[6] It follows that these two parts of Italy should now be explored, an inclusion that might lead to better understanding of the central government.

There are some important features of Italy that are still missing in these analyses. First, the role of small firms, industrial districts, and local systems in the country is bigger than acknowledged. These concentrations of light industry have a central role in industrial production and trade—particularly for the principal "Made in Italy" products (i.e., commodities for the house and the person that together with mechanical goods are the very pillars of the Italian trade balance). The main "remaking of the Italian economy" actually occurred here. Their development should be connected to the crisis of Fordism and to other important developments—like the sliding equilibrium between local and imported knowledge, cooperation and competition, participation and conflict—that came out of them.

Moreover, together with a Mediterranean landscape, one driving south may notice many islands of progress (particularly in some hills—part of what Manlio Rossi Doria called the "bone"—of Abruzzo, Molise, Irpinia, Murge, etc.) and also signs of small-firm widespread industrialization—particularly in Puglia and Campania. One may also be surprised by the recent performance of some big firms, maybe related to the greater adaptability of southern workers to post-Fordism.

But one may also imagine another side of the coin. Italy is not only a country of multiplicity and fragmentation. It is also a country in which market- and democracy-friendly behaviors coexist with strong countervailing types—particularly in the South. Indeed, through the journey south one may realize the great impact of "assistenzialismo" and its multiple consequences.

The Political Landscape

Suppose that through this journey we reach a better understanding of the "other half" of the country and, therefore, are able to better evaluate Italy as a whole. This would help in drawing a useful picture for comparative analyses not only for developed countries (as Locke suggests, p. xii, 4, 184, etc.) but for Latin America and other countries as well. This is the reason for our exercise. Though a member of G7, Italy stands at the intersection among the variety of nations that should be put to work in the rapidly changing international society of today. From this point of view, the ambivalent and paradoxical situations that the country is going through become more relevant and sometimes ironic. On the one hand, the cornerstone of the political system—the Democrazia Cristiana—collapsed, together with its allied Partito Socialista. A political personnel that dominated Italian politics for decades was disbanded, and a large body of political and administrative clerks, technicians, and party members had to look elsewhere for political "recycling." On the other hand, we had four years and four governments of transition (Amato, Ciampi, Berlusconi, and Dini). The change was quick, produced under the pressure of judiciary activism, political referendums, and elections. But the new political setting that came out of a majority electoral law and the March 1994 elections created a standstill, which was broken only in April 1996.

The First Republic was studied by many people. After having described at length the Italian "chaos," Joseph La Palombara in his *Democracy Italian Style* (1987) discovered some rationalities of a political system that (retrospectively) was heading toward collapse. He unconsciously followed Hegel's law, which Albert Hirschman talks about: Social phenomena are bound to be understood on the brink of their disappearance. David Hine published *Governing Italy: The Politics of Bargained Pluralism* (1993) when it was already too late. In this volume, he describes the political system of the First Republic, its historical legacy, its social and economic foundations, its party structure, the constitutional order, and so forth.

With all of these previous studies, it is odd that one would revert—as Locke does—to stereotypes such as Byzantinism and bureaucratic sluggishness. It is true that in the 1980s, concealed by a social climate dominated by the desire to get rich, some previous trends were accelerated. These trends include the overlegislation by parliament (and practically no assessment of the results), the declining efficiency of an administrative machine characterized by patronage and corporativism, and the strenuous struggle among parties, groups, and personalities both inside and outside the government, which strengthened indirectly the power of different sections of Italian society—legitimate and illegitimate alike. Great politicians of the time, like Andreotti, De Mita, Craxi, or Gava, were indeed "virtuoso" in the day-to-day exercise of getting on top of this crisis-prone reality.

Therefore, the many reform efforts of the period produced by different quarters and often conceived "in vitro" had to pass through Hine's "politics of bargained pluralism." It is not so much that they failed; rather, they became what the sociopolitical conditions allowed them to be.

One may emphasize the contradictory policy visions of the Italian elite and the fragmentation and lack of coordination of the policies eventually adopted.[7] But one should also add that the dominant, power-minded section of the elite was interested in ideas that both looked palatable and opened the road to their consensus needs (in terms of, say, large-scale financing and massive increases in public employment). For example, if one scrutinizes the story of key reforms of the declining phase of the First Republic—such as the regional government and the national health system—it is clear that both requirements were met.[8]

The innovations through which the political system tamed social awakenings and nurtured parasitism left a big imprint in Italy. Public spending skyrocketed, forcing the country into huge internal borrowing and creating the debt and deficit problem that has dominated public life ever since. Year after year, many "ceilings" to the budget deficit were imposed and regularly disattended. The (compounded) interest rate and its variations gave the enormous debt a life of its own, reaching a level that is more than double the one allowed by the Maastrischt treaty.[9] Innumerable schemes and measures were crafted for taming the deficit-debt headache, both on the fiscal side and on the expenditure side. The welfare state was curtailed, public intervention in the South suspended, a program of privatizations set in motion, and managerial expertise called in to man some parts of the public system. With so many measures already taken, it is uncomfortable to realize that the headache is still with us.

"For quite some time the transition to the Second Republic was considered a problem of institutional reform. Traditional electoral laws based on proportional representation—so the argument runs—favored coalition clientelistic governments, discouraging 'de facto' alternations in power of two competing political poles, as in fully developed democracies. This in turn made stable and authoritative governments impossible. Hence, after a referendum, a majority electoral system was approved and the March 1994 elections based on it were thought to give birth to the Second Republic" (Pasquino 1994; further explanations in Lyttelton 1994 and Meldolesi 1994b).

Unfortunately, the process ended up being more complicated than expected. Part of the reason probably lies in the institutional reform.[10] But one should look also at other obstacles, such as the ones within the state that Hine documented,[11] the actual working of the administrative machine, or the conscious and unconscious drawbacks that exist in a country largely influenced in the north by the Lega movement and in the South by the still-powerful machinery of patronage.

Lessons from a Turning Point

The developments of the last few years provide a more encouraging note. At the moment, nobody can tell whether the Center-Left government headed by Romano Prodi, with his scanty majority in the Chamber of Deputees, will be another transitional government or a lasting one, as it would like to be. But it is true that, so far, the moral atmosphere of the country has improved. We are passing through a mild recession, under international pressure to match European standards and deadlines, with a threat of secession coming from the north and an unsettled policy for the South. All this notwithstanding, the Italian state, now in the hands of more able and honest ministers, seems to be making ground toward normality and decency. If this endures, retrospectively it would make the efforts that the country has undertaken—the many laws passed by parliament that only now find some implementation, as well as the need for transparency and evaluation of public expenditure, which is still missing—more understandable.

Less corruption, better accountability within the public domain, and the gradual consolidation of democracy no longer look like abstract

chimeras. At least some hope exists that the decapitation of the big criminal organizations and of the political and economic headquarters of corruption that have succeeded in the past few years will be followed, albeit
painstakingly, by a process of social regeneration. In turn, this may help
to mobilize social energies toward meaningful goals.

The decline of corruption and the remaking of Italian democracy has attracted much attention. Alessandro Pizzorno's well-known model (1992) on
the "vicious circle of arrogance" shows how, in conditions of political transition and of social crisis, business politicians interact with brokers and firms
to develop their arbitrary power. The model crafted on the Italian experience
was successfully exported to Brazil and Argentina by Luigi Manzetti (1996)
and now, *mutatis mutandis,* may be imported back to Italy; for example, it
may be useful to apply the model to the new scandal of Lorenzo Necci and
Pierfrancesco Pacini Battaglia, which broke late in September 1996.

But other questions remain. Is corruption reproducing itself spontaneously? Is there any anticorruption policy to be followed? Can we utilize
the very process of change from a corrupt regime to a new one to make
some improvements?

Undoubtedly, for Italians, Brazilians, and many others, these are relevant questions. Looking at the Italian cases, there are some simple points
around which a comparative analysis may develop. First, political change is
not a panacea. As stated above, for some time the Italian debate focused
on majority electoral laws and political "alternanza," but it later came to
focus on the social pathologies connected to the great unresolved issues of
the country: the southern dilemma and the state. True, business politicians
may collapse and the overall atmosphere of the country may improve, but
the social seedbed that nurtured corruption will not be easily disbanded.
A report issued late in October 1996 by a special committee appointed by
the president of the Chamber of Deputees (Arcidiacono, Cassese, and Pizzorno 1996) states that after nearly five years of Mani Pulite, episodes of
corruption continue to be "much more numerous than the ones discovered." Prosecutors and solicitory, the report explains, "unveiled a system
in which 'tangenti' were often used, as a general rule, to obtain subsidies
and seal contracts, to bribe inspectors, to illegally finance political parties,
or company black funds, raise illicit income for Public Administrators,"
and so forth. The episodes uncovered are not exceptions to the rule. Indeed, they "may represent a small part of a much wider pathology."

Second, to understand this pathology, one needs a firsthand knowledge
of the country and familiarity with previous studies and research. One
needs a dispassionate assessment of the historical record, both long and
short term, where the latter should particularly focus on the motives and

maneuverings that take place within the process of social transformation, many of which are not readily apparent. The renovation of a political system does not simply lead to the reassessment of the status quo, it entails openings and opportunities that must be recognized and acted on.

Third, in a semilegal–semi-illegal country like Italy, an anticorruption policy should be part of a more general policy of the regulation and structuring of private and public life. There is no simple recipe. Rather, one should learn thinking according to a double timetable. On one hand, one should keep in mind the wide range of issues involved; on the other, one should manage with great care and determination the political reforms necessary to tackle them.

A successful regulatory policy must be broad in scope. We badly need improvements in law and order. The priority rightly given to the fight of the Mafia and other criminal organizations has led to an apparent tolerance for ordinary crime, particularly in metropolitan areas and in the South. This jeopardizes the economy and public security at a local level.

Petty corruption and other illicit behavior like tax evasion, disregard for administrative regulations, and so forth is widespread at the very roots of Italian society.[12] There exists an underground economy that, more in the South but not only in the South, works beneath the official one. More precisely, between the formal economy and the black market, there are many shades of gray, of changing combinations of legal and illegal behavior that cover a considerable part of productive activities. Here, a policy for inducing the overall inclusion of this gray activity into the regulated formal economy is badly needed.

Basically, Mani Pulite revealed the presence of corruption at a higher level in the interaction between firms, parties, and administration. This "intreccio" exists also at a lower level but so far has scarcely been persecuted. The process of decentralization, now labeled federalism, and the rise of the young new mayors, directly elected by the population, may in time promote better regulation and normalization at these levels.

In the day-to-day life of the Italian South, petty corruption is not considered a criminal offense but an expedient for obtaining something that should be due—that otherwise would not be easily delivered or something that should not be due but can be afforded. As in the Latin American setting Michael Reisman examined (1981), we have here a double normative system: one official, the other operative. The latter probably reflects a historical legacy of the need for the subordinate classes to muddle though or circumvent official regulations.

This attitude, however, should not be seen only as a liability. If the criminal behavior is limited, southern ingenuity may be profitably channeled toward legitimate means. This requires, however, a policy of legalization[13] and a more effective administrative machine in a double direction: friendliness to the people since the state is still felt as "coming from the outside" and reliability in providing more and better services.

The worldwide process of reducing the role of the state in the economy was implemented slowly in Italy. We did not experience the rapid economic transformation that allegedly promulgated corruption in some Latin American countries. We have, however, a sort of deadlock in the reform of public administration at both local and national levels. Cultural backwardness, a propensity to shortcuts that turn out to be ineffective, corporativism, and bureaucratic sluggishness are only parts of the explanation. The development of Mani Pulite and the roles of the other actors—firms, political parties, and public institutions—are also important factors (see also n. 17).

Italy's current renaissance is following a tortuous path. One still cannot detect a definite direction in the remolding of the economic and political setting of the country.

New laws and regulations on public works have been implemented one after another, but no proper working of the sector is yet in sight.[14] The sort of guerrilla warfare of the Berlusconi group against the Milano judges shows that economic and political powers still interfere with law enforcement, while the behavior of Italian companies the world over is not scrutinized for potentially corrupt practices.

A law just approved by parliament will encourage private financing of political parties through partial tax exemption.[15] One cannot tell at the moment whether it will bring much needed transparency or whether it will become a fig leaf to cover bribes, as previous public subsidies did. The sensible proposal of the report mentioned above (p. 112) is passing through rather slowly.[16]

Previously, high corruption was oiling the wheels of the Italian economy. It is no longer, and some roughness and difficulty are included. After a traumatic period in which many economic and administrative activities suffered a standstill, something is fortunately moving again. But it is clear that only a prolonged effort on the part of the government and society, backed by a cultural awakening and based on broad social support—from the left but also from the right, from small firms and trade unions but also from the professional strata, corporations, and religious leaders—will bring results.[17]

Much of the misunderstandings about Italy that abound the world over (and frequently lead to irrational praise or condemnation of the country) come from unrealistic expectations based on a one-to-one comparison of, say, France and Italy, the United States and Italy, and so forth. To better understand the many ambivalences and paradoxes of Italian life, I suggest that the political economy of the country should be discussed in the light of multiple comparisons, placing Italy where she effectively belongs: that is, inside the Latin world.

Some particularly interesting issues for inter-Latino study include problems of democratic consolidation and the social psychology rooted in Latin realities—the influence that it has on economic and social development.

Notes

1. Understandably, the Italian-American community, who severely suffered in the past from the negative image of Italy that prevailed abroad, did not welcome Mani Pulite wholeheartedly. Less understandably, however, in a session on Italy of the yearly conference of the Political Science Association held in New York in September 1994, a few political scientists suggested that comparisons with the Italian experience were exasperating and that a "normal rate" of bribery also exists in New York, Toronto, and elsewhere.

2. The political split between North and South on regional government performance was, therefore, much wider than the economic one. Profiting from a new law, the rehabilitation of public service in the South started in the municipalities a few years ago and is now reaching the regions.

3. Industrial vitality and decline—Locke adds—are situated in different localities, characterized by different sociopolitical networks within which firms and unions are embedded. These networks create different mixes of resources and constraints that shape the understanding of the challenges and the capacity of local economic agents to respond to them.

4. *Remaking the Italian Economy* contains two chapters on the failed attempts of modernizing economic policy and industrial relations during the 1980s. Then it shifts to local stories, studying industrial adjustments and relations in the automobile industry of Torino and Milano and the textile industry of the Biellese. From the social and economic solutions found for industrial reconstructuring in these sectors and places, Locke finally concludes that in a loosely coordinated, fragmented picture of different local realities, the industrial successes of some of them compensated the many shortcomings of the country.

5. The central-south of Italy is indeed half of the country in terms of territory and population. But its economic base is relatively small (while the commodities and services it produces may be statistically underestimated; Meldolesi 1995b). Therefore, *Remaking the Italian Economy* need not come to the South.

6. The title of Locke's chapter 4 is "Industrial Adjustment and Industrial Relations in the Automobile Industry," but its content refers only to Fiat and Alfa Romeo in Torino and Milano.

7. As Albert Hirschman had already singled out in 1948, sometimes, however, dishomogeneity may help the country in adopting original solutions. (Locke writes on the postwar period [p. 34] that the combination of two very different strategies—a severe austerity and stabilization plan and active intervention of state company managers—"produced impressive rates of economic growth and development in the late 1950s and early 1960s.")

8. The same can be said for public works. (In this respect, Locke [pp. 44–46, 50] tells the story of Fondo Investimenti Occupazione (FIO). Unfortunately, more should be said, as for example in Meldolesi 1992, ch. 2.) The same is true for the Italian State enterprise

(pp. 52–64), the decline of which was obviously connected to the decline of the First Republic. But the reverse also occurred. Because of their pressures, electoral leverages, and ability in seizing the opportunities offered by the reforms, "government funds were allocated disproportionately in favor of stronger firms and more dynamic regions" (p. 66).

9. The Italian public debt (more than 120 percent of GDP) is so high and has been around for so long that Nobel Laureate Paul Samuelson in his New Year's interview to *Il Corriere della Sera* (1996) suggested that the United States and other countries should learn from Rome how to survive with it.

10. The majority system modified by a certain percentage of proportionality—the so-called Mattarellum, from the name of Mattarella, who sponsored it—did not produce a stable majority in parliament. A discussion on its reform arose again in autumn 1995 around the "Mulino lecture" by Giovanni Sartori (1995), who advocated the adoption of a French-like, semipresidential, two-rounds system. Moreover, a reform of the Costituzione is now considered necessary by leading political forces in the country and may be set in motion in the near future.

11. "Through a detailed account of such topics as the budgetary procedure or parliamentary regulations, prime ministerial authority or policy coordination," writes Mauro Calise in his review of *Governing Italy* (1994, p. 184), "Hine leads us well beyond the stereotype of Italian inefficiency to show the legal and political roots of the present fragmentation of the governmental process. In this respect, Hine is very cautious about the possibility of reforming the system by the mere adoption of a new electoral law."

12. According to an internal memo of SECIT—the top inspective body of the Ministry of Finance—the percentage of total value added (TVA) tax evasion in Italy may be 46 percent; 77 percent in the South (cf. SECIT 1995 quoted in Brunetta 1995, p. 22).

13. Morally, this policy should be uncompromising. Contrary to the political scientists quoted in n. 1, I believe that only a turn in attitude that aims at reconciling low and daily life may shift the balance in the right directions and push our society toward the gradual abolition of the "double normative system" that Moreno Ocampo describes in his chapter. As has already happened with "Mani Pulite," more courageous commitment may encourage many positive undertakings around the world.

14. One may notice that a part of the forementioned Pacini-Battaglia scandal is focused on the planned expansion of railways. However, the patrimonial control of officials and their families proposed by the then Minister of Public Works, Antonio Di Pietro, was quietly shelved.

15. In the past, political financing proved to be a major source of corruption. Mani Pulite brought with it the collapse of political courts: some electoral campaigns spent one-tenth of what they had previously, even if Berlusconi drew from his group and other private finances. This low level of spending, however, did not prove to be sustainable.

16. The only point of the report turned into a law regards the private financing of political parties. All the rest is still missing. For example, public officials found guilty of corruption are not dismissed. (Only one case was recorded at the Ministry of Finance!) Officials do not disclose their patrimonies and there is no (sample) checking of their declarations, and so on.

17. To make the point, let us look again at the most difficult matter of all, the reform of the state. Traditionally, the Italian State has been regulated by laws and inhabited by law-abiding officials who had no idea of transparency and performance. In the 1980s, the formal respect of the law went hand in hand with the rising tide of corruption, so that early in 1993, at the Corte dei Conti's 130th anniversary, its president announced that in the very year that Mani Pulite came into effect, the Corte had made one million and three hundred thousand formal controls. But a difficult evolution followed. Here again, lower corruption initially meant lower performance for an already highly inefficient state. After a few years, we still look off the mark, unable to enter the age of state reforms that are spreading across the world from

the U.S. model. Some reasons for this blockage probably lie in a "vicious circle" between the need to increase responsibility at lower levels—which presupposes transparency in account-ability—and the difficulty of introducing the latter in a period of emergency fiscal reduction.

References

Arcidiacono, L., S. Cassese, and A. Pizzorno. 1996. *Rapporto del Comitato di studio della prevenzione della corruzione*. Rome: Presidenza della Camera dei Deputati.

Becattini, G. 1995. "I sistemi locali come strumento interpretativo dello sviluppo econom-ico italiano." Prolusione alla V settimana sullo sviluppo locale. Prato-Artimino, Sep-tember 11–15.

Brunetta, R. 1995. *Sud*. Rome: Donzelli.

Calise, M. 1994. "Review of D. Hine's *Governing Italy*." *Political Science Quarterly* 109, no. 1.

della Porta, A. 1992. *Lo scambio occulto: Casi di corruzione in Italia*. Bologna: Il Mulino.

Falcone, G. 1991. *Cose di cosa nostra*. Milan: Rizzoli.

————. 1994. *Interventi e proposte (1982–1992)*. Milan: Sansoni.

Fayette, J.R. 1990. *L'Italie, un pays formule 1*. Paris: Hotier.

Hine, D. 1993. *Governing Italy: The Politics of Bargained Pluralism*. Oxford: Clarendon.

Hirschman, A.O. 1948. "Inflation and Deflation in Italy." *American Economic Review* 38, no. 4.

————. 1995. *A Propensity to Self-Subversion*. Cambridge, Mass.: Harvard University Press.

La Palombara, J. 1987. *Democracy Italian Style*. New Haven, Conn.: Yale University Press.

Locke, R.M. 1995. *Remaking the Italian Economy*. Ithaca, N.Y.: Cornell University Press.

Lucentini, P. 1994. *Paolo Borsellino: Il valore di una vita*. Milan: Mandadori.

Lyttelton, A. 1994. "Italy: The Triumph of TV." *The New York Review of Books*, September.

Mazzetti, L. 1996. "Market Reforms and Transparency." Mimeograph.

Meldolesi, L. 1992. *Spendere meglio è possibile*. Bologna: Il Mulino.

————. 1994a. Problemas de reforma do Estado: crime, corrupçao, trapaça, parasitismo, in-curia. Sucessos, limites e liçoes do caso italiano." *Revista Brasileira de Ciencias sociais* 9, no. 24.

————. 1994b. "Democrazia ed intrasigenza. Un lamento post elettorale." *Il Mulino*, 3.

————. 1995a. *Discovering the Possible: The Surprising World of Albert O. Hirschman*. Notre Dame, Ind.: Notre Dame University Press.

————. 1995b. "L'elevata mobilità del lavoro nel Mezzogiorno della speranza." In *La mo-bilità della società italiana*, edited by P. Galli. Rome: Sipi.

————. 1995–96. "Mezzogiorno perduto e ritrovato." *Sviluppo locale*, 2–3.

Pasquino, G. 1994. "The Birth of the 'Second Republic.' " *Journal of Democracy* 5, no. 3.

Piore, M.J., and C.F. Sabel. 1984. *The Second Industrial Divide: Possibilities for Prosperity*. New York: Basic Books.

Pyke F., G. Becattini, and W. Sengenberger. 1990. *Industrial Districts and Interfirm Co-operation in Italy*. Geneve: International Institute for Labor Studies.

Porter, M. 1990. *The Competitive Advantage of Nations*. New York: Macmillan.

Putnam, R.D. 1993. *Making Democracy Work*. Princeton, N.J.: Princeton University Press.

Samuelson, P. 1996. "New Year Interview." *Il Corriere della Sera*, 1.

Sartori, G. 1995. "Democrazia in Italia." *Lezione*. 1995.

Pizzorno, A. 1992. "La corruzione nel sistema politico." *Lo scambio occulto*, edited by A. della Porta.

Reisman, M. 1981. *Remedios contra la Corrupción*. México City: Fondo de Cultura Economica.

4

Is Leaner Government Necessarily Cleaner Government?

SUSAN ROSE-ACKERMAN[1]

Corruption incentives occur whenever public or private agents have monopoly power over the distribution of valuable benefits. The impact of
public-sector corruption depends not only on the size of the payoff, but
also on the distortionary effects of payoffs on the economy. Common incentives for corruption occur when government is a buyer of goods and
services or a provider of scarce benefits. Also common are payments to
avoid the costs of regulation, to reduce tax and customs burdens, and to
expedite service. Most of these opportunities are reduced if the role of the
state in the economy is reduced. A small government needs to let fewer
building contracts, purchase less equipment, and can lower taxes.

Deregulation reduces the number of permissions needed from the state
by private firms. The elimination of subsidy programs eliminates the incentive to bribe to qualify for the benefit. Privatization of state firms removes bureaucrats from a wide range of day-to-day interactions with private individuals and firms. If the shrinkage of the state is not carefully
managed, however, corruption incentives may increase in some old areas
and arise in new ones. This chapter considers, in turn, (1) budget cutbacks
in (a) spending programs and (b) regulatory programs; (2) privatization;
and (3) the links between organized crime and corruption as governments
reduce their role in the economy.

I. Budget Cutbacks

Reductions in government spending can produce scarcity that encourages corrupt payoffs. This result can occur both when spending programs are cut back and when regulatory budgets are cut with no change in the substantive statutes. Furthermore, when a government that faces fiscal pressures cuts back spending, it may at the same time seek to maintain its influence by increasing regulations and mandates. The result can be increased corruption.

A. Cuts in Spending Programs

Although program elimination removes the corruption incentives that accompanied it, budget cutbacks that leave the program intact may not. For example, suppose that in the past subsidies for higher education were available to all students who had passed an entrance exam. Suppose a reform government eliminates the entitlement and states that only 50 percent of those who pass the exam will be eligible for subsidy. The scarcity created by the cutbacks creates corruption incentives where none existed before. The corruption-reducing solution here is to raise the passing grade so that the shrunken program retains its entitlement character. Alternatively, the quality of higher education could be lowered to reduce demand. Other ways of reducing demand such as complex applications, long queues, and cutoffs based on need all generate corruption incentives.

When government spending falls, the contractors who benefited in the past from public contracts may suffer. If the private sector expands as the public sector shrinks, many firms will simply redirect their business. Some firms, however, may be so specialized that they cannot change direction easily. Domestic military contractors are usually in this category. Multinationals are likely to be less affected both because of their diversified product mix and because they can sell in other countries. Firms that have trouble shifting the direction of their business may bribe to obtain a share of the shrinking pie of government business. The total quantity of bribes might fall, but the bribe per project will rise. Furthermore, once the government is locked into dealing with a particular contractor, bribery can still be used to get inflated prices, to overcharge for materials, or to skimp on quality.

B. Cuts in Regulatory Programs

Suppose budget cutters halve the budget of a regulatory agency with no change in the underlying statute. First, suppose that the statute permits firms to act unless the state finds a violation. Here we need to distinguish between regulations, such as environmental rules, that do not control product quality, and those that do. In the former case, few business-people will complain about budget cutbacks because inspections and other checks will be reduced, a benefit for firms. A firm's manager still has an incentive to bribe an inspector, but will do it less often simply because inspectors come less often. The same firms, however, may object to regulatory reforms that in less corrupt countries would be viewed as cost-reducing reforms by business firms. Thus in Mexico businesses have not generally endorsed proposals to substitute incentive-based schemes for command and control regulation of environmental pollution. According to the *Financial Times* ("Passage to Cleaner Air," April 10, 1996), "Widespread alleged corruption among environmental inspectors means, says one businessman, that 'usually it is cheaper to pay off the official than to make the improvements.' "

The case of product quality regulation is more complex. Although some firms may welcome the reduced scrutiny, high-quality firms may worry about the general loss of reputation of the industry in the newly lax regulatory environment. However, such firms will usually be able to fund their own efforts to convince customers of the continued high quality of their own products or support voluntary industry-wide standards. The firms lose simply because the costs of maintaining quality and of guaranteeing quality to customers have been shifted from the government to them. As an alternative, they could bribe officials to come to their place of business to certify product quality. This seems a risky and unlikely option, however, given the private alternatives.

Second, suppose that the law states that firms cannot operate or individuals cannot take some action, such as foreign travel, unless they obtain a license (e.g., a passport). Then a budget cutback with no change in the underlying statute increases corruption incentives. Firms and individuals will be encouraged to pay bribes to get the scarce attention of the regulatory authorities or to get to the head of a long queue. Bribes paid by some lead to more delays for nonbribers, a result that may induce more to pay bribes, and so on—producing a vicious cycle (Rose-Ackerman 1978).

Just as in the case of cutbacks in subsidy programs, shrinking government regulatory activity may increase, not decrease, corruption unless the statutes are changed to reflect the lower budget totals. There are several ways to do this short of outright repeal. (1) The regulatory process can be simplified so the reduced workforce can process more applications or inspect more producers. Some regulatory reforms that improve allocative efficiency can reduce corruption incentives as well. For example, the use of tradable pollution rights or effluent charges for environmental control not only will produce a more efficient distribution of regulatory burdens, but also will contain fewer corruption incentives than a command-and-control regime. And the sale of scarce regulatory permissions, such as import and export quotas, converts illegal payoffs into legal payments. (2) For open-ended programs, the law can establish a stronger burden of proof on an official who wishes to deny permission. (3) Fewer firms can be made subject to the regulations or several categories of regulatory approvals can be established so detailed scrutiny is given only to the most important cases. (4) Private rights of action can be created so citizens can help assure enforcement of the law by bringing suits against violators.

C. Shrinking Budgets While Increasing Controls

Suppose that a corrupt government suddenly faces a fiscal crisis. For example, suppose a government dependent on oil revenues must cope with a decline in the price of petroleum. Until the crisis, the nation's rulers have siphoned off funds for themselves while also spending public funds on programs with broad popular support. The crisis forces the regime to cut back public spending and the rent-seeking opportunities it generates. In addition, the government may privatize state enterprises reducing patronage and payoff opportunities. To compensate for these lost corrupt opportunities, the rulers may, however, increase the regulatory burden on the private sector.

This, argues Chhibber (1996), is what happened in Algeria in the late 1980s as oil revenues fell. According to him (p. 127), the ruling party "responded to the fiscal crisis by signaling a partial opening up of the market and a downsizing of the public sector. The proposed liberalization, ironically, led to increased financial and political corruption and larger transaction costs for small business." When an increased role for the private sector is combined with increased regulation, the result can be an increase in corruption. Chhibber argues that in Algeria the attempt to preserve the corrupt opportunities of the ruling elite and their allies contributed to the subsequent regime change. One reason for this political fallout was the increased burden on the small-business sector faced with a costly choice between increased regulatory strictures and heightened bribery demands (p. 133). Chhibber also suggests that a similar dynamic operated in India and Pakistan in the 1980s and in Iran before the fall of the shah (p. 145).

In short, shrinking the government budget can reduce corruption if it eliminates programs and reduces discretion. If, however, it simply makes government benefits scarcer without changing the method of allocation, corruption may increase as potential beneficiaries compete for the increasingly scarce pool of benefits. Spending cuts accompanied by increases in regulations may simply shift the locus of corruption. These conclusions suggest both that substantive statutory reform should accompany budget cuts and that internal government reform should be a high priority. It is not sufficient to get the macroeconomic totals in line with IMF and World Bank guidelines, nations should also be concerned with their performance under conditions of stringency. In those areas where scarcity cannot be eliminated, civil-service reform and strong financial management are especially necessary.

II. Privatization

Privatization can reduce corruption by removing certain assets from state control and converting discretionary official actions into private market-driven choices. However, the process of transferring assets from public to private ownership is fraught with opportunities for corruption and self-dealing. Corruption has frequently determined how the monopoly rents of the public firm are divided between bidders and the government.[2]

The first set of opportunities for corruption arises in determining the list of prequalified bidders. Bribes may be solicited for inclusion on the list, and firms may also pay to restrict the number of other bidders.

The second set arises when large state enterprises are privatized. As there may be no reliable way to value their assets, the tax and regulatory regime that will prevail ex post facto may be poorly specified. The uncertainties of the process create opportunities for favoring corrupt insiders by giving them information not available to the public, providing information early in return for payoffs, or giving corrupt firms special treatment in the bidding process. In extreme cases no auction occurs. The firm is simply awarded to those with excellent political connections. As John Nellis and Sunita Kikeri (1989, 668) state: "Sales, at unstated prices, have sometimes been made to dubious purchasers, such as ruling party politicians and others lacking in business experience."

For example, before an overhaul of the procedures, privatizations in Argentina were apparently accompanied by favoritism and payoffs (Manzetti 1996). In Brazil, when it became clear that an ally of President Fernando Collor de Mello was in line to receive the privatized firm, others withdrew their offers (Manzetti and Blake 1996). Collor sought to use market reforms to create a financial empire of his own (Manzetti 1996). Similar examples come from Zaire, Ivory Coast, Thailand, and Slovakia (Van de Walle 1989; Phongpaichit and Piriyarangsan 1994). Although competitive bidding is not always the preferred method of carrying out a privatization, when negotiated deals are used, the above examples suggest the importance of transparency and clarity in the privatization process.

Weak conflict of interest laws make insider dealing easy. In Argentina, several officials that designed the highway privatization bidding process were on the staff of companies that acquired the highways (Manzetti 1996). In Venezuela, First Boston organized the privatization of the state airline in spite of its close ties to the Spanish airline Iberia (Manzetti and Blake 1996). Iberia was involved in valuing the airline in spite of the fact that it also planned to bid on the company and did eventually end up purchasing the airline (Celarier 1996, 65). According to Russia's senior prosecutor, the privatization process in that country has been undermined by bid-rigging by banks that both arranged and won privatization auctions.[3]

There arises a third set of opportunities for corruption when the winning firm would like to obtain the firm at the lowest possible price. Corrupt officials may present information to the public that makes the company look weak while revealing to favored insiders that it is actually doing well. The insiders then are the high bidders in what appears to be an open and aboveboard bidding process. Similarly, corrupt bidders may be assured of the leniency of regulatory oversight, something an outsider cannot rely upon. Ex post facto evaluations reveal that the privatization was a huge success with the newly private company earning very high rates of return. Observers in both China and Ecuador have noted cases of this type. A Venezuela major bank was undervalued by the minister of national investment amid payoff allegations (Manzetti and Blake 1996).

A fourth set of opportunities may arise when a privatized firm is worth more if it retains whatever monopoly power was available to the public firm. To an economist, the retention of monopoly rents undermines the justification for privatization. To an impecunious state and its bidders, assuring monopoly power is in the interest of both. Thus the conflict between revenue maximization and market competition arises for all privatization deals. When a state gives lip service to competitive principles, however, it may be unable to endorse monopolization openly. Corrupt, back-channel deals can then accomplish that objective, but with some of the benefits transferred to individuals rather than the government. Luigi Manzetti (1996) argues that many Latin American privatizations increased, rather than decreased, market concentration. Although they provide no direct evidence of corruption, John Nellis and Sunita Kikeri (1989, 668) list several examples of special benefits firms may obtain. In one African country, the new private cigarette manufacturer received heavy protection, with confiscatory taxes on competing production and a monopoly on imports. An eleven-year monopoly on the sale of Coca Cola was obtained by a privatized distributing firm, and production limits on other soft drinks were imposed on competitors. High rates of protection have been granted to a leased (and thus partially privatized) steel mill in another country.

What do these opportunities for corruption suggest about how much and what kind of firms will be privatized? Will kleptocrats always want a larger state sector than an honest ruler? The answer is no. A corrupt ruler is likely to be especially eager to privatize monopolies that earn excess profits so long as he can extract a share of the gains. He may even seek to privatize more firms than a ruler whose only goal is efficiency if the corrupt one-shot gains from a sell-off are large.

Although corruption can occur at all these points in the privatization process, the desired end result is a private firm subject to market discipline and removed from corruption incentives. This does not mean, however, that once privatized, a reduction in corruption is assured. First, the firm, especially if it retains some monopoly power, is likely to retain a close relationship to the state. After all, outside the former socialist countries, most public enterprises are in industries with substantial economies of scale and in areas that are viewed as being closely associated with the national interest, such as public utilities or transportation (Yotopoulos 1989, 698). Sometimes the privatization contract explicitly requires the government to revisit the deal in a few years. This may be a good strategy if it permits the government to increase competition in the industry, but it also creates another opportunity for corrupt transactions. Those monitoring the process must be alert for situations where self-dealing has simply been replaced by bribery.

Second, frequently the state sells off only a portion of the state firm, often retaining control, at least in the early years. Such hybrids may be especially subject to corrupt inside arrangements. For example, a private firm with partial ownership of a former state enterprise may attempt to shift losses onto the state with the connivance of public officials. In Italy a joint public-private venture in the chemical industry allegedly involved just such a transfer. Bribes were apparently paid both to benefit the private firm when the venture was formed and to obtain a high price for the same assets when the venture broke down and the firm was nationalized (Colazingari and Rose-Ackerman 1995). These corruption incentives may mean that the most efficient firm manager loses out to a corrupt insider. They may also mean that the company continues to receive favors from the state even after nominal privatization has occurred. Even if the end result is an efficiently operating private firm, however, corruption in the tendering process assures that the government receives too little from the sale, a result that implies higher taxes or lower spending for ordinary citizens and other businesses.

These possibilities thus suggest the importance of designing the privatization process to assure the widest level of participation rather than favoring consortia with strong ties to local elites. They also imply that the process needs to be transparent, especially the evaluation of the assets.[4] The use of outside assessors to enhance transparency may not solve the problem, however, if they themselves have close ties with multinationals seeking to bid on the assets. This is an issue that is of increasing salience to international lenders such as the World Bank that are trying to assure competitive privatization processes.[5]

One option is to require all bidders to take a no bribery pledge as a condition for participation (Transparency International 1995). This is an ex ante version of the prequalification processes used by procurement offices in many jurisdictions. The number of bidders may be reduced, but the selective elimination of corrupt firms will enhance the competitive nature of the process, not reduce it.

An implication of this discussion is the value of setting up the regulatory framework in a credible way before the tendering process begins. This will both reduce the uncertainty associated with the tendering process and reduce the possibility that the winning bidder can manipulate the process by which regulatory institutions are created (Nellis and Kikeri 1989, 670). Unfortunately, clarity concerning the regulatory framework is often not provided.[6]

Alternatively, the international community could establish a forum, perhaps within the World Trade Organization or the World Bank, that could review cases of suspected corruption in privatization processes. Disappointed bidders could bring cases that would require the country involved to make a transparent accounting of their behavior. Such a process would, of course, discourage some privatizations from going ahead in the first place, but that might not be such a bad thing. When an inside deal appears inevitable, privatization should be delayed since a public firm is much easier to monitor than a private one. In this proposal, the cost of the proceeding might be subsidized by the international community if a country emerges victorious from a challenge. Also, the jurisdiction of the tribunal could be limited to countries that volunteer to join the process if, in return, they can receive World Bank technical advice and other support for the process of carrying out a privatization and establishing a reformed regulatory system. This proposal is an example of the more general principle that one way to fight corruption is to give losers a means of lodging a complaint, whether the harm they have suffered is a lost contract, control of a privatized company, or access to subsidized housing for the poor (Alam 1995).

III. Organized Crime and Corruption

Illegal businesses have a corrupting influence on government. Even when government's role in legitimate business activities shrinks, the state continues efforts against criminal businesses and their infiltration into legal markets. Criminals bribe both to keep their own businesses operating and to induce the police to shut down the businesses of their rivals.[7]

Of course, here too, the option of shrinking government exists. After a short experiment with Prohibition, the United States repealed the Eighteenth Amendment to the Constitution outlawing the manufacture and sale of "intoxicating liquors." Its time in force, between 1919 and 1933, was a period of widespread illegal production and sale of alcohol and corruption of law enforcement officers. The debate over legalizing drugs in the developed world turns on the feasibility of controlling the industry through the criminal law. Gambling, formerly outlawed in many jurisdictions, has recently become a legal business in many countries and in parts of the United States, albeit under heavy state supervision and even, at times, state ownership. Nevertheless, wholesale legalization of drugs, gambling, and vice seems unlikely in the near future, leaving a protected field of operation for criminal groups sheltered from competition from legitimate business. In corrupt systems, criminal groups also operate safe from legal prosecutions by paying off the police and politicians or including them directly in their businesses.

The danger for economic development arises when organized crime groups begin to dominate otherwise legal business. Southern Italy, several Latin American countries, the countries of Eastern Europe, and the former Soviet Union are cases in point. Organized crime groups can use the profits of illegal enterprise not only to assure the complicity of public officials in their illegal activities, but also to infiltrate legal businesses. The profits generated by illegal businesses, earned without paying taxes, can then be reinvested in legitimate business and in obtaining public contracts (Gambetta 1993; Varese 1994). If criminal groups can create an atmosphere of uncertainty and the threat of violence, they will drive competitors, especially competitors from developed countries, away, leaving the criminal organizations with a free field of operation. The risk of organized crime driving away legitimate investment suggests that great care ought to be taken to establish a transparent and reliable legal environment before privatization is undertaken. In many countries in Eastern Europe and the former Soviet Union this was not done with predictable results (Rose-Ackerman 1994; Shelley 1994). In Latin America, regulatory agencies were frequently created only after firms were privatized (Manzetti 1996). Although the influence of organized crime in Latin American privatizations has only infrequently been alleged, the opportunities for special treatment created by the uncertain legal environment create risks in those countries where drug money is an important source of wealth.

Even in developed countries, some legitimate businesses are especially vulnerable to criminal infiltration. Organized crime is both wealthy and unscrupulous. It is willing to use not only bribery, but also threats and violence to enforce its contracts and get its way. This gives it a competitive advantage in several fields. The first area open to the influence of organized crime includes businesses where entry is relatively inexpensive but can be discouraged by threats. Private garbage collection provides a good example. Entry is inexpensive—one need only purchase a truck. However, garbage trucks operate alone on the public streets. Thus is it relatively easy to intimidate unwanted rivals by attacking their trucks without attracting police attention. To assure even less risk of the involvement of law enforcement, but at a cost, the police can be paid to look the other way. Similarly, whenever a business needs a license to operate, the ability of corrupt officials to gain a license for yourself and deny one to your rivals gives one an obvious competitive advantage.

Second, legal businesses that benefit from prime urban locations are especially at risk of the influence of organized crime in countries with weak or corrupt police forces. This includes restaurants and shops serving tourists and business travelers. Manufacturers can hide in out-of-the-way locations (Charap and Webster 1993), but these service businesses cannot "go underground" to avoid notice. If the police are unreliable, criminal groups may demand protection money from the funds assigned to protect the businesses, in effect protecting the business from attacks by the group itself (De Melo, Ofer, and Sandler 1995; Webster 1993; Webster and Charap 1993).

Third, in communities or whole countries where capital is scarce or underpriced, organized crime may fill the gap by providing funds at high rates and by being willing to use threats and violence to enforce loan contracts (Webster 1993; Webster and Charap 1993; Yabrak and Webster 1995).

Fourth, businesses such as banks and casinos, which are effective venues for money laundering, risk criminal takeovers. In all countries, casinos are at risk. In countries such as those in the former Soviet Union, where banking regulations are lax or poorly enforced, financial institutions have been established and taken over by organized crime groups (Shelley 1994).

Fifth, businesses, such as road repair and building construction, that do a heavy business with the state are also prime candidates for the influence of organized crime. If a government has been corrupted by organized crime in connection with its illegal businesses, it may be a relatively short step to make payoffs to obtain public contracts on favorable terms. In the extreme, organized crime groups manage cartels that share contracts and pay off public officials to buy their complicity or at least their silence. In southern Italy, for example, over half of the small- and medium-sized businesses interviewed reported withdrawing from a public tender after pressure from criminal groups or their political allies. (See "Still Crooked," *The Economist*, February 5, 1994.)

Wealthy criminal groups may find it too risky to invest their earnings directly in the country where they were earned. Such funds might raise questions about their origin and if a criminal investigation is launched could be seized by the state. Thus criminal groups may seek to launder the funds abroad and then invest them at high returns either outside the country or as new "clean" investments in the country of origin. Many experts claim, for example, that a share of the "foreign" investment entering Russia is actually money controlled by Russian criminals that has been laundered to disguise its origin. Laundering both hides the funds' origins in organized crime and makes the investors eligible for special subsidies only available to outside funds (Shelley 1994).

The wealth, unscrupulousness, and international connections of many organized crime groups suggest the difficulty of control by any one country. The danger is that, rather than being a stage of development that will wither away over time, criminal activity becomes so intertwined with politics that it is difficult to tell them apart. The state then has little interest in controlling criminal influence and can descend into kleptocracy. Since criminals are as interested in getting rich as anyone, optimists might contend that if criminals actually control the government they will modify their ways; but this seems utopian. One would expect that those in control would seek to limit entry through threats of violence and the elimination of rivals as they have done in the drug business. These regimes are what Mancur Olson (1993) calls "stationary bandits." Furthermore, organized crime bosses may be more interested in quick profits through the export of a country's assets and raw materials than in the difficult task of building up a modern industrial base. The end result is the delegitimization of the democratic enterprise and the undermining of capitalist institutions.

When corruption is combined with organized crime, the problem for reform-minded governments and international-aid donors is made more difficult. If the entire state is permeated with crime, there is probably not much outside organizations can do except wait in the wings and hope for the best. In less extreme cases, the experience of developed countries in fighting organized crime may be useful. One strategy is to isolate criminal groups so that their influence does not extend outside of illegal businesses. In the New York City School Board, for example, this involves prequalification procedures for contracts that disqualify firms associated with criminal groups for several years (Thacher 1995). Also needed are active efforts to rout out corruption in the law enforcement and criminal justice systems in an effort to make payoffs more risky and difficult. One possibility is the creation of law enforcement authorities at different levels of government with overlapping authority. That way, if any one authority is honest, criminal influence can be limited. Corruption in drug enforcement in the United States, for example, is limited by the existence of federal, state, and city law enforcement, so corrupting any one organization is not worth very much (Rose-Ackerman 1978). In developing countries unused to confronting organized crime, a combination of training and law reform is likely to be needed. Civil service employment conditions must be improved, especially in police departments and customs services, so that collaboration with criminals is not an economic necessity. The compensation package should include some benefits, such as pensions, that only accrue if one is not discharged for dishonesty (Becker and Stigler 1974).

Such reforms are, however, unlikely to be sufficient unless the economy is strong and competitive. The state may need to make more direct efforts to reduce the excess profits available to criminal entrepreneurs in legitimate business. One solution is promoting the entry of well-capitalized legitimate businesses that, with some state help on the law enforcement side, can compete with mob-dominated firms. Although it is too early to judge the success of the effort, this is what Browning-Ferris, a large multinational waste management firm is doing in the trash hauling industry in

New York City.[8] Countries facing widespread criminal influence need to act decisively to limit the influence of entrenched criminal networks based on trust and family ties.

A country's links to the broader world can either limit or expand the scope for organized crime. On the one hand, an open trading and investment regime can make it easy for both contraband and the profits of crime to flow across borders. The existence of numerous "financial paradises" where illicit money can come to rest makes domestic criminal activity less risky since money can easily be hidden abroad. To counteract the negative impact of openness requires international efforts to "follow the money" and isolate those countries willing to provide safe havens for illicit funds. This suggests that international organizations ought to focus on international banking disclosure standards that make it more difficult to hide illicit funds.

On the other hand, open borders facilitate the investment by outsiders in a country. If these outsiders are not part of the domestic criminal bodies and are not associated with such groups elsewhere, they may challenge entrenched groups. Of course, if such investments are costly and dangerous enough, few may make the effort, but the lack of regulatory controls at least makes such investments possible.

IV. Lessons for Latin America

Although smaller government may indeed be cleaner government, this result is not inevitable. The cooperative efforts of officials and corrupt outsiders to gain at public expense will continue to be a problem, even in a shrunken government, unless legal and institutional reforms limit opportunities for corruption. Otherwise, incentives to divide the existing benefits or to create new ones will still exist. If government budgetary cutbacks simply produce scarcity with no corresponding change in the underlying substantive statutes, a government on an austerity plan may generate more opportunities for corruption than a less constrained one. The combination of poorly paid public officials and a scarcity of public benefits can increase both the supply and the demand for payoffs. Furthermore, the process of shrinking government by selling off state enterprises creates its own opportunities for corruption even if the end result is a day-to-day reduction of those opportunities.

Latin American regimes engaged in shrinking and streamlining government activities face all of the difficulties outlined above. Austerity budgets increase the competition for scarce public services and for the limited number of government contracts. Payoffs can play a role in the allocation of these benefits. Privatization of public firms has led to accusations of corruption and insider dealings. Regulatory agencies created to oversee the newly private firms have sometimes had difficulty establishing themselves as competent, apolitical bodies. A burgeoning private sector often makes illegal payoffs to limit bureaucratic red tape. The continuing importance of the drug trade in a number of Latin American countries has produced corruption scandals involving high-level politicians and law enforcement officers. Opportunities to resist corrupt demands and to report the corruption of others are limited by the ineffectiveness and corruption of the courts and law enforcement systems in some countries.

Latin American countries are at a turning point. It is not sufficient to limit inflation, set a realistic exchange rate, and bring the fiscal system into balance. Macroeconomic reform is only a first step. A number of countries such as Argentina, Chile, Mexico, and Peru have privatized a portion of the state enterprise sector and eliminated some costly regulatory structures (Manzetti 1996). But more needs to be done if reform is to produce growth that is broadly shared. The continuing existence of corruption in Latin American governments is one of the problems of political systems with strong executives, close-knit political-economic elites, low levels of transparency, and a highly unequal distribution of income and wealth. As I have tried to demonstrate, simply shrinking the size of the state is not sufficient. To limit corruption, other, more fundamental changes must occur in the relationship between the government, the private sector, and ordinary citizens.

The move to privatize and deregulate in some Latin American countries is, as I have argued, an important first step, but one that will fail to improve governmental integrity unless carried out with an awareness for the new opportunities for corruption created by the reforms. Remaining government responsibilities can often be reorganized to reduce corruption incentives, but more generic reforms are needed as well.[9] These include policies that make it easier for outsiders to monitor and discipline government, and policies that reduce the benefits and increase the risks to civil servants and politicians. The government must provide information about its behavior, including consolidated budgets and legal and regulatory texts, and must be required to explain its actions and open its procedures to the public. Nonprofits, the press, and ordinary citizens must be able to freely criticize state actions. To do this responsibly, they must have access to information about state actions and be able to lodge complaints and bring legal actions (Coronel 1996). Civil service reform is needed to make government work sufficiently remunerative to reduce corruption incentives and to reward people for a career of effective service. The carrot of better pay and benefits, however, must be supplemented with credible punishments for those who violate legal norms, otherwise government jobs will simply become rewards for loyal supporters.[10]

Reform does appear to be possible although it requires a long-term commitment to change that is often not easy to achieve. Chile was a very corrupt country in the period 1891–1924 but is now viewed as relatively clean by Latin American experts (Montinola 1996). Deregulation in Chile has produced a marked difference in how businesses view the state in Chile as compared to other Latin American countries such as Brazil (Stone, Levy, Paredes 1992). And even in Brazil attitudes may be changing. The independent behavior of the Supreme Court helped assure that the recent impeachment of the president occurred with little corruption of the legislature (Geddes and Ribeiro Neto 1992, 658). In Argentina under Carlos Menem, the second round of privatization was more transparent and less marred by allegations of corruption than the first (Manzetti 1996).

The reform of individual sectors or subnational governments can occur even without overall change. Thus the customs service in Mexico, the reinsurance system in Argentina, and the city government of La Paz all experienced successful cleanups (*El Economista*, February 13, 1992; Moreno Ocampo 1995; Klitgaard 1996). Reform in Mexico was based on simplifying procedures and improving pay and monitoring; in Argentina publicity led to changes in accounting practices and replacement of the board of the public company; in La Paz a reform mayor introduced a composite package of projects that began with efforts to remove the worst offenders but went on to include more fundamental changes. Several Latin American countries are considering judicial system reforms (Buscaglia 1995; Rowat, Malik, and Dakolias 1995). Nevertheless, the durability of partial reforms is questionable. In La Paz the government slid back into corrupt practices after a reform mayor left office. When he returned to power in 1995, he found that many of his anticorruption policies had been undermined (Klitgaard 1996, 116–125).

In those Latin American countries where the corruption of public officials is part of the illegal drug business, fundamental questions are raised about the independence and integrity of the state. An anticorruption effort cannot succeed apart from a more general attempt to limit the extent of illegal business activity. The profits from the illegal drug trade are so large that reforms such as improved pay and working conditions for law enforcement officials, although necessary, are unlikely to be sufficient. If illegal businesses cannot be eliminated, they can at least be contained and their impact on the state minimized. This involves not only limiting corruption in law enforcement, but also increasing the transparency and accountability of politicians and enhancing the competitiveness of the economy by removing government restrictions. The interrelationship between the illegal drug business and politics in some Latin American countries argues for strengthening state organizations designed to control this activity, limiting other state interventions that create corrupt opportunities, and protecting legitimate business from the threats of organized criminal groups. Legitimate businesses must have a way to seek redress from the state against the pressure exerted by criminal enterprises.

In general, reform governments should not focus exclusively on removing those accused of corruption. Campaigns against "rotten apples" are never sufficient. Simply removing one set of corrupt officials and replacing them with another is unlikely to improve matters much unless the underlying incentives for paying and accepting bribes are removed or reduced. The new recruits are likely to pick up where the old ones left off. The basic lesson of the economic analysis is that corruption can best be fought by limiting the opportunities and rewards for paying and receiving payoffs, not by searching for saintly people to staff government offices and run for office.

Notes

1. Susan Rose-Ackerman is Luce Professor of Law and Political Science, Yale University, and the author of *Corruption: A Study in Political Economy* (N.Y.: Academic Press, 1978). An earlier version of this chapter was presented at a World Bank Symposium on Public Sector Management, "Toward a New Paradigm of the State—Building a New Partnership for Development," November 1995 and was circulated as a background paper for the USAID-IRIS Seminar on Good Governance and Regional Economy, Dakar, Senegal, March 1996. A Spanish translation has been published as "¿Una Administración Reducida Significa una Administración más Limpia?" *Nueva Sociedad,* No. 145 (September–October 1996), pp. 66–79.

2. Celarier (1996) provides several examples from Latin America especially Mexico. Manzetti (1996) argues that the privatization of public enterprises in Peru reduced corruption in the public sector, but then goes on to detail several problems in the privatization process itself including lack of transparency. His studies of Argentina and Brazil contain similar examples.

3. "Russian Privatizations Face Crime Probe," *Financial Times,* 6 February 1996. See also Celarier (1996, 66).

4. Nellis and Kikeri (1989, 669). The costs to a country of lack of transparency are illustrated by the case of privatization in Brazil as described in a speech by Chase Manhattan managing director Charles Wortman. He advises foreign investors to take on local partners because little public information is available. According to Wortman, "Investors typically re-

ceive the bid package . . . 30 to 45 days and sometimes as little as 15 days before a company is sold. The information is skimpy and not necessarily reliable. Not much due diligence is allowed. Don't expect a company to open its books and allow your accountants to come in. Few representations and warranties are given. If surprises come up later, they are your problem." Based on a report on the speech in Rosemary H. Werrett, "Brazil: Privatization Program Throws New Curves at Foreign Investors," *Development Business*, 16 January 1996.

5. See Antonia Sharpe, "CVRD Sale Shows Limits of World Bank Adviser Rules," *Financial Times*, 18 December 1995.

6. See, for example, "Malaysian Privatization Loses Allure," *Financial Times*, 13 October 1995.

7. See "Bribes and Publicity Mark Fall of Mexican Drug Lord," *New York Times*, 12 May 1996; "Mexican Connection Grows as Cocaine Supplier to U.S.," *New York Times*, 30 July 1996; "Popular Revulsion Is New Factor in Chronic Colombian Drug Scandal," *Washington Post*, 28 January 1996.

8. "Judge Backs Competition in Trash-Hauling Industry," *New York Times*, 28 February 1994; "The Garbage Wars: Cracking the Cartel," *New York Times*, 30 July 1995; "Monitors Appointed for Trash Haulers," *New York Times*, 23 December 1995.

9. Such reforms are discussed in Klitgaard (1988), Pope (1996), and Rose-Ackerman (1997).

10. Klitgaard (1996, 118) mentions that after the reform mayor of La Paz left office, salaries remained high, but political appointments increased dramatically.

References

Alam, M. S. 1995. A Theory of Limits on Corruption and Some Applications. *Kyklos* 48: 419–35.

Becker, Gary, and George Stigler. 1974. Law Enforcement, Malfeasance, and Compensation of Enforcers. *Journal of Legal Studies* 3:1–19.

Buscaglia, Edgardo, Jr. 1995. Judicial Reform in Latin America: The Obstacles Ahead. *Journal of Latin American Affairs* Fall/Winter: 8–13.

Celarier, Michelle. 1996. Stealing the Family Silver. *Euromoney* February: 62–66.

Chhibber, Pradeep K. 1995. State Policy, Rent Seeking, and the Electoral Success of a Religious Party in Algeria. *Journal of Politics* 58:126–48.

Colazingari, Silvia, and Susan Rose-Ackerman. 1995. Corruption in a Paternalistic Democracy: Lessons from Italy for Latin America. Draft prepared for a lecture in the Trinity College Italian Programs, Hartford, Conn.

Coronel, Gustavo. 1996. Curbing Corruption in Venezuela. *Journal of Democracy* 7:157–63.

De Melo, Martha, Gur Ofer, and Olga Sandler. 1995. Pioneers for Profit: St. Petersburg Entrepreneurs in Services. *World Bank Economic Review* 9:425–50.

Gambetta, Diego. 1993. *The Sicilian Mafia*. Cambridge Mass.: Harvard University Press.

Geddes, Barbara, and Artur Ribeiro Neto. 1992. Institutional Sources of Corruption in Brazil. *Third World Quarterly* 13:641–61.

Klitgaard, Robert. 1988. *Controlling Corruption*. Berkeley Calif.: University of California Press.

———. 1996. Bolivia: Healing Sick Institutions in La Paz. In Center for Institutional Reform and the Informal Sector, *Governance and the Economy in Africa: Tools for the Analysis of Corruption and the Reform of Corruption*. University of Maryland, College Park, Md., 112–26.

Manzetti, Luigi. 1996. *Privatization South American Style*. Draft book manuscript. Southern Methodist University, Dallas, Tex.

Manzetti, Luigi, and Charles Blake. 1996. Market Reforms and Corruption in Latin America: New Means for Old Ways. *Review of International Political Economy* (forthcoming).

Montinola, Gabriella R. 1996. The Efficient Secret Revisited. Draft. Department of Politics, New York University, New York, N.Y.

Moreno Ocampo, Luis Gabriel. 1995. Hyper-Corruption: Concept and Solutions. Presented at the Latin American Studies Association, Washington D.C., September 29.

Nellis, John, and Sunita Kikeri. 1989. Public Enterprise Reform: Privatization and the World Bank. *World Development* 17:659–72.

Olson, Mancur. 1993. Dictatorship, Democracy, and Development. *American Political Science Review* 87:567–75.

Phongpaichit, Pasuk, and Sungsidh Piriyarangsan. 1994. *Corruption and Democracy in Thailand*. Bangkok: Political Economy Centre, Faculty of Economics, Chulalongkorn University.

Pope, Jeremy, ed. 1996. *National Integrity Systems: The TI Source Book*. Berlin: Transparency International.

Rose-Ackerman, Susan. 1978. *Corruption: A Study in Political Economy*. N.Y.: Academic Press.

———. 1994. Reducing Bribery in the Public Sector. In *Corruption and Democracy: Political Institutions, Processes, and Corruption in Transition States in East-Central Europe and in the Former Soviet Union*, edited by Duc V. Trang. Budapest: Institute for Constitutional and Legislative Policy, 21–28.

———. 1997. The Political Economy of Corruption. In *Corruption in the World Economy*, edited by Kimberly Elliott. Washington, D.C.: Institute for International Economics, forthcoming.

Rowat, Malcolm, Waleed H. Malik, and Maria Dakolias, eds. 1995. *Judicial Reform in Latin America and the Caribbean: Proceedings of a World Bank Conference*. World Bank Technical Paper 280.

Shelley, Louise. 1994. Post-Soviet Organized Crime. *Demokratizatsiya* 2:341–58.

Stone, Andrew, Brian Levy, and Ricardo Paredes. 1992. *Public Institutions and Private Transactions: The Legal and Regulatory Environment for Business Transactions in Brazil and Chile*. Policy Research Working Paper 891. World Bank, Washington D.C.

Thacher, Thomas D. II. 1995. *The New York City School Construction Authority's Office of the Inspector General: A Successful New Strategy for Reforming Public Contracting in the Construction Industry*. Draft. New York.

Transparency International. 1995. *Building a Global Coalition against Corruption*. TI Annual Report. Berlin.

Van de Walle, Nicolas. 1989. Privatization in Developing Countries: A Review of the Issues. *World Development* 17:601–15.

Varese, Federico. 1994. Is Sicily the Future of Russia? Private Protection and the Rise of the Russian Mafia. *Archives of European Sociology* 35:224–58.

Webster, Leila M. 1993. *The Emergence of Private Sector Manufacturing in Hungary*. World Bank Technical Paper 229. World Bank, Washington, D.C.

Webster, Leila M., and Joshua Charap. 1993. *The Emergence of Private Sector Manufacturing in St. Petersburg*. World Bank Technical Paper 228. World Bank, Washington, D.C.

Yabrak, Isil, and Leila Webster. 1995. *Small and Medium Enterprises in Lebanon: A Survey*. World Bank. Private Sector Development Department and Industry and Energy Division, Middle East and North Africa Country Department II. Final report.

Yotopoulos, Pan A. 1989. The (Rip)Tide of Privatization: Lessons from Chile. *World Development* 17:683–702.

Part 2

Theory Meets Reality:
Reducing Corruption in Latin America

5

High-Level Political Corruption in Latin America: A "Transitional" Phenomenon?

LAURENCE WHITEHEAD

Introduction

This chapter first sets out the theoretical basis for the claim that even if high-level political corruption appears to increase in the early stages of an economic-cum-political liberalization, it should be durably curbed once the transition is completed. This loosely neoliberal proposition has been used by Western experts to buttress their case for rapid and wholesale programs of liberalization. This chapter argues that neither the theoretical nor the empirical grounds for this contention are very convincing, at least so far as contemporary Latin America is concerned.

The missing ingredients are analysis of monitoring mechanisms, accountability, and the "rule of law." Western policymakers may now be in danger of swinging from one extreme to the other, pressing indiscriminate reregulation where previously their only concern had been with deregulation. At least in Latin America, the battle against high-level corruption will require time, patience, and domestic support. Cookbook prescriptions imposed from without could easily prove counterproductive.

In principle, high-level political corruption[1] is to be expected under authoritarian rule, where those in power enjoy impunity and are sheltered from public criticism. By the same token, a transition to democracy should lead to the emergence of a free press and independent media; the creation of competitive parties and counterbalanced institutions; and the subordination of all citizens (including the most powerful) to an impersonal constitution and the rule of law, administered by an independent judiciary. All this can be expected, *pari passu*, to discourage high-level political corruption by increasing the likelihood of exposure and punishment, and by reducing expectations that the perpetrators of such crimes will retain the freedom to reward their loyal followers and to retaliate against those who stand against them.

This dichotomous political analysis (authoritarian rule favors high-level corruption; democracy discourages it) has an exact counterpart in the realm of economic analysis. Here the argument is that a statist, interventionist, or politicized system of economic management favors high-level political corruption by distorting the market and so creating monopoly profits or rents that can be allocated with discretion by public office-holders. Such cross-subsidies and rentier incomes are nontransparent, and therefore escape public inspection and control. By the same token, a transition to an open, competitive market economy without politicized distortions can be expected, *pari passu,* to reduce the range of illicit and concealed profit opportunities available to the holders of political power; and to subject economic policymaking to more effective public scrutiny and control, backed up by the force of an independent business community, which can be presumed to favor transparent institutional procedures and legal accountability for the use of public monies. This dichotomous economic analysis, therefore, postulates that interventionist policies favor high-level corruption, whereas free markets discourage it.

Although these two hypotheses concerning the incidence of high-level political corruption are parallel and overlapping, they are in principle distinct. Latin America certainly provides clear examples of authoritarian rule combined with market economics (e.g., Pinochet's Chile) and also of interventionist economics combined with political democracy (most recently Caldera's Venezuela). The political diagnosis of corruption emphasizes simple abuse of public office, whereas the economic diagnosis points toward a more complex, discriminating, and enterprise-related account of surplus misappropriation. The anticorruption mechanisms postulated by political liberalism assume an empowered citizenry or electorate, whereas economic liberals rely more on an autonomous private sector pursuing its interests through the market. In practice, nearly all of Latin America has recently experienced both types of liberalization, usually proceeding more or less in tandem. Even Pinochet's Chile proceeded to a democratic transition after a decade or so of economic liberalization, and even Caldera's Venezuela seems to have returned to economic liberalization after its brief experiment with democratic interventionism. So, although our two initial hypotheses are, in principle, distinct, most of the available Latin American evidence relates somewhat indistinctly to both.

What follows, therefore, is a provisional review of the relationship between high-level political corruption in Latin America and the region's recent shift to political-cum-economic liberalization (without much disaggregation of the two). Although the two initial hypotheses are fairly clear and cogent, it is not a straightforward matter to relate them to the (no doubt highly incomplete) evidence presently available. Like most dichotomous analyses, the postulated contrasts are stylized and overstated. Yet in contrast to these neat theoretical constructs, the evidence refers to a range of intermediate or partial regimes that may contain elements from both sides of the dichotomy bound together in various combinations. In Brazil, for example, although military rule was unquestionably authoritarian, some elements of impersonal constitutionalism and a division of powers was always retained. Likewise, an interventionist style of economic policymaking was always operated in conjunction with a relatively strong and autonomous private sector, largely coordinated through the market.

In Peru, over the same period, both authoritarian military rule and economic interventionism took much more drastic forms. Even within Brazil, economic-cum-political liberalization has affected the calculus of corruption very differently in, for example, the northeastern state of Alagoas on the one hand, and the federal capital of Brasilia on the other. (Local power structures and institutional practices vary widely across the huge subcontinent that is Brazil.) Without further multiplying these examples, it can be seen that all evidence concerning the scale and distribution of political corruption needs to be interpreted within a context that is too elaborate to be captured by the two initial dichotomies.

A second limitation of the two opening hypotheses is equally severe. They are exercises in "comparative statistics," that is to say, they refer to a stable initial condition (authoritarian rule, interventionist economics), which can be contrasted with a stable alternative condition (democracy, a market economy). Such evidence as we have, however, refers to dynamic or unstable situations between these two poles ("transition to democracy"). However convincing may be the arguments from first principles linking a consolidated democracy and a secure market economy to the control of high-level corruption (and the evidence from Italy and elsewhere indicates that this is not, in fact, a straightforward link), it in no way follows that such malfeasance will diminish before those desired states are irreversibly entrenched.

On the contrary, both theory and experience offer good grounds for anticipating that the transition may be associated with an increase in the frequency and intensity of illicit enrichment. On precautionary grounds, those who had previously enjoyed impunity and immunity from public criticism can be expected to step up their acts of malfeasance when these defenses begin to crumble during periods of regime breakdown and uncertainty over the stability of the rules of the game (either economic or political). During periods of transition, the time horizons of many actors are foreshortened by uncertainties concerning their career prospects and by fears of regression. Hence new actors too may have precautionary motives for seizing immediate opportunities of self-enrichment. Also, when new rules of the game are still fresh and untested, it is easy through inexperience or lack of clear guidance to commit acts that will be interpreted by competitors as corrupt. The main monitoring and control mechanisms postulated by the theorists of economic-cum-political liberalization (a vigilant press, a well-organized private sector, a reliable justice system, an informed public opinion) cannot emerge overnight. If they do eventually become established, it can only be after a protracted process of testing and learning. Until then, the transition from an illiberal to a more liberal order may increase rather than diminish the opportunities and incentives for high-level political corruption.

Since such reasoning from first principles about high-level political corruption seems to generate inconclusive results, the obvious alternative is to appeal to the evidence and to construct generalizations inductively, but unfortunately there are also serious impediments to empirical work in this area. Individual, sometimes spectacular, episodes of high-level corruption may be well-documented through investigative journalism, congressional hearings, and indeed judicial processes, but even in the most visible and well-documented of cases, large areas of vagueness typically remain.

For example, as Luigi Manzetti describes elsewhere in this volume, Brazil's first democratically elected civilian president in thirty years, Fernando Collor de Mello, was forced to resign after less than three years in office as congressional inquiries uncovered the scale of his illicit fund-raising activities. On some key questions of responsibility and illegality, the public record seems incontrovertible. Yet it was only through an improbable succession of accidents that so much came to light in this case. Even then, it remains uncertain how much other evidence was effectively suppressed and at what point and by what mechanisms the spreading circle of complicities was limited. Subsequently, the very Congress that had championed the anticorruption case against an unpopular president was, in turn, exposed as riddled with comparable abuses.

A close relative of the disgraced president remains on the Supreme Court bench to which he was nominated by the chief executive before the impeachment vote. In any case, the evidence uncovered in this case is mostly concerned with narrow issues of criminal liability. It does not address the broader questions of political strategy or economic motivation that would need to be uncovered in order to construct a broad-gauge analysis of high-level political corruption in the course of Brazil's liberalization experience.

Objective and dispassionate data collection on the topic of political corruption is an inherently problematic enterprise.[2] The very term "corruption" denotes passion and subjectivity, and the charges and countercharges surrounding each case are infused with partisanship. This is hardly surprising when the stakes are so high for the powerful actors involved and when the control mechanisms are as controversial and distrusted as they are in contemporary Latin America. In relation to almost every case, it will be possible to find well-informed sources that will claim defamation and the planting of evidence, together with equally articulate exponents of the doctrine of the cover-up. The imperfections of Latin American mechanisms for the monitoring and control of public-office holders more or less ensure that for every convincingly proven case of high-level corruption there must be multiple others that could not be conclusively documented.

Some observers will tend to conclude from this fact that most unproven allegations are also probably true, whereas others will argue that in such circumstances unfounded accusations of corruption constitute a virtually costless instrument of political warfare.

It is small wonder, then, that many political scientists and academic observers of liberalization and transition tend to shrink away from this aspect and focus instead on other topics.

For my part, about twenty years ago, well before the latest cluster of transitions to democracy and economic liberalization, I attempted a synoptic survey of the available evidence concerning systematic and macroeconomically significant corruption in twentieth-century Latin America.[3] In contrast to alternative literature concerned with low-level corruption and inclined to rely on explanations based on various more or less cultural or traditional features of Latin American society, my chapter stressed hyperpresidentialism and executive impunity as the key explanatory variables, and it paraded a wide range of examples in which consciously designed strategies of illegal rent seeking and extortion were orchestrated from the very top of the political system.

The evidence assembled was approximate and impressionistic, but sufficient to suggest that: this had been a recurrent pattern in the region's political economy; the magnitudes involved were often highly significant in macro terms; a top-down institutional analysis was warranted; and rather than serving some functional purpose, such large-scale presidential corruption was potentially highly destabilizing. During the cold war, it was tempting for some political scientists to implicitly condone such corruption, either on the grounds that the detached observer should eschew value judgments, or in the belief that corruption assisted economic growth and provided an alternative to communism. Since 1990 both of these assumptions have been abandoned, and most political scientists are now normatively committed to honest markets and good government. But as Luigi Manzetti shows elsewhere in this volume, economic-cum-political liberalization can also be associated with high-level political corruption orchestrated from the presidential palace.

Manzetti may be right to assert that new forms of corruption appeared and corruption intensified as Brazil and Argentina democratized. But as he also recognizes, the evidence for such assertions is problematic. In order to judge just how new or increased the corruption was under President Collor, one would need comparable evidence concerning his predecessors (both military and civilian) and successors. Perhaps the Collor scandals were an aberration. Perhaps behind the regression and censorship of the military dictatorship even larger illicit fortunes were politically sanctioned.

Certainly after the 1964 coup, great publicity was given to allegations concerning the corruption that had occurred during the final years of the preceding and discredited democratic regime. Yet some business observers commented in the late 1960s that the only real difference was that pre-1964, Brazilian corruption had been chaotic and decentralized, whereas under military control it was methodical and concentrated at the top. In a similar vein, business informants in Argentina explained to me (anecdotally, of course) that in the 1980s, under the first democratic administration of President Alfonsín, it was difficult to know when a bribe was expected, which officials were or were not corrupt, or what the appropriate tariff might be. In the 1990s, under President Menem and the Peronists by contrast, there was, according to these sources, no ambiguity or embarrassment, and the rates and procedures were clear-cut and predictable.

Finally, still at this anecdotal level, it was common in 1990 and 1991 to hear American businesspeople gushing about the way the Salinas administration in Mexico had put an end to the extortion of foreign investors and had installed a new cohort of well-educated, properly paid public officials with good command of English and a commitment to transparency. The *Wall Street Journal* was so impressed that it put Salinas on the board of its management company, Dow Jones. These U.S. businesspeople and the *Journal* were apparently among the last to awaken to the sorry truth revealed at the end of that administration.

Indeed, the Clinton administration was still pressing for Salinas to be appointed director general of the World Trade Organization (against resistance from almost all of Washington's allies) as late as the end of January 1995, even after the scandals had become public.

Transparency International is making a systematic effort to tabulate this hitherto merely anecdotal information. It assembles various sources of information, mainly derived from the perceptions of international businesspeople whose companies operate in a variety of countries. The result is a "corruption perception index," with an annual rating of 0–10 (high corruption at the bottom, low at the top). Although this method is open to criticism, it does provide a series of judgments over time. Table 5.1 reports the tabulations from 1995–98, covering only the neodemocracies.

This is a useful compilation and will become more so as the time series build up. But for the purposes of this chapter, several qualifications are in order. First, foreign businesspeople have a more complete picture of the situation in some countries—the more liberalized, those with a high exposure to foreign trade, those with a long-established foreign investment community—than in others. Second, the type of businesspeople sampled may vary across countries; some samples may therefore have higher expectations of political probity than others. Third, this chapter concerns high-level political corruption in Latin America, a region characterized by hyperpresidential forms of government. Where presidentialism is strongest (e.g., in Mexico or Argentina), if businesspeople report widespread corruption it almost certainly reflects a strategy orchestrated from near the top of the political system. In other neodemocracies listed in Table 5.1, it may be that weak central authority is incapable of disciplining regional or local levels of corruption, and it may even be that the higher levels of political authority are doing all they can to combat such practices. In certain laissez-faire regimes, perceptions of corruption may refer to collusive business practices in the private sector that are largely beyond the reach of the formal political system, either central or local. The foreign business observers sampled by Transparency International would not necessarily observe or report these nuances. Finally, to some extent respondents may score on the basis of secondary impressions (e.g.,

Table 5.1
Corruption Perceptions Index

1998 Ranking	1998	1997	1996	1995
20 Chile	6.8	6.1	6.8	7.9
22 Portugal	6.5	7.0	6.5	5.6
23 Spain	6.1	—	—	—
26 Estonia	5.7	—	—	—
27 Costa Rica	5.6	6.5	—	—
29 Taiwan	5.3	—	—	—
32 South Africa	5.2	5.0	5.7	5.6
33 Hungary	5.0	5.2	4.9	4.1
36 Greece	4.9	—	—	—
37 Czech Republic	4.8	5.2	5.4	—
39 Poland	4.6	5.1	5.6	—
41 Peru	4.5	—	—	—
42 Uruguay	4.3	—	—	—
43 South Korea	4.2	4.3	5.0	4.3
46 Brazil	4.0	3.6	3.0	2.7
51 El Salvador	3.6	—	—	—
54 Turkey	3.4	3.2	3.5	4.1
55 Mexico	3.3	2.7	3.3	3.2
55 Philippines	3.3	3.1	2.7	2.8
59 Guatemala	3.1	—	—	—
61 Argentina	3.0	2.8	3.4	3.2
61 Nicaragua	3.0	—	—	—
61 Romania	3.0	3.4	—	—
61 Thailand	3.0	3.1	3.3	2.8
66 Bulgaria	2.9	—	—	—
69 Bolivia	2.8	2.1	3.4	—
71 Latvia	2.7	—	—	—
71 Pakistan	2.7	2.5	1.0	2.3
76 Russia	2.4	2.3	2.6	—
77 Ecuador	2.3	—	3.2	—
77 Venezuela	2.3	2.8	2.5	2.7
79 Colombia	2.2	2.2	2.7	3.4
83 Honduras	1.7	—	—	—
84 Paraguay	1.5	—	—	—

Note: The table only ranks the 34 "new democracies" included in the 85 countries surveyed. (In 1998 Denmark ranked first, with a "perfect" 10, the USA came 17th with 7.5 and Cameroon came last with 1.4.)

the level of polemic over corruption in the media) rather than from direct experience alone.

Yet averting one's gaze is hardly an option for anyone seriously concerned with the task of examining how Latin America's economic-cum-political liberalizations are actually proceeding and where they may be leading. Any list of the most prominent figureheads in Latin America's recent liberalization drive would necessarily include ex-Presidents Collor and Pérez (both impeached); ex-President Salinas (disgraced); and incumbent Presidents Fujimori and Menem (both surrounded by associates facing serious charges of dishonesty).[4] Whatever one's judgment of each individual leader on this list, taken as a group, their achievements and limitations can hardly be evaluated without considering the problems of malfeasance and inadequate accountability. Current tendencies to amend Latin America's constitutions in order to permit the reelection of incumbent chief executives cannot be adequately assessed without regard to these issues. Nor can the stability and legitimacy of a wider range of liberalizing reforms (including privatization) be determined in isolation from the controversies that have arisen concerning alleged political corruption in these areas.

In global terms, the most important consideration is to explain what almost derailed the liberalization process associated with the Salinas administration and caused the resulting crisis of the Mexican regime (and perhaps even the North American Free Trade Agreement model), thereby casting a deep shadow across all similar experiments. At least within Mexico, it is widely believed that discredit of the Salinas style of reform can be attributed in substantial measure to his administration's immersion in high-level political corruption. In view of this, serious empirically based work on economic-cum-political liberalization cannot afford to disregard the subject.

One way of advancing the analysis, given the limitations of the available theory and the inadequacies of the empirical data, would be to distinguish more precisely between various alternative patterns of behavior that may all be subsumed under the vague rubric of high-level political corruption. For example, the political rationale and institutional logic for amassing hidden funds that can be used to influence election outcomes should not be confused with that for arms trafficking, or for blocking judicial investigations into the narcotics industry, or for manipulating central bank assistance to insolvent privatized banks.

Each of these potential patterns of illicit behavior stands in its own distinctive relation to economic-cum-political processes of liberalization, and each may therefore either be curbed or facilitated by relatively specific public policy decisions. Admittedly, in practice, the recently uncovered scandals in Brazil, Mexico, Argentina, and elsewhere indicate how easily one variety of high-level political corruption runs into another: how electoral corruption can lead to money laundering, complicity with *narcotraficantes,* and eventually court rigging and even political assassination. But even if there is a corrosive logic to the dynamics of complicity and impunity that often overruns the neat boundaries that analysts try to erect between one type of illicit practice and the next, it may still help to illuminate this murky subworld if we separate out the various component elements and examine them one by one.

Fund-raising for political parties to finance election campaigns is a good place to start. Under authoritarian rule, political parties were often supervised or even banned, and electoral contests were frequently manipulated by those in power. But even then, most countries held periodic elections and these were often rather expensive affairs. Typically, the incumbent authorities would favor a particular party or slate of candidates and would provide abundant resources to pay for the associated campaigning and publicity. Such resources would come, in part, from the public sector and might include the support of public employees, deductions from employee payrolls to finance more or less compulsory party membership subscriptions, free advertising and unrestricted access to the (normally censored) media, the loan of official premises and vehicles, and so forth. Obviously, approved parties could run well-financed election campaigns while opposition parties were denied official resources and were often starved even of private funds. Whereas private donors were officially encouraged and rewarded if they contributed to approved campaigns, they were liable to penalties if they supported opposition candidates. The ARENA party in Brazil, Mexico's PRI, and the Colorado party of Paraguay all exemplified this authoritarian style of electioneering.

Following the transition to a more authentically competitive and genuinely multiparty electoral democracy, new systems of party fund-raising and campaign financing would be required. But old reflexes, assumptions, and the vested interests created by the previous history were not likely to disappear overnight. Nor was it usually a straightforward matter to agree on a new "level playing field" of rules governing political financing, let alone to establish the effective monitoring and reliable implementation of such rules once they were adopted. When, for example, the Colorado party of Paraguay mounts a strong and well-financed election campaign under democratic auspices, it is hardly surprising if some sections of the electorate find it hard to believe that all its campaign contributions are now voluntary and aboveboard. This is valid, especially considering that many contributors and beneficiaries are the same people who previously engaged in antidemocratic styles of electioneering.

In addition to the legacy of suspicion and distrust that may arise from predemocratic experiences of party fund-raising, new sources of unease about election finances may arise during democratization from the emerging posttransition incentive structure. As elections become more competitive, the stakes rise for the rival contenders. Incumbents may fear that if they lose office their chances of return will be severely impaired by the emergence of new options. Opposition politicians may also regard defeat in a competitive election as far more damaging to their reputations and prospects than previous defeats incurred against overwhelming odds. Thus early postdemocratization elections may arouse both more hopes and more fears than conventional campaigns in stable balance of party contests. This may help to explain why allegations of high-level corruption linked to campaign financing have proved a recurrent feature of democratization experiments in contemporary Latin America.

This short chapter is not the place for an exhaustive survey of the evidence concerning party financing in democratic Latin America.[5] A few highlights must suffice, simply in order to indicate the magnitudes of the sums allegedly misappropriated for this purpose and the widespread nature of the phenomenon. In accordance with my emphasis on high-level corruption, and in consonance with the presidentialism that characterizes most Latin American neodemocracies, the examples given below refer to the national levels of party leadership. Regional and local party financing also deserve careful scrutiny, however.

By the time he was impeached in December 1992, President Collor de Mello of Brazil had amassed secret funds, reportedly in excess of $1 billion dollars, through a systematic program of taking commission on public contracts organized by his financial henchman, P.C. Farias (the treasurer of his 1989 presidential campaign). Lacking a strong party of his own or a solid base in Congress, the president nevertheless expected to build up a loyal political following and secure passage of his preferred legislation by making judicious payments from this slush fund. As Brazilian election campaigns are both frequent and costly, and party discipline is weak, one of the most plausible uses for these secret funds was to bankroll the election of candidates who would vote as the president required on key measures.

When he was forced from office in May 1993, President Carlos Andrés Pérez of Venezuela was no longer on good terms with the party he had headed since the 1970s. Acción Democrática was a well-funded social democratic party that had repeatedly mounted lavish, and often highly successful election campaigns. Venezuela was accustomed to competitive elections but not to transparent rules on party financing. The charge against Pérez was that he had diverted $17 million of secret government funds intended for security and defense into the black market where it had been used to finance the president's political campaigns, thus freeing him from dependence on his party machine.

In February 1993 the Mexican PRI's secretary of finance organized a private dinner, attended by President Salinas, at which the twenty-five prominent guests were each "invited" to contribute $25 million to the funds of the ruling party in order to cover its expenses in the forthcoming 1994 election campaign.

In July 1995 the treasurer of the Colombian Liberal party was arrested and admitted to receiving $6 million from the Cali drug cartel as a contribution toward the second-round campaign of Ernesto Samper, the party's standard-bearer who had secured the presidency after a close race in June 1994.

As these miscellaneous examples make clear, various elected presidents of Latin America seem to require control over large sums of money of questionable provenance in order to win elections and reward loyal followers. Here we are not dealing with funds collected in small trenches from the rank-and-file of the ruling party. On the contrary, part of the objective seems to be to free the head of state from undue dependence upon independent party structures. When individual donations are for sums in excess of a million dollars apiece, it is difficult to believe that they express unrequited loyalty alone.

When the funds are secretly managed and are only provided to incumbents, a presumption of high-level political corruption is difficult to avoid. What could wealthy donors hope to obtain in return for secretly financing the election or reelection of certain candidates or parties? All of the four leaders reviewed above were identified with politics of economic liberalization and state reform in their respective countries. It is difficult to escape the inference that wealthy donors might hope to profit from inside information or privileged access regarding such liberalizing reforms.

As Susan Rose-Ackerman and Luigi Manzetti both argue elsewhere in this volume, shrinking the state can provide opportunities for rent seekers no less rewarding than those previously associated with state expansion. Although this type of corruption may be connected with election finances, the two are not necessarily linked and should be kept analytically distinct as the range of possible countermeasures are quite different. We now briefly review the theory and evidence relating high political corruption to programs of economic liberalization and "state shrinking." This discussion draws attention to an intervening variable—the rule of law, or independence and effectiveness of the justice system—which goes far to explain why in some countries, policies of state reform can be implemented without extremes of high-level corruption, whereas in others this is much harder.

According to prevailing neoliberal orthodoxies, corruption is inherently built into the incentive structure of state interventionism (which stimulates rent seeking) and becomes a marginal or inexpedient activity in a fully competitive market economy (based on profit seeking). The conclusion drawn is that the best antidote to corruption is to proceed at maximum speed with a strategy of wholesale economic liberalization and privatization. One line of cautious criticism has been to accept the basic premises of the argument (without necessarily endorsing its binary extremism), while arguing for a gradualist approach to reform, since too much haste itself could provide additional incentives and excuses for misappropriation.

But true believers in neoliberal doctrine have always tended to reject gradualism and prefer "shock treatment." On the corruption issue, they argued that even if rapid privatization did create additional transient opportunities for corruption, the speedy adoption of free-market disciplines would soon extinguish such incentives. They argued that protracted methods of privatization would be worse, in that during the interim the "insiders" controlling the state assets would have the time and motive to "loot" the enterprises in their care. This would both weaken state finances and undermine the momentum needed to make privatization irreversible.

It is not easy to reconcile this theoretical position with the comparative and historical evidence on high-level corruption available from Latin America. For example, comparing Costa Rica and Nicaragua, it would be hard to deny that the former had a long and effective record of broadly social democratic economic interventionism, while under the Somoza dictatorship, the latter eschewed public ownership or welfare provision and allowed prices to be set by world markets. Yet, in interventionist Costa Rica, the incentives for high-level political corruption were tempered by an independent and vigilant justice system, a free press, and a constitutional division of powers that normally held successive single-term presidents to account for the performance of their public duties. In less interventionist Nicaragua, by contrast, the ruling dynasty amassed a fortune, which, on the eve of the 1979 Revolution, was worth at least several hundred million dollars and included the most strategic and dominant industries of the republic's small economy. None of the constitutional checks and balances that worked so powerfully in neighboring Costa Rica provided restraints on the power of the Somoza family. The family had maintained effective political control for over forty years, either through presidential reelection or the nomination of puppet leaders, and operated in a "sultanistic" manner, that is, without recognizing a distinction between public property and the private wealth of the rulers.

Generalizing from these two polar cases, one can list a succession of Latin American regimes with small state sectors that practiced high-level corruption of the Nicaraguan type (from Plattist Cuba and Stoessner's Paraguay, onward). There is also a significant cluster of social democratic or interventionist regimes with institutional defenses against high-level corruption of a Costa Rican caliber (in Chile and Uruguay most notably). Between these two clusters, we can find a wide variety of hybrid cases, but in any case, comparative analysis of high-level corruption in pre–debt-crisis Latin American history offers scant support for the simple binary opposition between rent-seeking interventionists and profit-seeking markets postulated by neoliberal theory.

In defense of the neoliberal position, it might be argued that pre-1990s history is irrelevant to the new structure of incentives and disciplines arising from a globalized market economy after the end of the cold war. International markets and the standards of government demanded by foreign investors are now far more transparent than in the past (as Table 5.1 exemplifies). At least in this new setting, it can still be argued that the best way to curb high-level political corruption is to privatize and liberalize as fast and as thoroughly as possible. Inevitably, this argument will have to rest as much on deduction as on induction, at least until sufficient time has elapsed to confront the theory with conclusive evidence. But unless the theory is very compelling, this lack of historical confirmation or of corroborative pilot studies ought to incline practitioners and analysts toward gradualism and caution rather than root-and-branch constructivism. So just how compelling is the theory that urges shock treatment as a cure for corruption, and what provisional evidence can it invoke so far?

Neoliberal reform characteristically requires concentration of discretionary power in the hands of a well-insulated team of economic technocrats, usually acting on authority delegated by a powerful president. This is true of most neoliberal reform programs, but it is especially true of those geared to wholesale and irreversible institutional change in the short run (i.e., shock treatment state reforms). The theory underlying such reforms is that since economic agents are generally self-regarding, the rules of the economic game must be authoritatively redesigned from above, by those best equipped to understand the logic of alternative incentive structures.

Discretionary executive power should be used to dismantle those institutions and rules of the game that encourage self-interested agents to engage in rent seeking and to create or reinforce those that favor profit seeking. However, if it is assumed that all economic agents are self-regarding, how can one exempt the economic technocrats who are most committed to this theory from falling prey to the conduct they detect in others? And if institutions and rules of the game are to be evaluated according to the incentives for corruption they create, can the prescription that discretionary power should be concentrated in the hands of a well-insulated group within the most powerful branch of the state apparatus be exempted from that type of evaluation? In purely theoretical terms these seem troubling lacunae in the neoliberal analysis.

The evidence available so far is inconclusive and not reassuring. Reference has already been made to the disputed allegations concerning Cavallo, Salinas, and others. Conversely, it can be argued that the "Chicago Boys" in Chile broadly lived up to the promise of neoliberal theory, and that neoliberal reformism in Bolivia was also relatively clean and successful (particularly since some of the key reformers were themselves already very wealthy as private mine-owners). On the empirical side, the most disconcerting indicators relate to a succession of experiences of bank privatization. The Mexican example is extreme, but by no means unique. Over the past fifteen years, the main banks of Mexico have been successively nationalized, privatized, and, most recently, bailed out at great taxpayer expense. (The 1995 rescue effort is currently estimated to have cost around 12 percent of Mexico's annual GNP.) In each case a small group of well-insulated technocrats, acting under the protection of an imperial presidency, have deployed discretionary power on a massive scale. It does not seem very important whether private assets are being seized, public assets are being sold off, state subsidies are being granted, or uncollectable debts are being written off. Whichever of these activities happen to be engaging the energies of Mexico's bank regulators at any specific moment, they are allowed to act nontransparently and without much in the way of effective legal or political accountability. Neoliberal theory would predict that if this is the incentive structure then the agents in question will abuse their huge financial power and act in such a way as to ensure that financial crises keep recurring so that their privileges remain in place. Strategies of financial shock treatment have been justified on the grounds that the quickest route to a stable market economy is the strongest guarantee against future corruption. However, just as plausibly, it can be argued that reckless and indiscriminate bank privatizations ensure that the resulting privatized financial system will not be solid, and that the neoliberal insiders in charge of the process will also enjoy future opportunities for discretionary abuse of power to sort out the consequences of their own imprudencies.

Similar issues arise with regard to one of the latest neoliberal prescriptions: the need to entrench central bank independence following democratization and financial liberalization. The theory is that a legally and institutionally untouchable central bank can be mandated to protect the integrity of the currency and to shield the financial system from the temptations to engage in monetary manipulation that afflicts election-driven politicians. Yet the available evidence from neodemocracies in general, and from Latin America's experiments with central bank independence in particular, suggests that if these huge powers of financial supervision are insulated from democratic accountability, it is likely that those entrusted with them will succumb to other, more concealed forms of societal influence. In the absence of effective public accountability, strong legal supervision, or a vigilant public opinion, independent central banks can themselves become an institutionally secure base for high-level political corruption.[6]

Election financing and corruption arising from the discretionary implementation of liberalizing economic reforms may be the two forms of high-level political corruption most obviously associated with economic-cum-political liberalization projects, but they are not the only forms that require investigation here. More briefly, then, we also need to consider arms trafficking, money laundering, narcotics-related corruption, and finally abuse of the justice system. All of these take distinctive forms as a consequence of the contemporary liberalization trends in Latin America.

With the end of the cold war and the shift to fiscal austerity, the shrinking military and security establishments of the subhemisphere have lost much of their former raison d'être and their political protection against budget cuts. This situation creates new pressures and incentives, as institutional protections weaken and the time horizons of defense ministers and senior military personnel are shortened. Expensive weaponry may become surplus to requirements or become impossible to service and update. In a liberalized and internationalized environment, however, there are usually eager buyers for modern military equipment, especially if it can be delivered clandestinely.

In mid-1996 the Argentine minister of defense was forced to resign when it became apparent that his department had secretly supplied Ecuador with weapons used in its border dispute with Peru, despite Argentina's official status as guarantor of the cease-fire between these two sister republics. Whether the motive was simply personal enrichment or included some intention to supplement the resources available to the military establishment remains to be clarified, as do the broader political ramifications. Perhaps this was an unrepresentative incident, but it would be rash to assume that economic-cum-political liberalization necessarily diminishes the scope for this type of high-level corruption, either in the short run or over the long run.

Another feature of a liberalized international environment is that it can increase the opportunities for money laundering. The International Monetary Fund (IMF) seems to accept that the twin forces of economic liberalization and technological innovation have boosted this activity to an (conservatively estimated) annual turnover of $300–$500 billion. According to Vito Tanzi, a senior economist at the fund, both the rapid growth of loosely regulated emerging financial markets and the expansion of private financing operations conducted by companies technically headquartered in tax havens (notably in the Caribbean) have made it is easier to invest large amounts of anonymous capital without raising suspicion. He also argues that such laundered funds tend to work against the goal of economic efficiency. This is because their distribution is not driven by economic fundamentals (e.g., after-tax rates of return or real interest rates), but by differences in the degree of regulatory oversight in different markets, which accordingly attracts these type of funds regardless of the associated inefficiency and misallocation of resources. Governments that are not greatly concerned about the provenance of the funds they receive thereby secure a margin of freedom to pursue wasteful economic policies of the kind that the IMF is always trying to curb.[7]

Nothing in this analysis suggests that the growth of money laundering is a purely transitional phenomenon that can be relied on to go into reverse once liberalization programs have been completed. Only some form of reregulation, presumably with enhanced powers of intervention from the IMF or related international bodies, would be likely to promote such a reversal.

The question of deregulation versus reregulation is closely connected to the issues arising from the proliferation of international drug-related business, politics, and criminality. In Latin America the central issue concerns the cocaine trade, which has been primarily geared to supplying the huge U.S. domestic market for narcotics. Authoritarian military regimes, such as the García Meza dictatorship in Bolivia and the Noriega dictatorship in Panama, were initially the most visible culprits in this area of high-level criminality. (Both these ex-presidents are currently serving jail sentences for their drug-related crimes.) But the economic-cum-political liberalization of the region has done nothing to reduce the scale of consumer demand for these illicit substances, and consequently has done nothing to curb the incentives for engaging in this type of transaction or indeed for providing political protection to the big players in the business. While on the one hand the financial community based in Washington has been strenuously promoting economic liberalization, and the Organization of American States–based political community has stepped up international support for democratization in the Americas, elsewhere in Washington other agencies have been more aggressive in trying to counter international drug-trafficking.

Thus, both deregulation and certain forms of reregulation are being promoted throughout Latin America at the same time.[8] In a number of cases the result has been that a democratically elected head of state with a clear commitment to economic reform may be simultaneously subjected to equal and, in a certain sense, opposite forms of pressure from the international community. For example, improve your human rights performance, but crush the drugs barons by any means necessary. Privatize and deregulate your banks, but vet them more intensively than ever before for illicit deposits. Allow more open and competitive elections, but stamp out all expression of narcotics-related interest in your political system—even from regions where the cultivation of cocaine provides the main source of livelihood for most small producers. Uphold the constitutional order, founded upon a commitment to national sovereignty, but accept external certification of your conduct concerning the most delicate questions of internal security and bow to foreign demands for extradition or for extraterritorial rights, whenever they serve the cause of narcotics control.

Despite economic-cum-political liberalization, a succession of Bolivian, Colombian, Mexican, and Peruvian presidents have struggled with limited success to reconcile these competing and insistent external demands. It is far from clear that narcotics-related corruption and political delegitimization proves a merely transitional phenomenon in such countries.

More generally, in much of Latin America, over long periods of time, substantial amounts of high-level political corruption have coexisted with substantial islands of institutional integrity, and with rather extensive and durable areas of conventional and respectable profit-driven economic activity. Only in relatively exceptional cases has the corruption run out of control to the point of overwhelming the institutional integrity. Equally, the neoliberal theory that the expansion of the market economy will drive back and eventually eliminate large-scale politicized misappropriation of resources can only invoke a limited range of supporting instances from this region. Comparative experience—including from the Anglo-Saxon democracies—suggests that where the progressive elimination of corruption has occurred, it has been an incremental process extending over various decades, requiring cumulative pressure from a variety of sources, usually internally driven, and by no means linear in character.[9] This chapter has reviewed a series of indications tending to cast doubt upon the view that in the near future the incidence of high-level political corruption in Latin America will be drastically different from in the past.

On a panel at the September 1996 Woodrow Wilson Center conference on political corruption, I found myself sandwiched between two well-informed analysts. One of these analysts portrayed an unremittingly bleak image of the disintegration taking place, with Western support, in the former Soviet Union, while the other argued that in Asia, and in China in particular, the dismantling of old systems of state regulation was opening up spaces for great economic creativity at the local and enterprise levels. It was argued that in the Asian case, the predominant form of what Western analysis would call corruption was really a type of illicit profit sharing that could be wealth-creating and could encourage improved public policies—quite the opposite to the destructive rapacity portrayed in the Commonwealth of Independent States (CIS) cases.

My impression is that Western policymakers have periodically veered from one extreme to the other in their attitudes toward corruption in the non-Western world. Whatever the truth about contemporary postcommunist states in Europe and Asia, my conclusion is that neither of these stereotypical images provides a consistently valid guide to Western policies in Latin America. Both of these contrasting images share one common characteristic—they simplify complex situations in a way that tends to encourage indiscriminate, one-sided, and potentially very intrusive Western policy responses.

The implication of this analysis for Western policymakers is that neither traditional complacency nor a new surge of righteousness is the appropriate reaction. To effectively combat such long-standing and deeply entrenched practices will require patience, vigilance, and discrimination. High-level political corruption may be a scourge in many parts of Latin America, but it is not generally a terminal affliction. Over time, with persistence and through cooperation with the extensive local professional and institutional groupings committed to the strengthening of the rule of law, it should be possible to make progress in promoting an ethos of public responsibility and accountability. But this will only be durable if it has solid domestic support. Flamboyant interventions from without can easily undercut the construction of such local coalitions, providing a nationalist cover for the reaction against them.

This is especially the case when outside policymakers are suspected of grandstanding for their own political advantage, and when short-term gestures are perceived as selective and unlikely to last. A dense network of interlocking formal and informal institutions enjoying external support but resting primarily on internal bases of legitimacy, would provide the most secure defense against the region's old habits of patrimonialism and abuse of power. In consequence, effective long-run reforms to curb high-level political corruption would need to be constructed in the interests of the home population, promoted in a spirit of self-respect, and guaranteed by institutions that are locally authentic. Where external support is provided, it will work better if it is multilateral, durable, predictable, and aimed at reinforcing well-established islands of integrity within the country concerned.

These closing observations are slightly out of harmony with much of the mood music to be heard in official Washington these days. At the October 1, 1996, annual meeting of the World Bank and the IMF, for example, IMF Managing Director Michel Camdessus flatly stated that member countries "must demonstrate that they have no tolerance for corruption in any form."[10] A few months earlier, James Wolfensohn, president of the World Bank, was quoted as saying, "countries that are fundamentally corrupt should be told that unless they can deal with that they are not getting any more money."[11] The World Bank recently revised its procurement guidelines so that it can bar companies from Bank financial projects if they engage in "corrupt or fraudulent practices." The Bank's 1996 *World Development Report* devoted special attention to rampant corruption in transition economies, arguing that this was undermining public support for the entire reform process and threatening economic growth.

This stress on the negative consequences of unfettered corruption is a remarkable change from the official line during much of the 1960s and 1970s when World Bank and IMF prescriptions often focused on the rigidities and economic distortions arising from excessive state intervention in market processes. This was when some forms of corruption were regarded quite benignly, perhaps seen in terms of "speed money" to circumvent stifling regulations. At that time some kinds of corruption were thought to produce potentially positive results, both in terms of accelerated growth and as a catalyst for liberalizing reforms. On a wider canvas, during the cold war high-level corruption by reliable anticommunist allies was to some extent condoned by many Western policymakers as the lesser of two evils.[12] The current zero tolerance doctrine is therefore a novelty, perhaps an understandable response to the uncontrolled criminality that has accompanied the adoption of Western policy prescriptions in many former Soviet states, but arguably an overreaction, at least as far as Latin America is concerned.

In conclusion, this chapter is not a policy paper. It argues against some hasty and politically convenient shortcuts in the analysis of high-level political corruption in Latin America. There is no automatic connection between the adoption of economic-cum-political liberalization measures and the elimination, or even the near-term reduction, of political corruption. Some forms of high-level misappropriations of resources become more difficult as liberalization proceeds, but others may become easier. It is not only the incentive structures that need to be considered, but also the monitoring procedures, notably the judicial system, the media, and the various audit and control agencies, all of which can be destabilized by shock treatment. We should not be overly impressed by sensational short-term developments when the processes that count are mostly long-term and multifaceted. There are, no doubt, some situations in which international financial institutions and others will have to practice zero tolerance and the harshest forms of conditionality. But most contemporary Latin American experience points in a different direction.

Effective long-term progress toward reducing and eventually perhaps even eliminating high-level corruption requires considerable local knowledge, patience, and staying power. Therefore the monitoring mechanisms that stand most chance of taking root will need to be home grown and locally legitimized. They can certainly be encouraged and supported from outside (revelations in foreign courts, pressures from the international media, even rounds of official decertification, may provide essential backup), but effective international coordination of anticorruption policies will require candor about the nature of the interdependencies and co-responsibilities involved.

Although my focus has been on domestic Latin American institutions and practices, we should never forget that in a liberalized and internationalized environment, corruption is unlikely to stay confined within narrow national boundaries. Drug trafficking, for example, requires an external market and some complicity by developed-country banks, custom officials, and law enforcement agencies. Arms trafficking requires manufacturers and pushers outside Latin America as well as within the region. There have to be bribe givers as well as bribe takers, and both seek the security provided by international banking safe havens. It is not a cultural inevitability that Latin Americans must continue to live under governments characterized by high levels of impunity and power abuse, but neither can these patterns be eliminated from one day to the next by "just saying no." Underlying incentive structures would have to be refashioned, and anticorruption monitoring reinforced. An ethos of public responsibility would have to be nurtured. Any progress on these fronts would take considerable time, would vary with complex local conditions, and would require seriousness of purpose from a wide array of actors and institutions, both locally and internationally. Such anticorruption networks will only be durable, credible, and eventually successful if they are willing to challenge entrenched interests and practices opposed to their agenda wherever they lurk—whether within Latin America or outside the region—whether condemned by international financial institutions or tacitly condoned by them. Reforms and adaptations are likely to be slow and uncertain. Before we lose patience with this, we all need to consider the hard cases. If our arms manufacturers need time and support to adjust to the disappearance of lucrative markets, than so do their coca growers. If we would not tolerate intrusive foreign monitoring of the projects of our own elected leaders, then we should not expect the citizens of other democracies to be that enthusiastic either.

Notes

1. This chapter is only concerned with "high level" and "political" corruption, and not with "societal" or economic corruption more generally. The distinction rests on the claim—abundantly supported by evidence from Latin America—that a substantial proportion of the resources that are illegally captured or misappropriated in these economies are handled by national level public officeholders. Various modalities are identified in the chapter. Given the executive dominance that characterizes these political systems, presidents and their immediate associates are particularly prone to such activities, which should not be confused with lower-level forms of clientalism or asymmetric exchange of favors.

2. Consider, for example, the problem of the time lags that may separate the commitment of an offense from its public exposure. To take a recent example, following the military coup of 1964 one of the key conspirators used his privileged access to the authoritarian regime to build up a major Brazilian private bank, Unibanco. For twenty years under the shelter of impunity and immunity, this enterprise seemed to prosper. But with the return to democracy its advantages ceased. By 1986 it was effectively bankrupt. Yet, through the negligence or connivance of its regulators and the inexperience of new democratic actors, it continued to take deposits and to roll over debts for a further ten years. It was not until February 1996 that the Central Bank uncovered the fraud (which by then had snowballed to around U\$5 billion of unbacked liabilities, currently loaded onto the Brazilian taxpayer). Thus the scandal that broke in 1996 referred to offences committed perhaps decades earlier. But of course the political fallout accrued to the present democratic administration. No one can be sure how many other long-buried corruption scandals await exposure in other Latin American market-based neodemocracies.

3. "On Presidential Graft: The Latin American Evidence" reprinted in Arnold J. Heidenheimer, Michael Johnston, and Victor T. LeVine (eds.), *Political Corruption: A Handbook* (New Jersey: Transaction Publishers, 1989).

4. Following his dismissal as economy minister in Argentina, in July 1996, Domingo Cavallo has used his inside knowledge of the Menem administration to unleash an extraordinary succession of accusations against his former colleagues. He has demanded the removal of three cabinet ministers, accused judges of protecting smugglers and tax evaders, and warned President Menem that many of his closest associates are "criminals" or some of his own close associates were deeply corrupt. Hundreds of millions of dollars have been misappropriated, at least according to these allegations.

5. For an up-to-date survey, see Eduardo Posada (ed.), *Party Finances in Europe and Latin America* (London: ILAS, 1997).

6. I have assembled some evidence on this in my "Models of Central Banking: How Much Convergence in Neo-Democracies?" (Paper presented at a conference on The Political Economy of Central Bank Independence, St. Peter's College, Oxford, September 21, 1996).

7. Vito Tanzi, "Money Laundering and the International Financial System," IMF Working Paper (Washington, D.C., May 1996).

8. In theory, both deregulation and some forms of reregulation can proceed in parallel. For example, price liberalization need not be incompatible with improved tax collection, far from it, in fact. But, in practice, recent Latin American experience includes all too may instances of indiscriminate deregulation, inspired by doctrinaire antistatism. This in due course, produces a predictable backlash of reregulation. Various Latin American countries are still some way from establishing a reasonably stable balance between these two tendencies.

9. On Britain, for example, see "The Decline of Patronage" in H. Parris, *Constitutional Bureaucracy* (London, 1969); and W. D. Rubinstein, "The End of 'Old Corruption' " in *Past and Present* (1983).

10. *Financial Times,* 2 October 1996.

11. *Financial Times,* 2 July 1996.

12. Joseph Nye, for example, published a much quoted "cost-benefit" analysis of the relationship between corruption and development in the *American Political Science Review* (June 1967).

6

Market Reforms without Transparency

LUIGI MANZETTI

I. Introduction

Corruption has plagued Latin America since colonial times. Many observers believed that the return to democratic forms of government in the
1980s and the rise of a new breed of civilian politicians would diminish
corruption in most of the region. In the 1990s we have grown wiser. We
now find that old forms of graft not only continue, but that new corrupt
practices have also emerged. The dramatic events that led to the impeachment of Fernando Collor de Mello in 1992 and Carlos Andrés Pérez
in 1993 were only the tip of the iceberg.

The main argument of this paper is that when Less Developed Countries (LDCs) face a situation marked by political transition and severe economic crises, it is likely that unscrupulous candidates will gain a broad
mandate to promote far reaching reforms, escaping the checks and balances of the democratic system and allowing them, in the process, to pursue corrupt practices to an unprecedented level. Oddly enough, economic
deregulation and privatization of state enterprises—when pursued in a
nontransparent political system—offer such an opportunity. Kickbacks are
sought in return for rigging bids, that is, manipulating the rules governing
the transfer of state assets to the private sector. Before economic reforms
are decreed by executive order, persons in positions of power or trust can
sell privileged information to entrepreneurs or make exceptions to the

130

rules in exchange for bribes. Thus, the heralded policies of economic deregulation and privatization, instead of promoting less government intervention and greater transparency in business activities, can turn into new means to pursue old ends. In 1994, *Newsweek* underscored that free-market economic reforms can make corruption worse.[1] A recent article appearing in the *Wall Street Journal* echoed similar misgivings, "corruption may be more prevalent than ever. It is just that the players have changed, from bureaucrats and military dictators to a new class of closely allied entrepreneurs and politicians. . . . Nowadays [corruption] is more opportunistic, institutionalized, and very close to the style of organized crime."[2]

II. Analytical Problems

Scholarly works on political corruption dealing with LDCs have been usually anecdotal in character and have primarily focused on the sociocultural aspects of the phenomenon.[3] In the 1960s and 1970s much of the academic debate revolved around the question of whether corruption was detrimental to LDCs.[4] Those who argued about its pernicious consequences, often dubbed the "moralists," underscored how corruption slowed down economic growth, squandered resources, deterred foreign and domestic investments, weakened professional standards among public officers, and ultimately undermined democracy, thus paving the way to military takeovers.[5] "Revisionists" or "functionalists," on the other hand, argued that, on balance, corruption could have positive effects in terms of political development (by bypassing bureaucratic red tape) and political mobilization (through the creation of party machines).[6] Other scholars pointed out that the pros and cons of corruption in LDCs often depended upon the characteristics and stage of development of the socioeconomic institutions of a given political system. Only after taking into account these factors, the argument was, could the causes and effects of corruption be fairly assessed.[7]

Yet the functional approach became itself the target of sharp criticisms. In fact, some analysts showed that the thesis according to which corruption played a positive role in the economic and political realms was not supported by strong evidence, nor did corruption disappear once it was no longer functional as had been hypothesized earlier.[8]

Despite some notable exceptions, most of the research that followed remained anchored to the case-study approach, which, although useful in defining corruption and teasing out its several dimensions, was unable to provide the analytical tools necessary for comparative analysis.[9] Moreover, much of the failure in developing a sophisticated theory of corruption rests on the fact that, due to its complex nature, the subject itself presents serious operational and analytical problems.[10] Operationally, researchers have usually encountered serious difficulties in finding reliable and/or sufficient data as cases of political corruption usually go unreported. This is because those involved in corrupt practices often have the ability to cover up scandals through a variety of means among which intimidation is the most obvious. As a matter of fact, even when corruption cases are reported by the media or denounced by private citizens, few of them actually go to court.

Comparatively speaking, the study of corruption poses both "normative and positive questions which are difficult to disentangle."[11] Moreover, it is problematic to compare nations that have different standards of office holding and that enjoy different levels of economic development and public involvement in the market economy. Finally, there is considerable debate about how to define corruption.

Some have argued that corruption takes place when it violates the public interest,[12] yet this line of argument has been scarcely used due to the loose nature of the public interest concept itself. Adding to the confusion, not only the notion of public interest varies widely from culture to culture but, as we have seen, the revisionist camp actually considered corruption as performing a positive role for the achievement of public goods. Other scholars have looked at public opinion as a more useful criterion. This is because by asking people what they regard as corruption, we can both quantify the problem and avoid imposing a priori value judgments, as in the case of public interest. However, public opinion on issues of this nature is hardly unanimous, which begs the question: in the case of a divided public opinion, should we take the majority point of view as the one setting the standard criterion? If we did, we would impose the same value judgment that flawed the notion of public interest.[13] The third, and most used criterion, is the one based on the violation of legal norms of conduct in public office. Within this context, corruption is understood as implying the exchange of money or other material benefits in order to obtain a preferential treatment from public officials.[14] The most frequently employed legal definition of corruption has been Joseph Nye's: "Corruption is a behavior which deviates from the formal duties of a public role because of private-regarding (personal, close family, private clique) pecuniary or status gains: or violates rules against the exercise of certain types of private-regarding influence."[15]

One criticism that has been commonly made regarding the legalistic criterion is that it is usually based upon Western values and, therefore, is culturally biased. Another criticism is that, in terms of comparative analysis, problems often arise due to the discrepancies between countries in defining in legal codes what constitutes a corrupt act. On the other hand, the strength of such a criterion rests in its easy operationalization as legal sanctions make the quantification and classification of corruption cases easier than the other two previously examined.[16]

From the 1970s on, many scholars concentrated their research on what factors created opportunities for political corruption. It was hypothesized that such opportunities were shaped by a number of independent variables such as the degree of state interventionism in the economy, the degree of governmental discretionary powers, intermediation costs, and the entry of new groups into the political arena. Moreover, to address the shortcomings of previous research some scholars adopted a public-choice approach that enhanced the level of abstraction and its potential use in different scenarios regardless of country-specific circumstances.

Indeed, compared to previous approaches, the public-choice approach has the merit of specifying more or less rigorously the payoff matrix of the rational decisionmaker, whether a politician or a bureaucrat. Models were developed leading to a series of testable hypotheses. Hence, explicit efforts were made to mold together the "economist's concern with modeling self-interested behavior with a political scientist's recognition that political and bureaucratic institutions provide incentive structures far different from those presupposed by the competitive market paradigm."[17] Nonetheless, as in its application in other fields of inquiry, the public-choice approach came under attack for its reductionistic nature as it tended to postulate what, in the view of many, would otherwise be in need of being explained.[18]

III. The Institutions

Corruption depends heavily on the nature and functioning of political and governmental institutions (i.e., the presidency or premiership, the legislature, parties, the public bureaucracy, government agencies, the judiciary), which can either amplify or diminish corrupt practices. In the past, scholars have highlighted the expanded role of government and the abuse of its institutions by politicians and bureaucrats as a source of corruption. In LDCs this trend has been even more acute than in developed nations, in part because the checks and balances among the different branches of power in LDCs have been weaker leaving a few institutions like the presidency with greater discretionary powers. For example, in the presidential systems of Latin America, executive orders have been the usual means to bypass congressional opposition. Similarly, the executive branch has often purged the Supreme Court and lower courts in order to brake the independence of the judiciary. In addition, electoral systems using proportional representation or privileging some regions over others in the same country have fueled pork-barrel politics.

However, it was recently argued that weak presidential systems also provide incentives for corruption. In a study of corruption in Brazil, Geddes and Ribeiro Neto contended that the 1988 constitution increased the likelihood of corruption in that country "by decreasing the ability of the executive to (1) build coalitions and (2) assure the loyalty of its supporters in Congress."[19]

Electoral rules have often been regarded as instrumental in creating the conditions conducive to corruption. Geddes and Ribeiro Neto showed that the Brazilian runoff presidential elections, open-list electoral rules for Congress, and loose requirements for registering parties introduced in 1988 were partly responsible for the increase in corruption in Brazil as they produced party fragmentation, decreased party discipline, and gave greater representation in Congress to states where patronage politics was endemic. The impact of electoral rules, mentioned above, on corruption is not peculiar to Brazil but also has been observed in Italy (high party fragmentation, open-list system, and low party discipline due to a strict proportional representation system) and France (runoff elections and overrepresentation of rural areas).

Other institutional factors relate to government intervention in the economy. Starting in the wake of the Great Depression, either because of necessity or ideology, many LDCs saw in state-led development the only way to promote progress in a quicker, if not fairer, way. Thus government not only began to regulate most socioeconomic activities, but also, through setting up special agencies and state-owned corporations, became the largest producer, employer, and consumer in many LDCs. James C. Scott underscored the importance that such developments had in LDCs in these terms, "Accounts of corruption . . . abound with instances from such branches of the public service as customs, public works, tender boards, excise and tax offices, loan agencies, foreign exchange control boards, and so forth. These all tend to be areas where the state dispenses valuable privileges or handles a great deal of money and where the nature of the task gives wide discretionary powers to those in authority."[20]

Therefore, in this way politicians acquired enormous economic clout, which enabled them, due to the minimal supervision exercised upon them, to establish government-created privileges for the private sector. Thus ambitious politicians used ministries and state corporations to establish corrupt practices with businesses dependent upon government contracts and protection for their survival.[21] This is true during good economic times when government could engage in unrestricted largesse and even more so when an economic crisis squeezed government spending, which exacerbated competition within the private sector for fewer contracts.

IV. The Actors

According to Alessandro Pizzorno, two major actors operate within corruption mechanisms. The first is the "broker." As the name suggests, the broker performs the role of mediator in business and political transactions. The broker per se does not have to belong to a political party and can usually be found within a variety of liberal professions. The broker's role is to connect businesspeople with public administrators and politicians who have a mutual interest in engaging in corrupt transactions. The broker's task is to find loopholes that allow the attainment of "particular administrative or legislative treatment, indicate the illegal transactions needed, find out who is available to take advantage of them, and facilitate contacts among public administrators, politicians, and the private citizens interested."[22] Indeed, because the transactions in question are illegal, the broker's expertise is that of how to make shady deals without compromising the parties concerned with the specifics of the dirty work.

The second main actor is the "business politician." For Pizzorno, business politicians are the new political elites that emerge during periods of profound socioeconomic crisis that the old political establishment has proven unable to address. The state of turmoil generated by the crisis provides business politicians with a window of opportunity for exploitation. Unlike the traditional politician, the business politician knows how to create and sustain clientalistic networks. As the name suggests, this is a person who engages in politics not only for self-aggrandizement, but also as a means to acquire personal wealth quickly.

Indeed, unrestrained greediness is what usually distinguishes business politicians. By the same token, business politicians are strong personalities who have few qualms in resorting to illegal means and networks. In fact, the benefits of corruption are the very means by which the business politician increases his or her own power over those people that recognize money and political influence as the standards of real power. Business politicians are ideologically weak and lack the ability to develop programs as their expertise is in managing power rather than in designing policies; they are power politicians in the crudest sense of the term.

The display of arbitrary power is key to their capacity to expand their corruption networks and, accordingly, their personal support. In fact, as long as they can demonstrate that through their public office they can privatize public goods (that is, allow private interests to pursue their goals by using public instruments) without being prosecuted, they can strengthen the general perception of their invulnerability. Thus, if in a society the boundaries between what constitutes a legal or illegal act fade away, the greater the incentive will be for the business politician to engage in corruption. This is because his or her activity will be perceived as legitimate by an increasing number of people who are favorably disposed to such influence. Moreover, as the business politician's political clout grows stronger, he or she starts to discriminate against those groups or individuals who fail to join in the corrupt practices by excluding them from the partition of the public good.

For instance, suppose that a mayor is corrupt. If the mayor is able to control the decision about a bid for road construction, then the contract would be awarded to the firm (or firms) included in the mayor's corrupt network while excluding those that refused to go along with the corrupt practices. Over time, if the mayor can demonstrate his or her capacity for abusing public authority and getting away with it, the condition of exclusion may become intolerable and force honest businesses to ask for inclusion into the network by paying a higher price of entry than would otherwise have been the case had they petitioned earlier. This pattern then leads to what Pizzorno calls the "vicious circle of arrogance." To sum up, the cycle takes this form:

(*) arrogance (display of arbitrary power), reputation of being powerful →

(**) concentration of petitions for favors and protection →

(***) consensus to be used in the political arena →

(*****) political power →

(******) increased arrogance (greater arbitrary powers).[23]

V. The Mechanisms

Pizzorno posits that in a political system penetrated by corruption, party politicians, rather than satisfying the demands for public goods coming from the population at large, will devote themselves to special-interest demands as they bring high monetary payoffs. To this end, business politicians can utilize brokers or keep mediation costs low by dealing with private parties directly. The process is fairly simple and feeds into itself. Either the broker contacts a corrupt politician on behalf of some business or the politician uses the broker to make propositions to business. The use of the broker is more frequent when multiple actors are involved and the stakes are higher. At a lower level of government, when deals are less complex, it is more likely that the corrupt politician will propose a deal directly to the interested businesses. Thus corrupt practices imply here the illegal association of politicians with businesspeople, possibly but not necessarily with the mediating role of a third party. The "commission" is the key element of corrupt transactions. It constitutes the payment that brokers and politicians, or politicians alone, receive from business to intercede in the latter's favor. For example, a company competing for a public contract may be asked for a commission of 20 percent, based upon the final contract value, in order to win the bid.

A direct consequence of this trend in the political system is that it alters the nature of parties. While in the classical model individuals join parties to aggregate and articulate interests and put forward policy proposals to pursue the public good, in a corrupt polity individuals ask for a party membership in order to attain private benefits through public office. Consequently, parties become less likely to expand their membership because, from the standpoint of older business politicians, newcomers could compete with them in the pursuit of private benefits. To avoid competition, business politicians engage in a "filtering process," which ensures that the newcomers are incorporated into the network of a given leader or a faction within the party to avoid the alteration of existing equilibria. Equally important, the filtering process makes sure that the newcomers are willing to engage in corrupt deals or at least accept them without raising moral questions. The more young business politicians pursue their ambitions, the more coopted they will become in corrupt deals whose stakes and payoffs will increase accordingly as their careers advance.[24]

Thus in a situation of this kind, the competition is not so much among parties that try to position themselves on a left-right continuum based upon issues and/or ideology. In a corrupt system, the competition becomes more personalized with business politicians and factions, even within the same party, scrambling to get ahead. This is particularly true of countries where proportional representation (PR) is used to select representatives and internal party discipline is weak. In a scenario of this kind, candidates within the same party are practically forced to compete against each other, although in theory they should compete against other parties. Brazil's open-list, PR-system is a case in point. In such a system, candidates for Congress are elected according to how many votes they have received, regardless of their position in the party list. This fact forces candidates to compete against members of other parties as well as against those candidates from their own party list. Thus candidates, "to distinguish themselves from competitors within their own parties . . . must rely on charisma and their records as distributors of largesse."[25]

Let us now return for a moment to the filtering process. By itself cooptation is not enough. There are additional specific criteria for entry that Pizzorno calls the "guarantee of silence." The first is the protection of those who expose themselves to legal sanctions by engaging in corruption exchanges. When a corruption case is uncovered by an independent source, the business politician and his or her associates must be able to mobilize high-ranking public officials in government, the judiciary, and the police, who are not necessarily part of the deal, to stop any investigation and safeguard their partners in crime. Second, the corrupt network headed by the business politician must establish severe sanctions against defectors (such as excluding defectors from future deals or even using violent means). Third, the guarantee of silence goes beyond the corrupt network as it may also entail the connivance of a third party. This is the case, for instance, when a politician who is not participating in a given deal but is aware of it, is rewarded for his or her silence in a "horse-trading" fashion.[26]

VI. Economic Crisis, Market Reforms, and Corruption

As the rational-choice literature emphasizes, the logic behind corruption tends to be roughly the same regardless of the environment in which it takes place. However, depending on the socioeconomic institutions of a given society, incentives and opportunities differ. This partly explains why corruption manifests itself differently around the world and why its degree of pervasiveness varies greatly. Broadly speaking, political systems can be characterized by low or high levels of corruption. Low corruption is characteristic of political systems where: (1) checks and balances among the three branches of government (executive, legislature, and judiciary) and institutional mechanisms to prevent and penalize corruption exist and work effectively; (2) there are some self-imposed restraints in profiting from corruption resulting in relatively small commissions; and (3) corruption is regarded by the society at large as an aberration. High corruption takes place when: (1) many checks and balances among the three branches of government and the institutional mechanisms to combat corruption are weak or are not used; (2) there are no self-restraints in profiting from corruption as commissions reach extremely high levels;[27] and (3) corruption is so widespread at any societal level as to be accepted and tolerated.[28] Traditionally, the first model seems to apply to Northern European and North American countries, whereas many LDCs are likely to fall into the second model.

In recent times, however, corruption in some Latin American democracies has taken a turn for the worse. In a study of corruption in Brazil, Geddes and Ribeiro Neto posited that, "traditional forms of corruption have been more extensive since 1985 than they were during the previous democratic period. In addition, a new pattern of corrupt practices involving the private accumulation of wealth by the president and his cronies developed under Collor."[29] Indeed, new types of corruption have emerged in the last few years. The incentive structure behind corruption has changed because the political economy of many countries has changed as well. In the political realm, corruption takes the form of the rise of a new type of politician and in the economic realm it takes the form of a new opportunity structure created by a far reaching process of economic reform. Thus political transitions punctuated by severe economic crises are conducive to the rise to power of new political elites represented by business politicians.

Business politicians, while portraying themselves as reform-minded leaders and national saviors untainted by the ineptness of their predecessors, aim ultimately to acquire, once in office, a broad mandate that will enable them to pursue their ruthless goals. In other words, the main hypothesis here is that if a country that is already affected by high levels of corruption enters into a deep socioeconomic crisis, the likelihood that the executive office will be entrusted to a business politician is high. Once in office, with the excuse of tackling the crisis, the business politician adopts emergency powers that allow him or her to pursue reform policies conducive to corrupt practices on an unprecedented scale.

The decision to engage in corruption can be analyzed using two organizing concepts, "willingness" and "opportunity." Willingness pertains to the decision processes occurring at the micro level resulting from the scrutiny of a range of options. Opportunity encompasses environmental and structural factors at the macro level. Willingness and opportunity are interactive concepts linked in several ways. "They do not create mutually exclusive categories. Anything that effects the structural possibilities of the environment or environments within which decisionmakers must act also affects the incentive structure for those decisionmakers . . . [they] take the theoretical characteristics when the understand that they describe the conditions that are necessary for the occurrence of events."[30]

In our particular case, the business politician's willingness is influenced by the perceived margin of advantage, that is, the degree to which the expected benefits of corruption are greater than the expected benefits of honest conduct while in office. Willingness to pursue corrupt practices is based mainly on three types of behavioral patterns: personal greediness, power-seeking, and the "get-it-while-you-can" attitude. As we noted earlier, a prime motivation for a business politician to enter politics is to make money through public office. By the same token, the accumulation of wealth through illegal means feeds into the public perception of a politician's invulnerability, provides additional resources to extend clientalistic networks, and, in the end, reinforces a politician's display of arbitrary power.

The "get-it-while-you-can" attitude is well documented in Latin America. In most of the regions, presidents are not allowed to run for a consecutive second term. Their ministers and political appointees are at a greater disadvantage as their tenure tends to be even shorter due to the fact that they are usually used as scapegoats any time things go wrong. Thus, due to their limited time in power, both elected and nonelected officials are potentially inclined to take advantage of their office while they can, particularly in systems experiencing high levels of corruption.

However, willingness per se is not sufficient unless it is accompanied by an opportunity to engage in corrupt deals. Opportunity delimits the range of possible options available to business politicians. Such opportunities are the high degree of discretionary power, the wide popular consensus on structural reforms creating loopholes for corrupt activities, the low possibility of "getting caught," and the drop in state resources. The high degree of discretionary power allows a president to act with a free hand as, by definition, it bypasses checks and balances. An unprecedented economic crisis gives a president a clear mandate to change.

The crisis and its most tangible consequence, hyperinflation, is instrumental in enabling a president to impose a more centralized decision-making process than allowed by the constitution. According to Schvarzer, the hyperinflation spiral creates a basic consensus across society about the need for economic stability, even at the price of higher unemployment and lower salaries; radical structural reforms, as half-hearted attempts had proven ineffective before; and the abandonment of the old welfare-state economic model in favor of free-market economics.[31] These factors are then conducive to strengthening the power of the executive. The outcome is what O'Donnell has defined as "delegative democracy."

"Delegative democracies are grounded on a basic premise: he . . . who wins a presidential election is enabled to govern the country as he sees fit, and to the extent that existing power relations allow, for the term to which he has been elected. The President is the embodiment of the nation and the custodian of the national interest, which it is incumbent upon him to define. What he does in government does not need to bear any resemblance of what he said or promised during the electoral campaign—he has been authorized to govern as he sees fit. Since this paternal figure has to take care of the whole nation, it is almost obvious that his support cannot come from the party; his political basis has to be the *movement*, the supposedly vibrant overcoming of the factionalism and conflicts that parties bring about. Typically, and consistently, winning presidential candidates in DDs present themselves as above all parties. . . . In this view other institutions—such as Congress and the Judiciary—are nuisance that come attached to the domestic and international advantages of being a democratically elected President. The idea of accountability to those institutions, or other private or semiprivate organizations, appears as an unnecessary impediment to the full authority that the President has been delegated to exercise."[32]

The low possibility of getting caught is closely related to the absence of checks and balances discussed above. With the powers of congress and the judiciary emasculated, whatever transparency in government action existed before becomes obsolete, thus fueling the perception that the likelihood of getting caught is or approximates zero. Finally, the fiscal crisis inherited from previous administrations reduces the business politician's traditional resources of patronage such as state corporations and government agencies, many of which are in a virtual state of bankruptcy. Thus the need to substitute old sources of illicit payments, based upon government intervention in the economy, with new means.

Oddly enough, economic deregulation and privatization of state enterprises offer such an opportunity when pursued within a political system lacking transparency. This can easily be accomplished by manipulating the norms for the transfer of government assets to the private sector in return for kickbacks. In addition, as many structural reforms are rushed through executive orders, business politicians can sell privileged information to entrepreneurs prior to a reform or solicit bribes from business in order to make exceptions to the new rules. The basic model of the new type of corruption through market reforms is outlined below.

VII. Assumptions

1. The official engaged in corruption is a profit-maximizer.
2. The official can adopt or pertain to any (or a combination) of the following behavioral patterns: (i) personal greediness, (ii) power-seeking, and (iii) "get-it-while-you-can" attitude.
3. Engagement in corruption is a function of willingness and opportunity; these variables are not mutually exclusive.

$$C(i) = C(W(i), O(i)) \qquad (1)$$

where,

$C(i)$ = Corruption;
$W(i)$ = Willingness to engage in corruption; and
$O(i)$ = Opportunities for engaging in corruption.

The analysis of the $W(i)$ component of $C(i)$ leads to

$$W(i) = W(BP(i)) \qquad (2)$$

where,

$BP(i)$ = Behavioral pattern of government official, which can pertain to (i) personal greediness, (ii) power-seeking, and (iii) "get-it-while-you-can" attitude. The adoption of a determined behavioral pattern will depend on the following variables:

$$BP(i) = BP(G(i), N(i), t(i)) \qquad (2')$$

where,

$G(i)$ = Gain if corruption scheme is carried out;
$N(i)$ = Expected expanded network available for corruption activities, resulting in increased source of power; and
$t(i)$ = Expected period in office.

The likelihood of the personal greediness behavioral pattern to prevail will be in direct relation to variable $G(i)$; in the case of power-seeking, this will be in direct relation to variable $N(i)$; the "get-it-while-you-can" attitude will be in inverse relation to variable 't'.

Analyzing the $G(i)$ component of equation (2), we get that

$$G(i) = X(i) - P(i) - M(i) \qquad (2'')$$

$X(i)$ = Monetary amount involved in corruption scheme;
$P(i)$ = Expected penalty if official is caught in corruption scheme; $P(i)$ tends to approximate 0.

$M(i)$ = Monetary moral costs of engaging in corruption scheme; $M(i)$ tends to approximate 0.

The analysis of component $O(i)$ of equation (1) brings that,

$$O(i) = O(DP(i), C(i), E) \qquad (3)$$

where,
$DP(i)$ = Discretionary power;
$C(i)$ = Popular consensus of structural reforms that allow loopholes for corruption; and
E = Indicator of availability of resources; approximate of resources going to the executive branch (e.g., tax incomes) can be used.

VIII. Methodology

In order to test our model we have chosen the cases of Argentina under President Carlos Menem and Brazil under President Fernando Collor de Mello. The case selection was based on a number of factors. First, both administrations were contemporaries of one another and faced similar economic (hyperinflation, budget deficit, high unemployment, and large foreign debt) and political (lack of congressional majority, popular disillusion with democracy's achievements) constraints. Second, both administrations took office promising to end widespread corruption but were later troubled, in varying degrees, by a wave of scandals, which in the case of Brazil ended with the impeachment of President Collor de Mello. Third, the unprecedented diligence exercised by the press and congressional inquiries to uncover corruption cases enabled us to have a wealth of data not available in other Latin American countries.[33] Fourth and last, the cases of corruption denounced in these countries could give us a clue about how corrupt mechanisms worked under two different presidential regimes (the executive is more powerful vis-à-vis the legislature in Argentina than in Brazil).

In operationalizing the concept of political corruption we have opted for a restrictive definition.[34] Corruption cases are here viewed as illegal exchanges within which public officials have obtained money (or other material benefits that can be monetized) from private citizens or groups in return for preferential treatment in governmental decision making.[35] In other words, commissions are paid to obtain favorable governmental decisions. To reiterate, the definition is restrictive, but it allows us to separate out cases of lobbying, nepotism, or cronysm.

IX. Setting the Stage

The ascendancy to power of Collor de Mello and Menem was typical of business politicians. To begin with, both presidents came from among the poorest states in their countries, Alagoas and La Rioja, respectively. Both states resembled the ideal type of patrimonial societies where small wealthy elites represented dominant groups capable of perpetuating their hold on local power through the manipulation of public institutions and resources. This allowed the elites to redistribute favors and wealth among the lower social strata in order to create stable, yet subordinated, clientales. Similarly, while hierarchical and authoritarian, the patrimonial power arrangements were flexible enough to accommodate newly emerging groups through the use of the spoils of office as a deterrent against radical demands. As long as the political system so established was capable of maintaining the status quo and was willing to cooperate with the elites of more powerful states that dominated the national government, local patrimonial elites were left ruling as they pleased within or above the law.

Collor de Mello and Menem grew up in political environments like the one just described.[36] Both came from up-and-coming families that through commercial wealth were quick in buying their entrance into the political circles of the local elites and gaining political prominence.[37] Only in his late thirties, was Collor de Mello able to defeat old political bosses like Guillerme Palmeira and Divaldo Suruguay and become governor of Alagoas in 1986. Instrumental in Collor de Mello's ascendancy to power was P.C. Farias, a former seminarian turned businessperson with a renowned appetite for money and a long history of legal charges.[38] As Collor de Mello's campaign treasurer, Farias engineered a complex web of alliances and shady deals behind the scenes.

Menem, on the other hand, was a young governor when the military deposed him after the 1976 coup. With the return to democracy in 1983, he regained the governorship of La Rioja and quit only after his presidential election in 1989. Yet, as governors, Collor de Mello and Menem hardly distinguished themselves save for their old-fashioned clientalistic and corrupt practices.[39] Coincidentally, in the late 1980s both Brazil and Argentina were in the midst of their worst economic crises in this century. Both countries were plagued by hyperinflation, the first and third largest foreign debt in the world respectively, capital flight, all-time low investments, huge fiscal deficits, and ballooning domestic debt. The first generation of democratic governments headed by Raúl Alfonsín and José Sarney, which had replaced the military dictatorships, failed miserably in their promises of restoring economic prosperity and upholding democratic principles.

Despite being experienced politicians and representing traditional political forces, Alfonsín and Sarney were unable to carry out any coherent socioeconomic policy. Besieged by stiff opposition in and outside congress, the two presidents became increasingly captive of powerful lobbies. To compound matters, in the case of Argentina, Alfonsín had to make several concessions to the armed forces after enduring three military uprisings. By the time they left office, the Alfonsín (July 1989) and Sarney (March 1990) administrations were fully discredited as reports of mismanagement and malfeasance became widespread.[40]

The general sense of social malaise and disillusion with traditional party politics therefore created the right conditions for the emergence of new political leaders who were not tied to the failures of their predecessors. Collor de Mello and Menem portrayed themselves as political outsiders and indeed were regarded as long-shot underdogs when they announced their presidential candidacies. After being a member of the right-wing Partido Democrático Social (PDS), Collor de Mello joined in 1986, like many other opportunist politicians, the Partido do Movimiento Demócratico Brasileiro (PMDB), the largest opposition party, which had won the presidency in 1985.

Later on, Collor de Mello created his own party, the Partido de Renovaçao Nacional to further his ambitions. Menem, in the 1988 primaries, had to compete against the chairman of his own party, the Partido Justicialista or Peronist Party. Both men adopted a charismatic style punctuated by catchy slogans like "Follow me, I am not going to betray you" or "Whoever steals goes to jail." Collor de Mello went so far as to describe himself as *caçador de marajás*, a hunter of overpaid political appointees and bureaucrats. At the same time, Collor de Mello and Menem, as typical of business politicians, remained ideologically weak and downplayed any details on clear policy proposals, but were quite keen in packaging their image as saviors of the public good, promoters of modernization, and deadly enemies of the corrupt political system. The stage was set for the emergence of protest candidates. As an observer pointed out prior to Collor's election, "people are not interested in ideologies, what they really want is something which promises to change everything, government parties, politicians, the source of their suffering."[41]

Once in power, Collor de Mello and Menem appointed to key government positions a substantial number of political cronies (as well as a few technocrats) who were virtually unknown to the general public. Many of these individuals came from the inner circles of the two former governors and had gone through the filtering process described by Pizzorno back in their home states. Collor de Mello, more than any other Brazilian president, brought with him so many of his former aides that his cabinet was quickly dubbed the "Republic of Alagoas." Menem awarded key posts to La Rioja's friends, political strongmen from Argentina's northwest, and allegedly corrupt union leaders, most of whom had belonged to marginal factions within the Peronist Party until 1989. One of them, Luis Barrionuevo, appointed to a government post shortly after Menem took office, publicly stated on television that to solve the fiscal crisis, "we have to stop stealing for at least two years."[42] Menem also appointed a number of independent technocrats closely tied with the most important business circles of the country with whom he had established contacts a few months prior to his election.

Yet, both administrations were characterized by ministers who had little or no previous experience at the national government level.[43] Unfortunately, as it became painfully evident thereafter, many of these appointees turned out to be not only incompetent, but also quite corrupt. An Argentine newspaper aptly summarized the situation as follows, "The president's inner circle . . . has largely been recruited through patronage for political services and is thus strong on allegiance to its boss but rather short elsewhere. The result of this ill-advised recruitment strategy has been to see dozens of close [advisers] step out of line, get caught and eventually get ditched."[44] As a matter of fact, political commentators have stressed the fact that both presidents and their associates assumed that they could continue to abuse their public authority as they had done back in Alagoas and La Rioja.[45] This underscores the arrogance and naiveté of the Collor de Mello and Menem administrations.

X. Argentina and Brazil in Comparative Perspective

In the preceding pages we have tried to show how Collor de Mello and Menem closely resembled Pizzorno's definition of business politician. Hereupon we shall see how the two presidents' corrupt behaviors fit the willingness and opportunity model.

Collor de Mello's willingness to engage in full-scale corruption was evident to a few well before 1990. During a trip to China in 1988, the future president had expressed to some close friends his intention to enter the upcoming presidential race in order to accumulate power and wealth quickly.[46] Although well-off, Collor de Mello had no control over his family's media empire, owned primarily by his mother and managed by his young brother Pedro with whom he had rocky relations. Through the abuse of public office, Collor de Mello could create a great financial empire, independent from his family. The Collor de Mello–Farias strategy consisted not only of remitting abroad some of the profits of corrupt practices. Even more important was, according to some, the "accumulation of capital and property that could guarantee to the new millionaires the respect among entrepreneurs, economic power, and the insertion in the market. To do this it was necessary to accumulate a lot of money in a small period of time and reinvest it."[47] The "get-it-while-you-can" attitude was also present as the Brazilian constitution forbids a president to run for a second term. Indeed, part of the haste in getting money was allegedly due to the fact that Congress was scheduled to discuss constitutional reform in 1992. The acquisition of large funds could then have enabled Collor de Mello to "buy" congressional support to modify the constitution and allow him to run for reelection.

Much of the same can be said about Menem. Although not tremendously wealthy, Menem, while governor, had distinguished himself by his constant pursuit to join the Argentine jet set. His flamboyant lifestyle and his passion for sports cars, ballerinas, and movie stars often made the headlines in national news. He also had gained a reputation for making unscrupulous political deals with whomever would be willing to further his political ambitions. His successful presidential bid was made possible through funds provided by notoriously corrupt union leaders like Luis Barrionuevo and Jorge Triaca. The latter gained prominent cabinet posts after the 1989 elections but was eventually forced to quit upon rumors of corrupt behavior while in office. Moreover, as in Brazil, the Argentine constitution precluded the possibility of reelection.

The opportunity structure was also similar in both Argentina and Brazil. After the failure of heterodox stabilization plans in the mid-1980s, there was substantial consensus in both countries that market-oriented reforms were the only alternative available. At the same time, Collor de Mello and Menem found the government coffers depleted, thus depriving them of traditional funds for patronage that had therefore to be replaced by other means. The societal support for bold action to tackle the hyperinflation spiral also enabled Collor de Mello and Menem to initially enjoy a honeymoon with the public and opposition parties. The explosiveness of the socioeconomic situation inherited by Collor de Mello and Menem offered them the opportunity to strengthen their executive powers and to eliminate transparency requirements, which dramatically diminished the chances of getting caught.

Thus, arguing that the magnitude of the crisis required an immediate response through emergency measures, both presidents swiftly moved to nullify the checks and balances exercised by Congress and the judiciary. Yet their initiatives were also dictated by the need to freely pursue their corrupt practices. Menem had Congress pass the Law of Economic Reform and the State Reform Law (which put up for sale all state enterprises) shortly after assuming office. The two laws practically gave him a blank check. Congress delegated to the president the authority of enforcing key structural reforms as he saw fit through decrees of necessity and urgency (similar to the U.S. executive orders). Menem made unprecedented use of such decrees, issuing one hundred of them between 1989 and 1992 as compared to twenty-three between 1853 and 1989.

Having muted congressional opposition to his policies, Menem proceeded with the emasculation of the judiciary's independence.[48] The Supreme Court was enlarged in size and "packed" with government appointees, thus preventing the administration's controversial socioeconomic policies from being challenged by the courts. In 1990, Menem, through an executive order, also removed four out of the five members of the Fiscal Tribunal (which oversees irregularities in the government accounts). In 1991, again by executive order, he removed the state attorney for Administrative Inquiries (in charge of prosecuting irregularities in the public administration). In 1993, Justice Minister Jorge Maiorano bluntly stated that the Supreme Court should feel "addicted" to the policies of the elected government. With Congress and the judiciary made subservient to the executive, Menem had acquired many of the discretionary powers last enjoyed by the military presidents of the 1976–83 dictatorship without resorting to a coup. Indeed, at the time many believed that Menem's authoritarian style was a necessary evil to tackle the crisis.

Collor de Mello, who took office nine months after Menem, tried to do much of the same. The president, who contrary to Menem lacked a strong congressional backing, began from the start to make indiscriminate use of *medidas provisorias* (141 were enacted in 1990 alone), or executive orders contemplated by the 1988 constitution. These medidas provisorias enable the executive to legislate quickly, although pending later congressional approval, under exceptional circumstances. He used such executive orders to enforce many of his policies early in the term. The Parliamentary Commission of Inquiry (PCI), which later investigated the corruption scandals under Collor de Mello, summarized the events in these terms:

"Attacked, the Brazilian State turned from passive into non-functioning. The Provisional Measure 150 (Law 8.028/90) created an administrative reform that opened profound fissures in the structure of the State and its operations. . . . Successive alterations of the reform . . . consecrated the politics of exchange of favors and of the protection of followers. Later administrative measures, labeled as reforms, gave a deadly blow to all that was developed up to then to establish an effective control of the executive power. The government measures enforced after 15 March 1990 created a gigantic umbrella, sheltering shady deals aimed at funneling money . . . unprecedented in breadth and scope, and fueled by the expectation of its beneficiaries that they would prosper because they could not be sanctioned."[49]

Through an executive order, Collor de Mello, on the day of his inauguration, launched his controversial anti-inflation plan, or *Plano Collor*. The plan froze all bank and savings accounts and overnight deposits. Interestingly enough, as federal auditors found out thereafter, Farias removed $250,000 a few days prior to the launching of the *Plano Collor*.[50] The freezing of bank accounts brought economic activity to a halt and ultimately proved ineffective but, most importantly, it gave Farias and his accomplice, Finance Minister Zélia Cardoso de Mello, a monopoly on the country's financial liquidity. This power was in turn used to solicit bribes from money-starved companies in order to get special government permission to "defrost" their accounts. "The price for 'commissions' rose steeply. Businessmen were forced to negotiate with government officials for use of their own money to pay salaries, taxes, and other necessary expenses . . . commissions, kickbacks, and the emergence of numerous collusions between businessmen and officials were the natural consequence of dependence and monopoly."[51]

Consistent with the early definition of broker, Farias was the accredited negotiator of the new ruling group in charge of arranging corrupt deals with businesspeople and politicians, collecting the money, and then depositing it in phantom accounts at the disposal of the president, cabinet ministers, and government bureaucrats. According to the PCI, Farias disbursed a total of $32.3 million, of which $6.5 million went to the president's family alone. With the president's blessing, Farias acted as the gray eminence behind the throne. While holding no official position in the administration, he set up a parallel government that was practically in charge of the most sensitive decisions. Through his direct involvement in the appointment of government officials, Farias placed in key positions trusted people (including his own brothers) willing to collaborate with his kickbacks and influence-peddling scheme. The three factors described by Pizzorno in the "guarantee of silence" could all be found in the Collor de Mello administration. First, those entering corrupt deals with Farias were assured that the president was personally involved and there was nothing to worry about. In those few instances when scandals erupted, the administration exercised strong pressure on the federal police and the judiciary to stop any investigation. Second, those who refused to collaborate were threatened and pushed aside. This was the fate of Brazil's state oil company chairman, Luís Octávio da Motta Veiga, who, after refusing Farias' request to grant a $40 million loan to a business associate, was forced to quit. Third, although many congressional representatives became increasingly aware of Farias' activities, none took the initiative to denounce them. In fact, the whole scandal would have probably not occurred if Pedro Collor de Mello had not denounced his brother due to a business dispute.

Both politicians and entrepreneurs quickly learned that the only way to do business with the administration was to deal directly with Farias, who had no qualms in describing himself as the president's "best friend." Those who tried to bypass and lobby the government directly were quickly turned down and sent back to Farias. With traditional lobbying forms shut down, Farias's consulting firm acquired a de facto monopoly and suddenly became the most sought after in the nation. Using loopholes in the law and government contracts, Farias fixed bidding procedures and government loans to "sympathetic" businesses worth hundreds of millions of dollars, in return for "salty" commissions. Such commissions, which averaged 15–20 percent under the Sarney administration, surged to 30–50 percent, leading the Collor de Mello–Farias duo to amass a fortune estimated by some to be worth $2 billion.[52]

According to a congressional investigative committee headed by Senator Amir Lando, privatization was used as a source for generating cash. Lando suspected the officer in charge of the privatization program under Collor, Eduardo Modiano, and his deputy Eduardo Leite, of having favored industrialists and banks who may have illicitly rewarded the administration.[53] João Agripino Maia, the former vice president of the government's Comissão Diretora do Programa de Privatização, charged that the Brazilian state had lost $3 billion due to the many "irregularities" that flawed the privatization process.[54]

Economic reforms were not the only means to further corrupt practices. In July 1990, three months after his inauguration, Collor de Mello dissolved the Serviço Nacional de Investigações (SNI), the military security agency equivalent to the Central Intelligence Agency in the United States. The SNI played a crucial role in the 1964–85 military regime and two of its former directors, Gustavo Garrastazu Medici and Joao Bautista Figuereido, eventually became presidents. To understand the pervasiveness of the SNI's controls, it is important to know that its agents were attached to each government department and special agency to oversee their operations. In theory, the dismantling of the SNI fulfilled a campaign promise and was presented as evidence of Collor de Mello's administration's commitment to political reform and modernization. In practice, it worked to destroy the only independent government institution left capable of uncovering and denouncing Farias's scheme.[55]

In their effort to create a financial empire, Collor de Mello and Farias concentrated primarily on three sectors: aviation, mining, and the media. Again, so-called economic reforms were used to this end. For instance, one of the administration's much-publicized policies to introduce structural reforms in Brazil consisted of the privatization of state enterprises. Viaçao Aérea de Sao Paulo, the country's second largest airline and the first company to be auctioned, was awarded to one of Collor de Mello's allies, Wagner Canhedo, thanks to illicit funds provided by Farias.[56] In the end, it seems that Canhedo was only a front man for Farias's plans to create the largest South American airline. Farias, who already owned a number of private jet companies and used to smuggle money abroad, had in fact established contacts for the purchase of two other flagships, Lloyd Aéreo Boliviano and Pluna of Uruguay.

The Collor de Mello–Farias venture in the media business was dictated by the president's concern of having a personal means to publicize his political plans in the future.[57] In fact, Brazilian all-powerful media conglomerate O Globo, the fourth largest in the world, was very ambivalent about the president's policies. Collor de Mello and Farias thus proceeded with the purchase of several broadcasting companies and newspapers. It was this initiative that eventually led to the president's downfall. Farias's attempt to create a rival newspaper in Alagoas, in direct competition with the one run by Pedro Collor de Mello, the president's brother, precipitated the events. As the president showed no willingness to compromise, Pedro disclosed the whole corrupt scheme to the weekly Veja whose revelations prompted the congressional investigation by the PCI.

Once the PCI report was made public in August 1992 and Congress set a deadline for December of that year to decide whether or not to impeach the president, the administration mounted a full-scale offensive. Government departments, special agencies, and government banks like the Caixa Econômica Federal and the Banco do Brasil were used by the administration as a resource for pork-barrel projects on behalf of congressional representatives willing to deny the two-third congressional majority needed for the impeachment. In the end, the whole effort was to no avail. Under pressure from outraged public opinion, the Brazilian Congress, which initially seemed inclined to simply take over many of the president's prerogatives while keeping him in place, decided to impeach Collor de Mello.

The events in Argentina were far less dramatic. As noted earlier, Menem, early in his term, succeeded in emasculating the traditional checks and balances of the democratic process. This allowed the pursuit of illicit government actions. However, during the administrations' first two years, public opinion polls clearly showed that people's concerns were primarily focusing on economic issues as inflation remained high and the economic recession continued. In 1991 the highly conservative and pro-establishment Argentine Catholic Church dared to say what many had been beginning to notice for quite some time: that while corruption had always existed in the country, it had recently skyrocketed.

Such statements were echoed by the president of the influential Asociación de Bancos de la República Argentina who announced that the country was in a virtual state of kleptocracy where government officials were engaged in full-scale corruption schemes. In less than four years, the Menem administration was rocked by nineteen major scandals resulting in the resignation of twenty ministers and senior presidential aides. Although no scandal directly involved President Menem, there is enough circumstantial evidence to make the conjecture. In early December 1989, Speaker of the House (and later interior minister) José Luis Manzano was confronted by fellow Peronist congressional representatives who raised questions on the whereabouts of some commissions. According to the daily *La Nuova Provincia,* an entrepreneurial consortium had paid a commission to the minister of public works, Roberto Dromi, the presidential chief of staff, Eduardo Bauzá, and Manzano in order to be awarded a contract from Petroquímica Bahía Blanca, a government-owned chemical company. The contract had been inflated by as much as $40 million, some of which had been taken by Dromi, Bauzá, and Manzano with the complicity of Petroquímica's president, Jorge Geraige. Upon asking for their slice of the commission, Manzano responded, "I have only one thing to say. I steal for the Crown. Is that clear or does someone need some further explanation?"[58] By the "Crown" Manzano seemed to imply that he was collecting on Menem's behalf and no more questions were asked. The clamor that the scandal raised thereafter ended with the firing of Garaige and the contract was not honored at due time.

Unlike Brazil, where the influence-peddling scheme was organized mostly by Farias, in Argentina there were several individuals occupying official posts who managed different "cajas," or cash boxes. Allegedly, these men were Manzano, Bauzá, and former Minister Erman González, all of whom were part of the president's inner circle.[59] All three seem to closely adhere to Pizzorno's definition of business politicians. Bauzá and Manzano were very ambitious men from the western region of Argentina. Both were born in middle-class families and worked their way up within the Peronist Party by allegedly engaging in corrupt practices, which made at least Manzano quite wealthy.[60] Erman González, an accountant by training, was Menem's finance minister in La Rioja in the 1980s. Virtually unknown to the general public when he joined the cabinet in 1989, González was one of the president's most trusted advisers and had allegedly run Menem's influence-peddling scheme in La Rioja.

Based on our interviews with state prosecutors, politicians, and foreign diplomats shortly after Menem announced his privatization plans, prospective buyers were told, through informal channels, to pay substantial commissions to government officials in order to receive preferential treatment. In fact, the first round of privatizations, worth about $7 billion, took place not by chance without any regulatory framework. The allegation of corruption that ensued forced a new economic team in early 1991 to revise the whole policy with the assistance of the World Bank.

The first of the many government scandals was the so-called Swiftgate. Swift-Armour, a subsidiary of Campbell Soup Co., taking advantage of new policies aimed at encouraging foreign investments and trade liberalization, decided to invest $115 million in capital equipment in Argentina in the late 1980s. However, at the end of 1990, Swift-Armour reported to the U.S. ambassador Terence Todman and to the foreign minister Domingo Cavallo (who later became economy minister) that government officials had solicited a bribe in order to approve the investment. The whole issue would have been quietly covered up had it not been for the independent daily *Página 12*, which started an aggressive investigation upon receiving, from undisclosed sources, a copy Ambassador Todman's written complaints to Menem.

In the end, it was ascertained that Menem's brother-in-law and economic adviser for economic affairs, Emir Yoma, was the one that had solicited the "commission" from Swift-Armour.[61] Emir Yoma came from the poor northwest of Argentina where his family had established a thriving leather tanning business. He had no previous experience in national government but had been a long-time adviser to Menem and worked hard on his brother-in-law's presidential campaign. After Menem's election, Emir Yoma, along with other members of the Yoma family, was rewarded with a high-ranking governmental post, which, obviously, he perceived as a payback opportunity.[62]

Privatization, as well as deregulation policies, were marred by scandals.[63] It was not by chance that the first round of privatizations, worth about $7 billion, took place within a very weak, and often contradictory, legal framework. A typical example of corruption via privatization was the sale of the flagship Aerolíneas Argentinas to the Spanish carrier Iberia. In its acquisition sheet, Iberia reported some $80 million in expenses under the invoice of "costs associated with the sale." Allegedly, this amount corresponded to the bribe paid to government officials.[64] When a state prosecutor tried to stop the sale in order to investigate its irregularities, Minister Dromi, the chief architect of the privatization program, appealed to the Supreme Court. Using an obscure procedure called *per saltum* (never used before), the Supreme Court ascribed to itself the jurisdiction over the case and took it away from the federal court.[65] To no one's surprise, it took a few minutes for the Supreme Court to rule in favor of the government.

The other major privatization of 1990, that of the national telephone company ENTel, is another case in point. María Julia Alsogaray, the ENTel trustee in charge of selling the company, paid $63 million and $3 million to Siemens and FECOM-NEC respectively, two of ENTel's suppliers, while ignoring debts of other suppliers. Alsogaray's collusion with Siemens and FECOM-NEC was denounced in Congress and prompted the federal accounting office, the Sindicatura General de Empresas Públicas (SIGEP), to start an internal investigation whose results were sent to the Fiscal Tribunal. The latter, however, having been made inoperative by Menem, failed to start legal proceedings against Alsogaray as solicited by the SIGEP's report. A few months later, the U.S. consortium Bell Atlantic–Manufacturers Hanover Trust, competing for the privatization of ENTel, announced that government officers had solicited a large bribe from government officials, which of course it was not allowed to pay.[66] In fact, the 1977 Foreign Corruption Act bars U.S. companies from paying bribes abroad. Although strongly endorsed by Alsogaray, in the end, the U.S. consortium failed to acquire ENTel. In fact, ENTel went to Telefónica of Spain and Telecom-Stet, a French-Italian consortium, whose bids had been supported by Dromi and Manzano. The result created a well-publicized rift between Alsogaray on the one hand and Dromi and Manzano on the other.

Notably, none of the European companies (all state owned) involved were barred from bribing by similar legislation at home. A year later, Italian state prosecutors filed corruption charges against the former minister of foreign affairs, Gianni de Michelis, who had lobbied strongly on Stet's behalf. According to the Italian magistrates, Stet had paid commissions to de Michelis for his "mediation" role as well as to Argentine officials.[67]

Highway privatization experienced many of the same problems. About Km 10,000 were privatized by the executive without telling who the private tenders involved were, which of those bidders won, and what the contents of the signed contracts were. Prior to the privatization the Bicameral Commission for the Reform of the State (monitoring the privatization process) was assured that the new private owners would be allowed to charge $1 per Km 100 *after* having repaired the roads, but congressional representatives later came to know that Minister Dromi had allowed the new private owners to charge $2.50 per Km 100 immediately and that road repairs had been postponed.[68] The many irregularities of the contracts had no explanation. Several of Dromi's technical staff that had designed the privatization bids were also on the payroll of the companies that eventually acquired the highways and went to work for such companies full time after the transfers were completed.[69]

Another major scandal, the so-called "Yomagate," took place a little later and involved other members of the Yoma family: Amira Yoma, Menem's audience secretary; Miss Yoma's former husband, Ibrahim al-Ibrahim, a former Syrian Colonel who spoke little Spanish but nonetheless was named head of customs at the Buenos Aires international airport; and Mario Caserta, chair of the federal water and sanitation council and a personal friend of Menem's. The three were accused by a Panamanian drug dealer, who was arrested in Spain, of using their official positions to launder drug money on behalf of the Colombian cocaine cartels.

The state prosecutor in charge of the case, Judge María Servini de Cubria, after talking to her Spanish colleagues who had requested the extradition of the three, passed the confidential information she had obtained in Madrid to the Menem administration in order to help the defense council. Collusion between the Menem administration and the federal prosecutor was leaked to the press by Servini de Cubria's secretary. Once the scheme appeared in the press, the outrage that it provoked among opposition parties and parts of the judiciary forced the dismissal of Servini de Cubria from the case. However, while the secretary that had denounced the scheme was eventually fired, Servini de Cubria suffered only a modest fine, and the free defendants avoided extradition to Spain while awaiting the results of a new investigation.[70] As in the previous case, the three individuals charged with corruption were recent political climbers who interpreted their role in government as a way of getting rich quickly.

Another policy area where corruption thrived was foreign loans. In 1987, the Alfonsín administration signed two cooperation agreements with Italy and Spain worth, respectively, $5 and $3 billion. Such agreements, implemented during the Menem administration, were loans meant to allow the Argentine government to promote technological and infrastructure development by contracting with Italian and Spanish firms. Additional money was also provided for Argentine private companies to purchase Italian and Spanish goods. In March 1993, former President Alfonsín told the press that in 1990 he had notified the government that Karim Yoma, then secretary for special affairs of the Argentine foreign ministry, Interior Minister Manzano, Chief of Staff Bauzá, and the then Argentine ambassador to Italy Carlos Ruckauf, had requested double-digit commissions from Italian, Spanish, and Argentine businesspeople applying for loans under the cooperation agreements. The government's response was to resurrect an old scandal concerning the sale of the state bank Banco de Italia y Río de la Plata to the Italian Banca Nazionale del Lavoro in 1987 and launch a prosecution against the whole economic team of the Alfonsín government that had negotiated the transfer.

These and many other scandals generated millions of dollars for corrupt politicians at a time when the government was asking the citizenry to tighten up their belts to bring inflation under control. In April 1993, Deputy Carlos Alvarez, a Peronist opposing Menem's policies, filed a petition to inquire into the illicit payments to fellow congressional representatives who, although earning $3,000 monthly, had an ostentatious lifestyle worth more $30,000. This denunciation confirmed an earlier press report that alleged a scheme, run by Chief of Staff Bauzá since July 1989, that complemented the salaries of government officials with additional "donations" provided by private businesses. Payments, which started out ranging from a monthly $1,000 for high-ranking civil servants to $3,000 for a minister, increased to $5,000 and $10,000 respectively.[71]

Menem's response to these scandals always followed the same pattern. First he openly defended his ministers and advisers only to dismiss them shortly thereafter in the hope of coming off clean of the situation. To fend off his critics, Menem, like Collor de Mello, announced a much publicized anticorruption bill in 1991, which never reached the floor of Congress. However, his sincerity remained suspicious. In fact, he continued to accuse the independent press that uncovered the wrongdoing as being "journalistic delinquents." At one point, he withdrew government paid advertisements from *Página 12,* which had led the anticorruption crusade. The decision was later reversed due to the public outcry it created but testifies to Menem's questionable behavior. In the meantime, scandals continued and none of the resulting investigations that ensued have ever ended in a trial. The executive's cooptation of Congress and the Supreme Court has de facto created a system of impunity.

Allegations of corruption in these and other early privatizations led to the resignation of Dromi in early 1991. To regain some credibility, Menem appointed Domingo Cavallo as his new minister of the economy in place of González in March 1991. Cavallo proceeded to overhaul the entire privatization framework, with the assistance of the World Bank, and was forced to renegotiate the Aerolíneas and highway privatizations.

However, Cavallo admitted in August 1995 that market reforms were being put to corrupt use. The economy minister, widely credited for the so-called "Argentine miracle," accused old-style Peronist politicians of derailing his policies to favor "Mafia-like cartels."[72] More specifically, Cavallo claimed that many legislators and prominent administration officials were trying to change the privatization of the national post office bill that was being discussed in Congress so that the only possible bidder could be Alfredo Yabram, a businessperson and personal friend of Menem's, who already controlled 70 percent of the private couriers working in Argentina.[73] If passed in the amended form, the bill would not only allow Yabram to acquire a virtual monopoly of mail service, but would also enable him to ship items in and out of the country without any control from law enforcement officials. For Cavallo this was most disturbing as he claimed to have evidence that Yabram was involved in trafficking narcotics.

The economy minister also charged that Yabram was thwarting the economy ministry's attempt to brake the monopoly on national customs that one of Yabram's companies and the air force jointly administered on behalf of the federal government. Cavallo added that Yabram had physically intimidated a former secretary in charge of deregulation and other senior officials in the national post office who acted against his interests. The minister lamented that senior officials in the justice ministry not only had ignored his previous denunciations but were actually part of the plot.[74] In fact, according to his thesis, some state prosecutors were investigating several of Cavallo's closest aides in key ministries and agencies, using false allegations to force their resignations. The ultimate goal of this strategy, according to former Public Revenues secretary Carlos Tacchi, was to get rid of Cavallo.[75]

Unlike previous corruption charges, Cavallo's accusations could not be dismissed easily. Although the minister did not mention names it was clear that his charges were aimed at Menem's inner circle, including his brother Eduardo (majority leader in the Senate), Eduardo Bauzá (chief of staff), Jorge Matzkin (Speaker of the House of Deputies), Carlos Corach (interior minister), Erman González (former economy and defense minister), and Raúl Granillo Ocampo (Argentine ambassador to Washington), all of whom had close ties to Yabram. In response, a furious Menem first announced that he was planning to reduce Cavallo's status as a super minister by breaking up the economy ministry into three smaller ones.[76] The president openly defended Yabram and even flew back to his home state of La Rioja on Yabram's personal jet days after the scandal erupted. However, domestic and foreign investors (who saw Cavallo as the best guarantee to keep economic reforms on track), the U.S. government, and some opposition leaders openly supported Cavallo. This support forced Menem to grudgingly reaffirm that the minister's job was safe. However, as the economic situation started to deteriorate, and with it Cavallo's prestige, Menem was able to fire the minister in July 1996.

In both the Brazilian and Argentine governments here examined, Pizzorno's "vicious circle of arrogance" seems to describe events quite accurately. Both Collor de Mello and Menem repeatedly made use of their arbitrary power to expand their corrupt networks and build up personal support. Traditional lobbying mechanisms were replaced by a concentration of petitions for special treatment by the president and his cronies. The president's ability to abuse government authority without other institutions restraining his illegal acts made political and economic exclusion intolerable for politicians and businesspeople alike and forced them to deal on the executive's terms.

This monopoly of power permitted the executive to raise the stakes of the game and charge higher commissions than usual to enter corrupt deals. In turn, this increased the confidence of the president and his associates in their invulnerability and, with it, their greediness and arrogance. The Brazilian PCI described this behavior as marked by the obstinate quest for quick and easy profit, no matter what means had to be used.[77]

Why then was Collor de Mello impeached while Menem is still in office? First, Argentina never had a member of the president's inner circle like Pedro Collor de Mello announcing in detail the administration's corruption. Second, Menem had greater control of Congress and the judiciary than his Brazilian counterpart. Third, Menem proved to be a much better politician. While Collor de Mello had virtually alienated everyone after only two and one-half years in office, Menem forged powerful alliances with big business and traditional foes of Peronism in Congress who were willing to tolerate corruption as long as the economic reforms they advocated were implemented. Fourth, Menem, unlike Collor de Mello, was able to control the judiciary whose prestige has steadily deteriorated since the former took office. Menem's decision to pack the Supreme

Court and numerous cases of government collusion with sympathetic fed-eral prosecutors and judges, some of whom have recently been denounced for illicit enrichment, have created what in Argentina is referred to as "ju-dicial insecurity." This came out in the open in October 1993 when two Supreme Court justices announced that a court ruling against the Menem administration had been snatched from the archives and wiped out from the computer system.

In a 1996 poll by Demoskopia, 76 percent of the respondents felt that the rule of law was absent in Argentina and that the government did not respect the constitution. Another poll taken by Gallup in January of that year showed that 47 percent of the interviewees believed that the fight against corruption of government officials and politicians had to take the highest priority. Perhaps the most eloquent statement of how corruption has become a serious threat to Argentine society came from the papacy, a notoriously cautious institution. In November 1995, Pope John Paul II stated that, "corruption and its impunity risk becoming generalized in Ar-gentina and are leading to social indifference and skepticism."

In both Argentina and Brazil it was the press, rather than the democra-tic institutions, that actively investigated corruption. Taking advantage of the unprecedented climate of political freedom and lack of censorship brought by the restoration of democracy, the Argentine and Brazilian press took the lead in the fight against corruption. The Brazilian Congress was initially inclined to cover up Collor de Mello's wrongdoing in ex-change for a greater involvement in the decision-making process and the end of ruling by executive decrees. However, the daily revelations appear-ing in the press created such a popular disgust that Congress, in the end, found it impossible to manage the situation without taking a strong stand against the president.

In Argentina the Radicals, the largest opposition party, remained am-bivalent about attacking the administration too strongly for a number of reasons. First, after they lost the presidency their reputation was in sham-bles. Second, upon taking office six months ahead of time, Menem re-ceived assurances from Alfonsín that the Radicals would cooperate with his reform agenda in Congress. Third, the Radicals feared that Menem could bring up the illicit business that took place under Alfonsín. Finally, there was no equivalent of Pedro Collor de Mello in Argentina to give de-tailed documentation of the Menem administration's corruption scheme (Cavallo stopped short from accusing the president in 1995).

To be sure, these are problems confined not just to Argentina and Brazil. An analysis of the privatization process in Mexico during President Carlos Salinas de Gortari (1988–1994) points to a similar pattern. The scandal in August 1995 involving former AereoMexico President Gerardo de Prevoisin and the ruling *Partido Revolucionario Institucional* (PRI) offers the first proof that nouveau-riche Mexican businessmen—many favored in government privatization auctions—pumped millions of dollars into the PRI's campaign war chest for the 1994 federal elections. The PRI spent more than 90 centavos of every peso that political parties paid out during the August 21 contest, winning the presidency and majorities in both houses of Congress. Rumors of multimillion dollar donations from privatization kingpins or their newly acquired companies began with reports that ex-President Carlos Salinas hosted a "millionaires' banquet" on February 23, 1993, to ask the entrepreneurs to organize businesspeople into groups donating $25 million each to the PRI. Salinas confirmed that the dinner occurred, but denied asking for million-dollar donations. The latest scandal (AeroMexico) shows otherwise.[78]

The press uncovered another major scandal when it found out that the private owners of the former telecommunication state monopoly paid Salinas's brother Raúl $50 million for a "venture capital fund." Subsequently, the justice department of Mexico traced $300 million in Raúl Salinas's bank transfers to foreign banks. "If the president's brother starts depositing millions of dollars at a time, you should certainly suspect that he did not make it from any legitimate business," said Tom Cash, a former senior U.S. Drug Enforcement Administration official.[79]

In Venezuela, the Supreme Court has recently found former President Carlos Andrés Pérez guilty of misappropriating $17 million of discretionary funds. Former Vice President Alberto Dahik fled from his native Ecuador before being apprehended on charges of embezzlement. Even Uruguay, a country considered less corrupt than its Latin American neighbors, seemed to face similar problems. In 1995, special congressional committees turned evidence over to the judiciary involving an influence-peddling scheme that occurred under former President Luis Alberto Lacalle. According to the inquiry, there was sufficient ground to link senior officials of the Lacalle administration with the irregularities committed in the privatization of the Banco Pan de Azúcar.

XI. Transparency and Regulation

What appears clear is that compensation mechanisms for the potential losers of privatization, as argued by Haggard and Webb in a 1992 World Bank study, are closely associated with the rapid implementation of privatization programs. In Argentina, such compensations, targeting big domestic conglomerates, were overt and suspect of corrupt activities. In other words, the Menem administration bought out some of the country's most important rent seekers and rent receivers by framing the first wave of privatization policies in a way that would benefit domestic conglomerates. Thus, at least in the Argentine case, Bates's hypothesis that economic reform in general is a means to change the groups for which the economic system is set up, rather than an effort to promote an open economic system, seems to be confirmed.[80] This raises some troublesome questions regarding the true nature of privatization in these countries. Vargas Llosa, the Peruvian privatization zealot, evaluated the results of state divestiture in Latin America in rather dark and alarming tones.

"What principally happened with the privatization efforts in Peru, Mexico, and Argentina does not differ much from the transfer of State monopolies into the hands of the large private entrepreneurs. This contradicts the moral reasoning behind privatization: opening the markets and beginning the competition that will lead to the process of wealth creation . . . privatization was used simply to inject fresh money into a bankrupt State through the corrupt sale of assets to the friends of the political leaders. Privatization should be, on the contrary, the key element toward social and economic reform. It should allow people to participate in the system and give them [economic] independence."[81]

Two major issues raised above deserve some discussion here, as the fact that they deal with the consequences of privatization means they will be the center of the academic debate in the next decade. The first is transparency and the second deals with regulation. As Devlin pointed out:

"Transparency improves social welfare because it reduces possibilities for corruption, collusion and the misuse of inside information, all of which permit privileged gains from the sale of public assets. It can also be complementary with many other objectives. Since transparency opens the process for more public scrutiny, errors can be checked more easily and fairer evaluations can be made as to whether the government's stated objectives—regarding the privatization process as well as its end product—are being reasonably fulfilled. The closer results are to objectives, the more likely it is that privatization will have a "happy ending" for the firms, the government, and the general public, which in turn reduces the risk of policy backlash. Transparency also enhances the efficiency of the "learning by doing" process which is an inevitable part of any government's privatization programme. An enhanced flow of information will obviously also contribute to overall market efficiency and price maximization."[82]

However, in Argentina, Brazil, and Peru, transparency was sorely missing, particularly in Argentina and Peru, where the disempowerment of the judiciary and other independent institutions made many feel uncomfortable. As even a pro-government analyst underscored, "the abuse of decrees of *need* and *urgency* from the part of the executive bring about worrisome questions. . . . Between the importance and the urgency, society (and the government) . . . must give top priority to the consensus over the importance of the changes introduced [by the economic reform program]."[83] This sentence, written to describe the situation in Argentina, could be easily applied to Brazil. In all three cases, policymakers reasoned that, "privatization should be implemented with less concern about the correct way to do it and more emphasis on getting it done quickly."[84]

Moreover, the need to act quickly regardless of the cost is no justification for macroeconomic mismanagement and collusive practices, both of which took place in these countries. Speed has more to do with political than economic reasons. As Devlin underscored, "most of the objectives that commonly drive privatization processes are not necessarily enhanced by speed; indeed many of them, such as productive and allocative efficiency, credibility, government revenue, catalytic effects, etc. . . . can be seriously compromised by a hasty privatization process."[85] Modiano, the former head of Collor's privatization program, went even further stating, "one can always choose urgency, make bad shareholder decisions, leave significant debts pending, reduce the minimum price, etc. These, however, are not good recipes for a successful privatization programme. Indeed, they are detrimental to the principles of oneness and transparency, as well as to the public wealth (represented by the assets being sold off)."[86]

For example, private enterprises that were transferred under time pressure, such as Aerolíneas Argentinas and ENTel Argentina, were plagued by technical and legal problems and marred by suspicions of corruption. In justifying the poor government record in these two cases, a senior Argentine official flatly stated that those were, "political privatizations." In Argentina and Brazil, whenever the government tried to rush sales, transfers were invariably problematic in one way or another, as had been the case in Chile during the late 1970s.

Moreover, the need to act quickly often seemed to be an excuse to cover up illegal practices. Lack of transparency resulted in cases of alleged wrongdoing, ranging from the sale of privileged information to outright bribes, which failed to be investigated simply because of the heavy government influence in the judiciary, particularly in Argentina and Peru. In

Brazil, where in the wake of Collor's impeachment Congress was under pressure to investigate alleged corruption cases in the privatization process, a special commission found evidence of collusion but its findings never led to criminal investigations for lack of political will.[87] In Argentina, where the press denounced repeated cases of corruption involving Menem's inner circle, all cases were dismissed by sympathetic judges.[88]

The second issue has to do with regulation. With antitrust legislation either weak (Brazil) or so rudimentary as to be ineffective (Argentina), privatizing under monopolistic/oligopolistic conditions raises serious doubts about the establishment of a true market economy, as Vargas Llosa's statement stressed before. As reported by the *Financial Times* in describing the Argentine situation after privatization, "the importance of effective regulation has become paramount: a perception that newly privatized utilities are using their monopoly positions to exploit the public could damage the government and its economic programme severely."[89] Indeed, it seems that the creation or strengthening of monopolistic/oligopolistic markets under private ownership was at best a marginal concern in all these countries. Actually, as I mentioned in the case of Argentina, the lack of a clear regulatory scheme in many sectors was a deliberate government action as part of the incentive package to lure investors such as Aerolíneas Argentinas, ENTel, and gas companies.

For instance, the Argentine Consumer Protection Law 24240 of 1995 did not apply to privatized companies. Complaints and legal charges against them were the jurisdiction of the regulatory agencies. This provision did not seem accidental. In fact, once regulatory agencies were set up after privatization, they found it difficult to effectively monitor the private operators of public services.[90] This occurred for two main reasons. First, the contract of transfer contained loopholes allowing the private companies to resist controls. Second, many agencies had little information about the way public services operated and private companies often withheld such information. When some regulatory agencies tried to defend consumers, private companies went on the attack charging that such agencies should instead "harmonize" consumer interests with "the rights of the private operators of public services."[91]

On one such occasion, Menem sided with the private telephone companies and reduced the prerogatives of the National Commission of Telecommunications by assigning some of them to the undersecretariat for telecommunications, which depended upon the executive branch. However, in Argentina, Brazil, and Peru, clashes between private companies and regulatory agencies were more the exception than the rule. In fact, regulatory agencies often went along with the executive wishes since most of their members were political appointees.

These facts do not invalidate the theoretical premises upon which privatization stands. However, they do indicate, in varying degrees, the extensive shortcomings of such policies if preliminary steps for economic deregulation and political transparency are not taken. The divestiture process often did not lead to greater competition but merely reassigned rents to the private sector without any regulatory structure for the supervision of the new monopolies' operations. The concern here is that there are not sufficient safeguards against the kinds of collusion and abuses that might give some small group of companies a stronghold on the markets they dominate.

Neo-orthodox economic theories do justify privatization as it increases economic efficiency through competition. The more competition, the better, and I fully agree with it. Yet when markets tend to be natural monopolies or become oligopolies for a variety of reasons, government regulation is necessary precisely because it guarantees competition by thwarting collusion and corrupt practices. What we need is not the old-style regulation that, in the past, allowed governments to impose arbitrary controls on the economy and reward special constituencies. What we need is instead a new-style regulation.

Private investment requires a new-style regulation that is limited, transparent, and allows individual managers flexibility and autonomy. The choice between old-style and new-style regulation is ultimately a pragmatic one. If a country really wants private investment in, for instance, its energy sector, it has no choice but to adopt a new regulatory system that keeps promises and exercises self-restraint. . . . Regulation, then, is simply a system that allows a government to formalize its commitments to protect consumers and investors.[92]

So far, at least in the countries examined, there has been little effort to promote new-style regulation. Yet, if no effort is made in this direction, it is hard to see how true competition can emerge under the present monopolistic or oligopolistic conditions characterizing many important sectors in Argentina and Brazil. If the issue is not resolved, it may become a political, as well as an economic, hot potato in the years to come.

XII. Conclusion

The goal of this paper has been to outline the close relationship among economic crisis, market reforms, and new forms of political corruption perpetrated by new political elites. Although the model we developed is far from conclusive, it tries to highlight in a systematic fashion the logic behind new types of corruption. Much of the difficulty of this kind of research is due to the lack of judicial evidence that will allow scholars to better define the phenomenon under study across countries.

One of the most troublesome aspects of those corrupt practices is the damage they wreak on public support to market reforms required for economic growth and investment. For example, in Brazil powerful lobbies attempted to thwart President Itamar Franco's proposal for modest reforms by associating it with his discredited predecessor, Collor de Mello.

Evidence suggests that as long as an administration is able to restore and maintain economic stability and growth, most citizens are prepared to tolerate corruption. If economic instability persists, however, corruption will gain prominence and may be used to oust ineffective administrations. Foreign dignitaries and observers were quick in labeling Collor de Mello and Menem as a new brand of great Latin American reformers only to be embarrassed by the facts later on. An Argentine newspaper put it best when it said, "Despite anything President Carlos Menem would like us to believe, pursuing the worthy goals of efficiency and productivity cannot be achieved if the cardinal virtue of Justice is neglected."

Curbing corruption requires action on several fronts. First, strong checks and balances among the three branches of government must be in place. As long as the executive wields extraordinary discretionary powers, opportunities for corruption will abound. Requiring the three branches of government to act transparently is essential.

A key area that would benefit from a transparent system is the election of judges and prosecutors. They must be hired on the basis of professional achievements, not political connections. However, hiring by merit is not enough. Judiciary budgets must afford competitive wages that attract top candidates at all levels. Court information systems need to be computerized, a factor that tremendously helped the Italian magistrates who started the *Mani Pulite* inquiry. Examining magistrates and prosecutors must have the resources to conduct in-depth investigations.

Penalties against corruption exist in many Latin American countries, but they are not enforced; they must be if people are to believe that the system works. As the twentieth century draws to a close, an individual's high status or political position must no longer be a shield of impunity, eliciting winks instead of active enforcement.

Public servants need to receive extensive training in the legal, administrative, and ethical choices that their work entails. On the legislative and constitutional fronts, steps should be taken to end all unwarranted secrecy in official business. Transparency is the best safeguard against arbitrary decisions and administrative abuses. The light of day is a powerful disinfectant.

In closing, the association between democratic government and corruption is unfortunate wherever it occurs. Political observers have raised warnings that corruption may endanger democracy in countries lacking longstanding democratic traditions.[93] When bribes are associated with painful policies like privatization and deregulation they can jeopardize the whole market reform agenda whose goal, in theory, is to create greater transparency, less government discretionality, and more economic opportunities for all.[94] Not surprisingly, some of the new anticorruption crusaders of today are using scandals to protect old privileges. As pointed out elsewhere, "Throughout the region, many self-appointed anticorruption crusaders tend to be supporters of statist policies, who possess doubtful credentials and self-serving motives."[95] Thus, in the end, everything is trivialized. "Everyone accuses and everyone is accused. If everyone is corrupt, no one is, thus no one goes to jail and everyone keeps stealing as usual."[96]

Summing up, there is nothing inherently wrong or corrupt with free-market economic policies; rather it is the way in which they are pursued that should be scrutinized. St. Augustine wrote that "States without Justice are but bands of robbers enlarged." A renewed focus on corruption has both theoretical and normative importance.

Notes

1. *Newsweek,* 14 November 1994, 40, p. 42.

2. *Wall Street Journal,* 1 July 1996, p. 1.

3. Some examples are Victor Le Vine, *Political Corruption: The Ghana Case* (Stanford: Hoover Institution Press, 1975); Leslie Palmier, *The Control of Bureaucratic Corruption: Case Studies in Asia (India, Hong Kong, Indonesia)* (New Delhi: Allied, 1986); Robert Wade, "The System of Administrative and Political Corruption: Canal Irrigation in South India," *Journal of Development Studies* 18 (April 1982):297–328; Eduardo Diaz Uribe, *El clientelismo en Colombia: un estudio exploratorio* (Bogotá: Ancora, 1986); Luís Pazos, *Democracia a la mexicana* (Mexico City: Diana, 1986); Alvaro Avila Bernal, *Corrupción y expoliación en America Latina: los casos de Colombia, Venezuela, Brasil* (Bogotá: Grijalbo, 1987); Gabriel Zaid, *La economía presidencial* (Mexico City: Vuelta, 1987); Carlos Elizondo, *La silla embrujada: historia de la corrupción en México* (Mexico City: ADAMEX, 1987); Francisco Leal Buitrago, *Clientelismo: el sistema político y su expresión regional* (Bogotá: Instituto de Estudios Políticos y Relaciones Internacionales, Editorial Tercer Mundo, 1990); Horacio Verbitsky, *Robo para la corona: Los frutos prohibidos del árbol de la corrupción* (Buenos Aires: Planeta, 1991); and Stephen Morris, *Corruption and Politics in Contemporary Mexico* (Tuscaloosa: University of Alabama Press, 1991).

4. For an overview of the debate see Michael Johnston, "The Political Consequences of Corruption: A Reassessment," *Comparative Politics* 18 (1986):459–77; and Robin Theo-

bald, *Corruption, Development, and Underdevelopment* (Durham, N.C.: Duke University Press, 1990), pp. 107–132.

5. Ronald Wraith and Edgar Simpkins, *Corruption in Developing Nations* (London: Allen and Unwin, 1963); James Wilson, "The Shame of States," *Public Interest* 2(1966):28–38; Stanislav Andreski, "Kleptocracy: Or, Corruption as a System of Government," in Stanislav Andreski ed., *The African Predicament: A Study in the Pathology of Modernization* (London: Michael Joseph, 1968), pp. 92–109; Gunnar Myrdal, "Corruption: Its Causes and Effects," in Gunnar Myrdal, *Asian Drama: An Enquiry into the Poverty of Nations,* vol. 2 (New York: Twentieth Century, 1968), pp. 937–58. More recently similar negative analyses have appeared in the David Gould, *The Effects of Corruption in Administrative Performance* (Washington, D.C.: World Bank, 1983); Richard Hodder-Williams, *An Introduction to the Politics of Tropical Africa* (London: Allen & Unwin, 1985), p.17; A. Riding, *Mexico: Inside the Volcano* (London: I.B. Tauris, 1987); and Robert Klitgaard, *Controlling Corruption* (Berkeley: University of California Press, 1988), among others.

6. Nathaniel Leff, "Economic Development through Bureaucratic Corruption," *American Behavioral Scientist* 8 (November 1964):8–14; Colin Leys, "What Is the Problem about Corruption?," *Journal of Modern African Studies* 3 (August 1965):215–30; José Abueva, "The Contribution of Nepotism, Spoils, and Graft to Political Development," *East-West Center Review* 3 (1966):45–54; David Bayley, "The Effects of Corruption in a Developing Nation," *Western Political Quarterly* 19 (December 1966):719–32.

7. Samuel Huntington, *Political Order in Changing Societies* (New Haven: Yale University Press, 1968); Joseph Nye, "Corruption and Political Development: A Cost-Benefit Analysis," *American Political Science Review* 61 (June 1967):417–27; Arnold Heidenheimer, ed., *Political Corruption: Readings in Comparative Analysis* (New York: Holt, Rinehart & Winston, 1970); Gabriel Ben-Dor, "Corruption, Institutionalization, and Political Development: The Revisionist Thesis Revisited," *Comparative Political Studies* 7 (April 1974): 68–83; John Waterbury, "Endemic and Planned Corruption in a Monarchial Regime," *World Politics* 25 (July 1973):533–55; John Waterbury, "Corruption, Political Stability, and Development: Comparative Evidence from Egypt and Morocco," *Government and Opposition* 11 (Autumn 1976):426–45.

8. R.O. Tilman, "Emergency of Black Market Bureaucracy: Administrative Corruption in the New States," *Public Administrative Review* 28 (1968):437–44.

9. Some exceptions can be found in Stephen Bunker and Lawrence Cohen, "Collaboration and Competition in Two Colonization Projects: Toward a General Theory of Official Corruption," *Human Organization* 42 (Summer 1983); Robert Wade, "The Market for Public Office: Why the Indian State is Not Better at Development," *World Development* 13 (April 1985):467–97; and Michael Johnston, "The Political Consequences of Corruption: A Reassessment," *Comparative Politics* 18 (1986):459–77.

10. For recent critiques of the political corruption literature see A. Deysine, "Political Corruption. A Review of the Literature,"*European Journal of Political Research* 8 (1980): 447–462; Tevfik Nas, Albert Price, and Charles Weber, "A Policy-Oriented Theory of Corruption," *American Political Science Review* 80, no. 1 (1986):107–8; Philip Oldenburg, "Middlemen in Third-World Corruption: Implications of an Indian Case," *World Politics* 39, no. 4 (1987):508–10; Robin Theobald, *Corruption, Development, and Underdevelopment* (Durham: Duke University Press, 1990), p. 80.

11. James C. Scott, *Comparative Political Corruption*, p. 5; and Johnston, "The Political Consequences of Corruption," p. 461.

12. Arnold Rogow and Harold Lasswell, *Power, Corruption, and Rectitude* (Englewood Cliffs, N.J.: Prentice-Hall, 1963), p. 132; C.J. Friedrich, "Political Pathology," *The Political Quarterly* XXXVII (January–March 1966):166; and J. Hurstfield, "Political Corruption in Modern England: The Historian's Problem," *History* 52 (1967):19.

13. The most important advocate of the public opinion criterion has been Heidenheimer who employed a sophisticated typology distinguishing between "white," "gray," and "black"

corruption, which tries to account for variations of public reactions depending on the so-cioeconomic context of a given society. Arnold Heidenheimer, "The Context of Analysis," in Arnold Heidenheimer, ed., *Political Corruption: Readings in Comparative Analysis* (New Brunswick, N.J.: Holt, Rinehart, and Winston, 1970), pp. 26–28.

14. John Gardiner and Theodore Lyman, *Decisions for Sale: Corruption in Local Land-Use Regulation* (New York: Praeger, 1978), p. 5.

15. Nye, "Corruption and Political Development," p. 565. Other commonly used legal definitions can be found in V.O. Key, *The Techniques of Political Graft in the United States* (Chicago: University of Chicago Libraries, 1936), pp. 386–401; Huntington, *Political Order in Changing Societies*, p. 59; Andreski, *The African Predicament* (New York: Atherton Press, 1968), p. 92.

16. For a summary of the pros and cons of the three criteria see Theobald, *Corruption, Development, and Underdevelopment*, pp. 1–7.

17. Susan Rose-Ackerman, *Corruption: A Study in Political Economy* (New York: Academic Press, 1978), pp. 3–4. The feasibility of rational choice has been tested almost exclusively in the cases of developed countries. See J.R. Shackleton, "Corruption: An Essay in Economic Analysis," *Political Quarterly* 49 (January 1978):25–37; Gordon Tullock, "The Backward Society: Static Inefficiency, Rent Seeking, and the Rule of Law," in J. Buchanan and R Tollison, *The Theory of Public Choice* (Ann Arbor: University of Michigan Press, 1984), pp. 224–37; G.C. Benson and J. Baden, "The Political Economy of Governmental Corruption: The Logic of Underground Government," *Journal of Legal Studies* 14 (1985):391–410; Tevkif Nas, Albert Price, and Charles Weber, "A Policy-Oriented Theory of Corruption," *American Political Science Review* 80, no. 1 (1986):107–119; Dennis Mueller, "The Economics of Special Privilege and Rent Seeking," *Economic Journal* 100, no. 402 (September 1990):976; and M.S. Alam, "Some Economic Costs of Corruption in LDCs," *The Journal of Development Studies* 27, no. 1 (1990):85–97. A noticeable exception is John Macrae, "Underdevelopment and the Economics of Corruption: A Game Theory Approach," *World Development* 10 (August 1982):677–87.

18. For instance, the existence of a common incentive structure and payoff matrix for both corrupt public officials and corrupting private individuals. On this criticism see Antonella della Porta, *Lo Scambio occulto: Casi di corruzione in Italia* (Bologna: Il Mulino, 1992), p. 81.

19. Barbara Geddes and Artur Ribeiro Neto, "Institutional Sources of Corruption in Brazil," p. 6, paper prepared for the conference Whither Brazil After Collor?: The Political, Economic, and Institutional Issues of the Transition, Miami, February 26–27, 1993.

20. Scott, *Comparative Political Corruption*, p. 14.

21. In the case of Brazil the most common forms of corruption among office holders come from: (1) overpricing the costs of services provided by private entrepreneurs to the government, with part of the money going to politicians and bureaucrats; (2) the facilitation of government payments to private contractors in return for kickbacks; (3) illegal fund-raising; (4) ignoring technical and price criteria in the selection of contractors for public projects; (5) selling government confidential information; (6) imposing a "mediation tax" on private business in order to win government contracts; and (7) manipulating government regulations to favor private citizens/companies. Geddes and Ribeiro Neto, "The Institutional Sources of Corruption," pp. 10–14.

22. Alessandro Pizzorno, "La corruzione nel sistema politico," pp. 22–23, in della Porta, *Lo scambio occulto.*

23. Ibid., pp. 25–26.

24. Ibid., p. 27.

25. Geddes and Ribeiro Neto, "Institutional Sources of Corruption in Brazil," p. 18.

26. Della Porta, *Lo scambio occulto*, pp. 29–30.

27. For instance, the former president and general manager of ELMA, an Argentine state company, were indicted for having purchased two ferryboats at a price worth about ten. Upon taking office, the former Argentine minister of health and social action, Avelino Porto, found out some 23,000 files showing that bureaucrats of his ministry had solicited commissions for the processing of paperwork. Rates for kickbacks ranged from $1,200 for a certificate necessary to import food to $50,000–80,000 for the authorization of new cosmetic products.

28. In a survey research conducted between 16–22 January 1992 in Buenos Aires and its metropolitan area by Mora Araujo, Noguera & Asociados, respondents identified in the state the main cause of corruption. The state, its institutions, and the public officers representing it, came out as essentially corrupt. Respondents believed that the high level of corruption in Argentine society was primarily an adaptive, functional behavior because "nothing can be obtained from the state without bribes." *Poder Ciudadano*, Buenos Aires, April 1991, p. 4. Similarly attitudes have been found in Brazil, Mexico, Peru, and Venezuela.

29. Geddes and Ribeiro Neto, "Institutional Sources of Corruption in Brazil," p. 4.

30. Randolph Siverson and Harvery Starr, "Opportunity, Willingness, and the Diffusion of War," *American Political Science Review* 84 (1990):49.

31. Jorge Schvarzer, "La reestructuración de la economía argentina en nuevas condiciones políticas," *Documento CISEA*, Buenos Aires, November 1992.

32. Guillermo O'Donnell, "Delegative Democracy?" *Kellog Institute Working Paper* 172 (March 1992), pp. 6–7.

33. Besides press coverage and congressional investigations, the research was based on extensive open-ended interviews carried out in the fall of 1992 in Argentina and Brazil with state prosecutors, members of congress, journalists, businessmen, and high-ranking government officials. Many interviewees, spoke on condition of anonymity and therefore they were not cited in this paper. However, whatever information was used in the text was thoroughly double-checked.

34. On the notion of exchange in corrupt practices, see Johnston, "The Political Consequences of Corruption," pp. 464–74.

35. This definition derives from Gardiner and Lyman, *Decisions for Sale*, p. 5, and della Porta's who selected cases were characterized by: "(a) public administrators who (b) have betrayed the public interest for private profit through (c) acts that have violated the law and have been condemned by the public opinion. Such acts have (d) taken place during shady transactions within which (e) money has been exchanged for influence in the behavior of the public administration." Della Porta, *Lo scambio occulto*, p. 83.

36. On Menem's patrimonialism, see Atilio Borón "'Los axiomas de Anillaco.' La visión de la política en el pensamiento y en la acción de Carlos Saúl Menem," in Atilio Boron, ed., *El Menemato: Radiografía de dos años de gobierno de Carlos Menem* (Buenos Aires: Letra Buena, 1991), pp. 55–56.

37. Collor de Mello's fortune was built around the media business (television and radio stations), while the Menems started as salesmen in the Northwest of Argentina to eventually gain prominence in the production of wine.

38. On the background of P.C Farias and his early political association with Collor de Mello see Gustavo Krieger, Luiz Antônio Novaes, and Tales Faria, *Todos os Socios do Presidente*, 3d ed. (San Paulo: Editorial Scritta, 1992), pp. 21–56. According to the CPI, Farias had 70 pending trials on a large array of illegal activities. All charges were mysteriously dropped in April 1990.

39. Collor de Mello was appointed mayor of Alagoas's capital, Maceió, by the military regime in the early 1980s. In 1982, he went on to run for Congress. At the time, he put thousands of campaign activists on the Maceió's payroll as school aides. In 1988, Collor de

Mello, in order to finance his campaign, returned some $100 million in taxes to sugar cane plantation owners who then returned 20 percent of that amount to Farias. Menem, on the other hand, put on the La Rioja's payroll as much as half of the working force in the 1980s. When the Radical administration of President Raúl Alfonsín decided to cut down federal funds to La Rioja, Menem began to print his own money to pay employees. It must be underscored that in Argentina states are called provinces and have less fiscal and political independence than their Brazilian counterparts. James Brooke, "Looting Brazil," *The New York Times Magazine,* 8 November 1992, p. 42.

40. In the case of Argentina, former state prosecutor Luis Moreno Ocampo found evidence about the involvement of president Alfonsín's brother, and many prominent members of the Radical Civic Union, had diverted government funds for their own personal profit as well as to their party and party supporters. In Brazil, Sarney used lavishly government funds to buy supporters in Congress (Sarney had no congressional majority) leaving the federal coffers in a state of chaos by the time he left office. Outrageous corruption scandals under his term, like the North-South Railway, were covered up.

41. *Brazilian Report,* 6 July 1989, p. 2.

42. Gabriela Cerruti and Sergio Ciancaglini, *El Octavo Círculo* (Buenos Aires: Planeta, 1991), p. 110.

43. The Collor de Mello administration's inner circle was so dominated by people from his home state to be nicknamed the "Republic of Alagoas." A year after his inauguration, the president was forced to dismiss most of these people due to charge of widespread corruption. *Latin American Weekly Report,* p. 2.

44. *Buenos Aires Herald,* 19 January 1992, p. 3.

45. *New York Times,* 7 August 1991, p. A4.

46. Krieger et al., *Todos os Socios do Presidente,* p. 44.

47. Ibid., p. 126.

48. Horacio Verbitsky, *Hacer la Corte: La construcción de un poder absoluto sin justicia ni control* (Buenos Aires: Planeta 1993).

49. Joao Batista Petersen Mendes, *A CPI do PC e os Crimes do Poder* (Rio De Janeiro: Foglio Editora, 1992), pp. 4–5.

50. Brooke, "Looting Brazil," p. 45.

51. Geddes and Ribeiro Neto, "Institutional Sources of Corruption in Brazil," p. 30.

52. Kenneth Serbin, "Collor Impeachment and the Struggle for Change," *North-South Center Focus,* University of Miami, vol. II, no. 2, 1993, p. 3.

53. *Brazil Watch,* 27 September–11 October, 1993, p. 16.

54. *Latin American Regional Reports: Brazil,* 8 July 1993, p. 6.

55. Krieger et al., *Todos os Socios do Presidente,* pp. 139–40.

56. *Veja,* 19 August 1992, pp. 24–25. Canhedo turned out to be the only bidder as other potential buyers withdrew their offers upon knowing that Farias was allegedly behind him.

57. Krieger et al., *Todos os Socios do Presidente,* p. 122.

58. Verbitsky, *Robo para la corona,* p. 114.

59. Gabriela Cerruti and Sergio Ciancaglini, *El Octavo Círculo* (Buenos Aires: Planeta, 1991), p. 103.

60. Manzano, for instance, failed to explain how he could afford a house believed to be worth over $3 million. See *Buenos Aires Herald,* 1 March 1992, p. 20. Minister Dromi also came from a middle-class background and made a brilliant career as a attorney specializing in corporate law and public administration. In that capacity he made a reputation for himself by representing private firms that had thrived under fat government contracts. Dromi, a former mayor of Mendoza (the same city of Manzano's) during the last years of the military dictatorship, in 1987 opened a branch of his law firm in Buenos Aires where he quickly gained a reputation of being one of the ablest wheeler-and-dealers.

61. Verbitsky, *Robo para la corona*, pp. 195–200. On González's responsibilities see also *Clarín* (Buenos Aires), 12 June 1991, pp. 6–7, and *Ambito Financiero* (Buenos Aires), 26 November 1991, pp. 21–22.

62. *Miami Herald*, 22 December 1991, p. 25A.

63. Luís Moreno Ocampo, *En defensa propia: Cómo salir de la corrupción* (Buenos Aires: Sudamericana, 1993), pp. 240–244.

64. Interviews with Horácio Verbitsky and Luís Moreno Ocampo, Buenos Aires, November 1992.

65. Roberto de Michele, "Serás Juez," *Sentencia* no. 9 (May 1993), p. 44.

66 On the Bell Atlantic–Manufactures Hanover Trust's charges, see Gabriela Cerruti and Sergio Ciancaglini, *El Octavo Círculo* (Buenos Aires: Planeta, 1991), p. 232.

67. Corrado Incerti, "Tanfo Argentino," *Panorama*, April 1993, p. 11.

68. Alberto Natale, *Privatizaciones en Privado: El testimonio de un protagonista que desnuda el laberinto de las adjudicaciones* (Buenos Aires: Planeta, 1993), pp. 141–158.

69. Archives of the Cámara de Diputados de la Nación Argentina, appeals presented by deputies German Abdala, Darío Alessandro, Carlos Alvarez, Alberto Aramouni, Juan Pablo Cafiero, Franco Caviglia, and Moisés Fontela, May 15, 1990.

70. A detailed account of the "Yomagate" can be found in *Somos* (Buenos Aires), "La mano negra," 12 August 1992, pp. 4–7.

71. *Latin American Regional Reports: Southern Cone*, 24 December 1992, p. 3.

72. Cavallo made the first allegations during the television program "Key Hour" anchored by journalist Mariano Grondona on August 17, 1995.

73. On Yabram's shady business deals see *Noticias*, 27 November 1994, p. 49.

74. Cavallo filed these accusations against Yabram to the Federal Court of Buenos Aires on September 14, 1995.

75. *Financial Times*, 24 September 1995, p. 6.

76. *El Expreso*, a paper close to Menem ran a headline stating "Cavallo's Days Are Numbered," which was echoed by Ambassador Granillo Ocampo in Washington. Granillo Ocampo had been attorney general of La Rioja when Menem was governor of that province.

77. *O Estado de S. Paulo*, 25 August 1992.

78. *Mexico Weekly Fax Bulletin*, Mexico City, 14 August 1995. Early warnings of such scandals were reported earlier by the *Miami Herald*, 26 September 1993, p. 27A.

79. *Miami Herald*, 25 march 1996, p. 6A.

80. Robert Bates, *Beyond the Miracle of the Market* (Cambridge: Cambridge University Press, 1991).

81. *Clarín*, 17 November 1993, p. 18.

82. Robert Devlin, "Privatization and Social Welfare," *Cepal Review* no. 49 (April 1993):169–70.

83. Enrique Bour, "El Programa argentino de la desregulación y privatización." In *Reforma y convergencia: Ensayos sobre la transformación de la ecnomía argentina* edited by Felipe de la Balze, (Buenos Aires: ADEBA, 1993), pp. 263–264.

84. Woodrow Wilson Center. *Noticias* (Spring), 1991.

85. Robert Devlin, "Privatization and Social Welfare," *Cepal Review* no. 49 (April 1993):170.

86. Statement delivered by Eduardo Modiano at the Seminar on the Politics and Economics of Public Revenues Expenditures, sponsored by the World Bank and the Ministry of Economics, Brasilia 10–12 June, 1992.

87. Commissão Parlamentar Mista de Inquérito, Relatório no. 3, De 1994-CN, Brasilia, National Congress, 21 July 1994.

88. Interview with journalist Hétor Ruiz Núñez, Buenos Aires, March 1995.

89. *Financial Times*, 27 May 1993. p. 3.

90. The only two exceptions are the electricity and gas regulatory agencies.

91. *Clarín*, 22 March 1995, p. 26.

92. Bernard Tenenbaum, "The Real World of Power Sector Regulation," *Viewpoint* no. 50 (June 1995), p. 1.

93. Georgie Anne Geyer, *World Monitor*, Sept. 1922, pp. 11–12; "The Politics of Corruption: And the Corruption of Politics," *NACLA Report on the Americas*, vol. XXVII, no. 3 (Nov/Dec. 1993), pp. 11–12; Timothy Goodman, "Political Corruption: The Payoff Diminishes," *The American Enterprise* (September/October 1994), pp. 19–27; and Dorinda Elliott et al., "Corruption," *Newsweek*, 14 November 1994, pp. 40–42.

94. Ken Silverstein, "Marketing Misery in Latin America," *The Nation*, 21 December 1992, p. 766.

95. *Wall Street Journal*, 1 July 1996, p. A7.

96. *Buenos Aires Herald*, 28 March 1993, p. 16. With inflation now under control and the economy growing again, the Argentine public is becoming much less tolerant about corruption than it was when Menem took office. In February 1990, a Gallup poll recorded that only 3 percent of the people interviewed mentioned corruption as the most urgent problem facing the country. In March 1992 corruption had become the number one priority. *Poder Ciudadano*, April 1992, p. 4.

7

Journalism and Corruption in Brazil

CARLOS EDUARDO LINS DA SILVA

The press has had an important role in denouncing corruption in Brazil, but it is not the sole institution responsible for initiating reforms, as many journalists who portray themselves as crusaders for morality like to claim. Neither have Brazilian social and political environments been rid of corruption as many analysts would hope. Corruption is still there in a wide variety of forms and areas, including journalism, and social tolerance toward it is still very high. Impunity continues to be the rule for those charged and convicted of corruption. But much has changed recently, particularly since 1991, and it is fair to acknowledge that the press has had something to do with it. This chapter will offer a broad view of how corruption practices became embedded in the Brazilian social fabric throughout its history and will concentrate on analyzing how the press has been covering political events in Brazil in the last few years, stressing the way it has been dealing with charges of corruption against high-level public officials.

It is well known that Brazilian national culture has been remarkably complacent with regard to corruption. The social anthropologist Roberto DaMatta, in his classic book, *Carnivals, Rogues, and Heroes,* includes the folkloric character of Pedro Malasartes among those who best help define the essential contradictions of the Brazilian "collective soul."[1]

"In the stories of Pedro Malasartes we are struck by the looseness of the narrative style, in which countless independent episodes are combined as the narrator sees it. These accounts—which define the character of the hero and the society in which he operates—depict Pedro deceiving or out-witting people in social positions of power and prestige, even selling feces to a very rich man. Others depict much more ambiguous situations where the distance between shrewdness and social offense is muddied, for example inducing a powerful plantation owner to murder, the use of a corpse to make money, and the conscious, deliberate, destruction of goods of production and consumption owned by a large proprietor. It is clear that we have a 'hero without any character.' To say it more clearly, we are dealing with a personage who characteristically knows how to transform every disadvantage into an advantage, which is the sign of any good rogue and all good roguery. . . . He teaches us . . . that money (and its corresponding social position) is rotten and disposable, like the feces he sells to a rich and conceited fool."[2]

Some attempt to explain the pervasiveness of tolerance toward corruption in Brazilian society by the fact that the country was colonized by "morally condescending" Catholics rather than by strict Puritans. Richard Morse, in his masterwork *O Espelho de Próspero*—by no means a glorification of the Protestant approach, quite the contrary—gives a notable historic review of how facets of each religion helped forge national values, behaviors, and attitudes in both the Iberian Peninsula and Anglo America, while helping us to understand some of the cultural roots of each subcontinent.[3]

Whether because of Catholicism or not, the unavoidable truth is that corruption has been a trademark in the Brazilian political system since its earliest origins. The first form of political organization imposed by the Portuguese authorities on their American colony was one known as "inheriting captaincies." Parallel strips of land bordered by the Atlantic Ocean to the east and by the line of the Treaty of Tordesillas (which in 1494 divided South America between Portugal and Spain) to the west were given out as property by the king of Portugal to noblemen or commoners who had provided good service. The captains had the right to do whatever they wanted in their captaincies, creating a quasi-feudal regime. Both the captaincies system and its successor, the general-governorship system, which centralized the management of the colony into the hands of one man, were undermined by incompetence and corruption in the top levels of the administration and among the very powerful landowners.

Being sent to Brazil was an attraction for the Portuguese for one reason: the opportunity to make a lot of money in a little time. In order to achieve this goal, almost anything would be considered acceptable both by the court and by the officials' peers. As noted by Joseph Page, the king "may have been pragmatic enough to realize the impossibility of subjecting them (the officials) to close and effective control."[4] The officials became very rich, and they were also important to Lisbon as a source of wealth from the New World. Although their standards of morality were not very high, the Crown could trust their loyalty to Portugal for the good reason that probably no other European power with interests in South America (France and the Netherlands, for instance, who attempted to seize parts of Brazil in the sixteenth and seventeenth centuries but were defeated by the Portuguese with the support of native Indians and Afro-brazilians) would allow them as much freedom of action as they enjoyed under Portuguese rule. "The administration of the colony became a paradigm not only of inefficiency but also of graft and corruption, as local officials siphoned off public funds and otherwise took financial advantage of their position. The pervasive presence of red tape survives to present day. Brazilians generally deal with it indirectly, by resorting to *jeitinhos*. Indeed, an entire profession—private facilitators known as *despachantes*—has emerged to guide people through bureaucratic mazes."[5]

Another characteristic of the colonization process in Brazil was that no press was allowed to be established in the country until November 1807, when the queen of Portugal, Maria I, and her court moved from Lisbon to Rio de Janeiro to escape the Napoleonic French troops. The prohibition of the press in Brazil was a unique trait in Latin America; mostly because of church initiative, most Spanish colonies had their first presses long before Brazil did (Mexico in 1538, Peru in 1684, Guatemala in 1660, Paraguay in 1700, and so on).

Even by Portuguese standards of colonization, the ban on the press was extraordinary: Jesuits from Portugal, with the approval of the court, established presses in the sixteenth century in Goa and Macao. José Marques de Melo, the most respected communication scholar in Brazil, has several explanations for the proscription of the press in the Brazilian colony: the fact that it was much cheaper to have books exported to America than produced there; the nonexistence of economic activities in large scale in the colony to justify the establishment of a typographical industry there; the small number of literate people living in Brazil at the time of the colonial regime; the fact that the indigenous societies in the country—contrary to other parts of Spanish America—did not constitute a threat to the colonizers and, thus, did not need to be "culturally tamed" by them; the obscurantism of the Portuguese court and its fear that a free press in the colony where it generated most of its wealth could disseminate the wish for independence, among others.[6] The few attempts to introduce presses in colonial Brazil (six in total) had short lives (the longest were led by the Dutch and Spanish in areas under their control). When the court established itself in Rio de Janeiro in 1808, a Regal Press was installed in that city and the first newspaper, the *Gazeta do Rio de Janeiro*, began to be published under the prince regent's auspices and with the primary goal of promoting the government. In truth, the very first Brazilian newspaper was the *Correio Brasiliense*, founded in London also in 1808 (three months before the first issue of the *Gazeta* was produced) by Hipólito José da Costa. Da Costa was a Brazilian who had spent two years in the United States and, after being prosecuted by the Portuguese government because of his religious beliefs, exiled himself to England under the protection of the Duke of Sussex. The *Correio* almost did not circulate in Brazil; its readers were mostly Portuguese exiled in London. Contrary to what many believe, the *Correio* was not an advocate for the independence of Brazil but just a newspaper with a strong stand of opposition to the Portuguese government.[7]

The *Gazeta* and the *Correio* were the founders of two of the most important traditions in Brazilian journalism: the sycophantic and the partisan. In subsequent years, the majority of the newspapers published in Brazil were either sponsored by the state in order to flatter it or by political parties or leaders in order to promote their ideas and to serve as vital pathways to power.

After independence (1822) and becoming a republic (1889), the general public's attitude toward corruption remained more or less the same as in the colonial period. It was assumed almost as an unchangeable fact that corruption should, in some way, permeate the relationships between the government and its agents and the civil society. In the microcosms, policemen, public controllers, and tax collection inspectors excused bribery— even among their very victims—as something justifiable vis-à-vis their very low salaries; in the macrocosms, powerful businesspeople established the rule that doing successful business with the government at any level (federal, state, or municipal) almost always involved some kind of kickbacks to high officials who, through these deals, enriched themselves. The "10 percent fee" was considered a fact of life in Brazil and was adopted not only in the public sphere, but also in several private institutions. In any bid the offer with the best chance to win was not necessarily the least expensive or the best qualified but the one that included the best fee to the right decisionmaker.

Many have noticed that in the federal government the average "commission" to be paid by the bidder or the supplier of goods or services to an officer in order to "facilitate" things has gone up. It was 5 percent in the 1950s, rose to 10 percent during the military regime, hit 15 percent when the civilians returned to power in 1984, and even reached 40 percent in the government of Collor de Mello in the 1990s. During the periods of the independent monarchy (1822–89) and the First Republic (1889–1965), most of the newspapers and magazines published in Brazil followed one of two models created by the *Gazeta* and the *Correio*: the state adulator and the ardent supporter of political causes. They were "vehicles for government platforms, opinions of groups, specific social programs."[8] The greatest Brazilian journalists from the nineteenth century were those who defended noble causes such as the abolition of slavery and republican ideals. But there was no newspaper, in the sense of a medium for disseminating news (such as existed in the United States), after 1830 because of the rise of what Michael Schudson called "a democratic market society," which "meant the expansion of a market economy and political democracy or, put another way, the democratization of business and politics sponsored by an urban middle class which trumpeted 'equality' in social life."[9]

In nineteenth-century Brazil, the social and economic reality was so vastly different from Schudson's description of the United States at the same time that it is hardly imaginable how anyone could have conceived of the establishment of a standard American-like newspaper in that country. Some dreamers even tried it. In 1887 José do Patrocínio thought he could create a tropical version of *The New York Herald* with his *Cidade do Rio* only to see it vanish after a few issues. The press had some social role, but was restricted to the dissemination of ideas among the very small political and economic elite. As beneficiaries of the social structures permeated by practices of corruption, those elite members would never have made any effort to combat them.

The first organized attempt to combat corruption occurred in the 1920s under the influence of the emerging urban classes eager to see the country modernized and the old rural oligarchies dismantled. The "tenentes" (lieutenants) movement, named after young army officers raised in cities by families without links with the traditional landlords of the agricultural sector, was very influential among the forces who overthrew the First Republic with the 1930 revolution led by Getúlio Vargas, and the fight against corruption was among its most important programmatic flagships. But as noted by Ronald Schneider among others, ". . . the civilian middle sectors could not hold on to political power in a still patrimonial society. Yet they could reap individual benefits from the clientalistic-*cartorial* system by agreeing, once again, to be coopted. Instead of a pluralistic democracy, the populist authoritarian regime of Getúlio Vargas emerged (from the 1930 revolution) and built up the urban working class as a potential power factor under a corporative institutional structure."[10] The result was not only the survival of corrupt practices in state and private sectors, but also the creation of newer forms, most of them as structural parts of the huge government-controlled workers' unions raised under Vargas's auspices, following the models of fascism and Nazism.

The 1920s and the Vargas era would also be the time when something vaguely similar to the American cultural industry began to be established in Brazil. The first advertising agencies were created, commercial radio stations were licensed by the state, and newspapers started to give priority to the news instead of opinion (the first one to subscribe to the services of a news agency, United Press International, was the *Jornal do Brasil* in 1922).[11] But those incipient steps would only be solidified in the 1950s. The newspapers of that period began to represent cautiously the interests and points of view of the emerging urban middle classes, including their dissatisfaction with the perceived arrogance and corruption of the elites. However, during most of the first period of Vargas's power (which lasted from 1930 to 1945 when he was ousted only to be restored by popular vote to the presidency in 1950), the press was submitted to a very harsh censorship system similar in the history of the country only to that imposed by the military regime from 1968 to 1975.

The Vargas era would end with his suicide in 1954, after a well-organized moralist campaign under the leadership of Carlos Lacerda, a journalist-politician who used his newspaper, *Tribuna da Imprensa*, and the airwaves of Radio Globo and Tupi TV to launch an endless series of charges against the "sea of mud" on which the government seemed to rest. But Vargas's death had the effect of transforming him overnight from the suspicious leader of a corrupt regime into a patriotic martyr who gave his life for the country. The headquarters of *Tribuna da Imprensa* were the target of popular riots led by Vargas's followers who blamed Lacerda for their leader's death. The end of the Vargas era also meant the weakening of one of the most successful daily newspapers of Brazilian history, *Última Hora,* founded in 1951 by Samuel Wainer, who introduced several modern practices to Brazilian journalism. Wainer was a close friend of Vargas and his paper relied heavily on the patronage of his government.

The president and vice president elected after Vargas's suicide (Juscelino Kubitschek, from the Social Democratic Party (PSD), and João Goulart, from the Workers Party of Brazil (PTB)) belonged to the political parties perceived by him to represent the left and center of the ideological spectrum. The PSD-PTB alliance easily won the election against Lacerda's party, the National Democratic Union (UDN), whose presidential candidate, Juarez Távora, had been one of the "tenentes" movement leaders thirty years before. UDN had as its motto the famous words of Thomas Jefferson: Eternal vigilance is the price of liberty.

The PSD-PTB coalition, which had controlled both Congress and the presidency since the elections of 1946, was finally defeated in 1960 but only for the presidency. Jânio Quadros, who used a broom during his presidential campaign as a symbol of how he would clean up the country (including corruption), was elected with the reluctant support of Lacerda and his UDN. Quadros was a beyond-parties, young, charismatic leader and the old-guard UDN would have rather had another veteran "tenente," Juracy Magalhães, as the party presidential candidate. But Lacerda saw Quadros as the only viable alternative to the continuation of the Vargas political scheme. He was right: Quadros got 5.6 million votes against 3.8 million given to Henrique Teixeira Lott. But at that time, the votes for president and vice president were independent from each other and João Goulart (PSD-PTB) beat Milton Campos (UDN) and was elected along with his foe, Quadros.

Despite the extraordinary popular mandate that he held, Quadros did not have the support of Congress, still under the control of the PSD-PTB alliance, and seven months after his inauguration resigned the presidency. Quadros would reappear in the political world twenty years later but this time no longer with any popular support; he became the leader of an allegedly corrupt political group. Goulart, an old Vargas protégé considered his political heir, became president. Lacerda, then governor of the newly created state of Guanabara, started a new campaign to undermine Goulart and the fight against corruption was, as in the 1950s, one of its main components. His newspaper, *Tribuna da Imprensa*, was once again instrumental in the success of the crusade.

The drive against Goulart was led by many conservative civilian leaders, including Lacerda, but the president was deposed in 1964 by a military coup. The coup was preceded by huge street demonstrations, promoted by the title the "Family Marches with God for Liberty," organized by middle-class sectors led by the conservative Catholic church. One of the key phrases heard in those demonstrations was the "fight against corruption" that allegedly had taken over the government. The most important newspapers in the country openly supported plots against Goulart and, in their editorials, argued that the country needed to get rid of the government to free itself altogether of corruption and the "communist threat."

Lacerda and his allies, among them the owners of some of the most important newspapers in the country such as *O Estado de S. Paulo,* attended meetings with army officials in order to conspire against the government. Lacerda imagined that, as had happened in 1945 and 1954, the military would give up power as soon as a popular election could be held. He thought he would be the strongest candidate in the already scheduled 1965 presidential elections, although former president Kubitschek also had the same ambition. But the military held on to power.

From that time until 1985 five generals succeeded each other as president, all of them elected by a puppet electoral college. Military leaders stressed that one of the justifications for their presence in power was the need to remove corruption from the state apparatus in Brazil. During the military's reign, all of the important civilian leaders, Kubitschek and Lacerda among them, were stripped of their political rights; Congress was kept open for most of the time during those twenty-one years but under strict control and submitted to continuous censorship of its most outspoken leaders (whenever government's positions were endangered in Congress, the military would intervene in order to restore its majority); an opposition party was allowed to exist but also under harsh limitations; the press was submitted to censorship (the very few media that did not abide by the daily orders—received by editors over the phone—for the censorship of certain subjects had all-powerful censors installed in their offices); and almost all civil liberties were abolished. But despite those measures, or perhaps because of them, corruption was not extinguished. On the contrary, in many ways it flourished as never before because it was difficult, if not impossible, to charge those responsible for it.

In the three decades between Vargas's suicide and the restoration of democracy, the country experienced an extraordinary phase of economic development: national industries rose, exports increased in size and were diversified, vast numbers of people moved from rural areas to the cities, the middle class became larger and stronger, and the average salaries went up. The media followed pace: newspapers became more modern and influential, television came into the era of national networks through microwaves and satellite communication, and weekly newsmagazines reached huge circulation figures. More and more, the mass media tried to match the aspirations and values of the urban middle class that constituted their public.

But much of the progress in the media sector was due to corruption. For instance, the state-held concession of radio and television licenses was governed by the traffic of political influence and sometimes by sheer financial transactions. The intimate relationship between the military governments and the largest media group in Brazil, Globo, was notorious and conspicuous. After 1965 Globo controlled a virtual monopoly of the television market in Brazil thanks to countless favors received from the state, including impunity for violating constitutional laws, such as those forbidding illegal agreements with foreign companies, among them the American Time-Life group.

In exchange, Globo Network was a faithful "spokesmedium" for the government throughout the military regime. In fairness, it is necessary to say that Globo is also a very professional and competent organization and much of its huge success is due to its own merits. Others, such as the Bloch group, also received state protection for decades and were not able to achieve anything comparable to what Globo has obtained in artistic, journalistic, or entrepreneurial terms. When, in the 1970s, the government had to give new concessions for the television stations of the failing group Diários e Emissoras Associados, the winners were not the most capable but were the two groups seen by the military as more in line with the regime. The Bloch group was one of them. Twenty years later, that group is on the verge on bankruptcy.

In the microcosm of the media, small acts of corruption were tolerated despite the improvements observed in this sector. Low salaries were considered a sufficient excuse for journalists to feel comfortable holding one job at a newspaper and another in the government or in a private company. The fact that the journalist would eventually have to cover the activities of the branch of government or the company he or she also worked for never seemed to matter much. The result, of course, was the production of a lot of biased material. In the police and sports desks, it was also very common for reporters, editors, and columnists to have their wages supplemented by different kinds of gifts (including money) from the very people or institutions covered by them. Most newspapers did not see anything wrong in letting their reporters accept nice trips, fancy meals, or expensive tickets from their sources of information. Some would even nurture those practices because they could help them save money.

Another effect of the military regime was the creation of a rabid loyalty among journalists. Because the media were victims of censorship and some distinguished newspeople had been arrested, tortured, and even killed because of their ideas, any criticism against the predominant practices in the media was seen as offensive and needing to be silenced in the name of democratic values. Such attitudes helped to maintain the status quo; bad ethical behavior among journalism professionals was adopted

and considered natural. Even today, more than ten years after democratization, much of this rabid loyalty and many of the practices described
above survive intact. The *jabás,* or expensive material gifts from sources to
journalists, continue to be received; journalists with double (or triple) employment, employment in industries and government agencies that they
cover, are still common around the country (in 1989, there were at least
3,652 journalists on the federal government payroll and in some of the
poorest states of Brazil; 99 percent of the journalists were paid by the state
government[12]); the auto industry in Brazil sells new cars to journalists
with substantial discounts; blackmail against businesspeople and politicians is still practiced by journalists, particularly in the poorest areas of the
country; and editors who are put in charge of both the newsroom and the
advertising department still exist, and not only in small newspapers from
poor areas of Brazil. It is true that such rabid loyalty is not as strong nowadays as it was in the past. Some journalism union leaders even support
public hearings being held in Congress to investigate charges against journalists.[13] However, they are still the minority.

The military regime came to an end partly because of the growing popular feeling against corruption in the government, which became apparent with the gradual end of censorship. Two corruption cases (the Coroa-
Brastel and the Delfin, both involving financial operations) were
particularly highlighted in the press in the early 1980s. But the main reasons for the demise of the military regime were dissatisfaction with increasing inflation and the wish for the restoration of democracy. In 1985,
after ten years of political dissension, Congress, the press, the workers'
unions, and civil-society organizations were allowed more freedom than
ever before. The military, nevertheless, was still strong enough to contain
a movement that called for a direct presidential election in 1984. But although the movement's supporters had the majority in Congress, the
candidate of its party, the civilian Paulo Maluf, was defeated by another
civilian, Tancredo Neves, an opposition leader who gained the endorse-
ment of a group of dissidents from the government and was considered
admissible by the most prominent military leaders.

Maluf had been appointed in 1969 by the military as the mayor of São
Paulo, the largest and most important city in Brazil (during most of the military regime, there was no election for mayors of the states capitals and of the
largest cities in the country). Very entrepreneurial and assertive, he followed
the classic Brazilian political advice that "governing is building highways."
His methods, however, were the epitome of old-fashioned clientalism and,
although very few charges have ever been proved in the courts against him,

his name was closely associated with the practices of corruption. Very few other politicians in Brazilian history have been popularly considered as corrupt as Maluf. Many military leaders disliked and even despised him mostly because of his notoriety for corruption. But following the rules imposed by the regime, he became governor of São Paulo in 1979 and was elected to Congress in 1982 with wide popular support.

Against the wishes of then-President João Batista Figueiredo, who favored his fellow army officer Mario Andreazza, Maluf was able (possibly with the help of his enormous personal fortune) to get the majority of the votes at the national convention of the Democratic Socialist Party (PSD), (the party that supported the military) and became its presidential candidate. President Figueiredo, a very mercurial man, was upset with Andreazza's defeat and decided that the military, this time, should not intervene in the electoral college decision process. Neves, who had been closely associated with Getúlio Vargas in the 1950s (he was attorney general in the beginning of Vargas's constitutional government) and a member of the PSD-PTB coalition who never lost his political rights under the military regime, was able to capitalize on the strong desire of the populace to put an end to the military regime. He allied himself with some of the most prominent civilian leaders of that regime, among them José Sarney, his running mate, and was elected president by a vote of 480 to 180 in the electoral college. Neves was seen as a moderate and did not raise fears among the military and his conservative supporters.

On January 15, 1985, the eve of his inauguration, Neves fell gravely ill. Sarney took over in his place, although the constitutional provisions on what to do in such a situation were not clear. Figueiredo, who felt personally betrayed by Sarney, refused to be present at the ceremony of transference of power. Neves never recovered, underwent seven surgeries, and died on April 21, in the midst of a national commotion on one of the most important Brazilian civic holidays.

Sarney's government did not fare much better than his predecessors' at fighting corruption. The press, enjoying absolute freedom for the first time in two decades, published a lengthy list of various scandals, most of them typical of those occurring during the military regime and the previous republican period: public bids the results of which were decided even before the offers had been open; large official delegations composed of friends and relatives of the president and his ministers sent on questionable missions abroad; and exchange of personal favors to congressional representatives for votes in legislative battles. The two most important candidates to succeed Sarney, the neoconservative Fernando Collor de Mello (who was elected) and the old-fashioned leftist Luiz Inacio Lula da Silva, made combating corruption a very important theme in their campaigns.

Even though Sarney had been a prominent civilian leader of the military regime, he came into power as the inheritor of another man's government. Neves had already made public the names of the people who would form his cabinet when he fell ill. Sarney had to accept them because it was uncertain if Neves would recover or not. The agony of the president-elect made him extremely popular as he had never been in health; he became a kind of "martyr of democracy." Sarney was not able to dismantle the complex alliance that Neves had put together in order to win the vote in the electoral college. For most of his term, Sarney was a hostage of Neves's legacy.

In December 1992, Brazil missed the opportunity to become the first country in history to remove a president from office through a peaceful impeachment process. Fernando Collor de Mello resigned as president twenty-two minutes after the Senate had begun his final political trial. However, by a vote of 73 to 8, the senators decided to continue the impeachment process in order to strip Collor of his political rights until the year 2001. But as of today, Collor de Mello has not been brought to justice for the financial corruption within his government.

It is true that his friend Paulo Cesar Farias, who was one of the group of businesspeople charged with receiving millions of dollars in exchange for government favors, served some months in prison, although a very privileged kind of prison (in the headquarters of a military command, with all kinds of amenities), but he was the only scapegoat. In 1996, a few days before the last suit against him was to be dismissed, and a few weeks before his new newspaper was set to be launched, and after having promised that he would write a "kiss and tell" book about his experiences with the government, Farias was shot to death. His body was found along with his girlfriend's. Police concluded that she killed him and then committed suicide.

Collor de Mello had been the mayor of Maceió, the capital of the very poor state of Alagoas, in the northeast of Brazil (by appointment of the military) and the governor of Alagoas (with the support of the military) before being elected president in 1989. He built up his image as a "maharajah hunter," meaning an official that combats public servants who are paid high salaries but do no work, although, as it was later proved, he did nothing against those persons besides getting benefits from them. The press in Alagoas, much of it controlled by his own family, never investigated his claims. Neither did the national press when he became the front-runner candidate for the presidency.

Collor de Mello was supported by most of the press during the campaign because his rival in the runoff, the leftist and former workers' union leader Luiz Inacio Lula da Silva, scared conservatives. Collor de Mello's main issue in his electoral platform was his promise to fight corruption. And again, despite the very clear fact that he was receiving multimillion dollar illegal contributions to run against Lula, no newspaper or TV network raised this subject. At most, some dirty tricks (such as huge payments made by his supporters to Lula's former lover in exchange for testimony on video that Lula had suggested she abort a child of his, a practice illegal in Brazil) were denounced by some papers. Collor de Mello won the election with 52 percent of the vote; Lula got 48 percent.

Most of the press, with one notable exception, continued treating Collor de Mello softly after his inauguration. His flamboyant style was, if not praised, at least registered with positive association, particularly by television networks. In his first months in power, the president acted in a very authoritarian fashion; he ordered the federal police to invade the headquarters of the only important newspaper that opposed him, *Folha de S. Paulo*, and sued it (with no success). Even after his attempts to curb the freedom of the press, the president continued receiving the support of most of the press.

It was only after his brother, Pedro, decided to denounce the president in an interview in the newsweekly magazine *Veja* that the press started making space for investigative reporting on Collor de Mello's alleged corruption schemes. Some of the most prestigious newspapers in the country, such as *Jornal do Brasil*, which was heavily indebted to state-owned financial institutions, however, maintained their support for Collor de Mello for several months.[15] The public resentment against the president (who had frozen Brazilians' saving accounts without prior notice, leading thousands to desperation) and the arrogance of Collor in dealing with Congress during his first eighteen months in office, were both very important factors in the development of the impeachment process.

As in 1964, the fall of the president in 1992 was preceded by street demonstrations organized by middle-class leadership. This time, however, corruption was not just one of the reasons, it was the only reason for mobilizing public opinion to achieve Collor de Mello's impeachment or resignation. Contrary to 1954 and 1964 when there was a clear ideological division between those who supported Vargas and Goulart and those who did not (the left was in favor and the conservatives in opposition to both presidents), in 1992 there was a virtual consensus: almost the whole country was against Collor de Mello and the reason was corruption.

Today, Collor de Mello lives in a very comfortable house in Miami and maintains the playboy lifestyle that made him famous. In an interview with CNN in October 1996, he said that he intended to be a candidate for the presidency of Brazil in the 1998 elections, declaring that "it will only depend on Congress's decision to restitute to me my political rights."[14] He argued that "the people must judge me," and that such a verdict will only be possible through an election. [Editor's note: currently Collor de Mello is attempting to position himself for a run at the presidency in 2002, but so far with scarce national-level support.]

As defined by Joseph Page, "Collor's demise was not just a political milestone in Brazilian history; it also laid bare, in the most vivid way imaginable, the corruption that defined the symbiotic relationship between the government and the nation's elite."[16] The public impeachment hearings in Congress were so devastatingly revealing of the century-old schemes of corruption, that powerful public figures such as Mario Amato, the president of São Paulo's Federation of Industries, had to admit: "We are all corrupt." The richest businessperson in the country and political hopeful, Antônio Ermírio de Morais, also candidly acknowledged that he and his family had paid bribes to secure favors from the government. Paulo Cesar Farias said in his testimony to the impeachment committee, facing the congressional representatives who denounced Collor de Mello's campaign financing: "This is sheer hypocrisy." Everything that most people knew but never confessed in public was overtly exposed: that companies often overcharged government for goods and services provided by them (including in the administration of health care), that public officials constantly accepted kickbacks from individuals and corporations, that congressional representatives were elected with illegal contributions made by businesspeople who later would receive their compensation in the form of favors from their protégés acting as lawmakers, and that journalists also benefited from all sorts of exchanges between them and powerful politicians.

Public opinion pushed at least part of the press to put pressure on Collor. It was more or less the same thing that had happened in 1984 during the popular campaign for direct elections: some media, especially the most powerful among them, Globo Network Television, only became critical of the president after hundreds of thousands had demonstrated on the streets. The absence of legislative support for the president was a key element in his fall. If he had built a strong legislative block behind him, Collor de Mello could have survived. In 1984, when the military regime still had control of Congress, the constitutional amendment to hold direct election was defeated despite huge public demonstrations in its favor. In 1992 the same could have happened with the impeachment of Collor de

Mello as it happened in Colombia with Semper in 1996. Even the consensual support of the press for an idea is not enough to make it happen; other actors have to perform their role. Congress acted against Collor de Mello mostly because it felt that it was mistreated by him. He offended, despised, and humiliated several congressional representatives who paid him back during the impeachment process.

Back in the Neves administration, several ministers were chosen from among a group of lifelong adversaries of the military regime. The fact that those men, who had countless admirers and friends among journalists, were now in power created an ethical problem for Brazilian journalism. For the first time in more than a generation, journalists had ideological fellows in government, and many acted with the objective of favoring them. This phenomenon occurred again quite dramatically when Fernando Henrique Cardoso was elected president in 1994. Cardoso himself and several of his closest associates were in opposition to the military regime and had used the press and his journalist friends as tools to promote their ideas (and, by extension, their political careers). Once in power they counted on them once again and unfortunately for the quality of journalism in Brazil, most of them did not fail the president's expectations.

It is the same in the United States and everywhere else. The press is often given the credit for the downfall of President Richard Nixon in 1974. But if Congress and the justice department had not proceeded as they did, all the investigative work done by journalists, the editorials, the columns in papers, and the commentary on television would not have been sufficient to force Nixon's impeachment or resignation.

There are several examples in Brazil of investigative stories that went nowhere because of the inaction of other institutions such as the judicial system. In 1987, for example, the winners of a public bid for the construction of a huge railway, the Norte-Sul, one of the most expensive projects of the Sarney government, were published in code by a journalist, Janio de Freitas, in the classified ads of the daily newspaper where he had worked for weeks before all the proposals had been received. The "ad" proved correct. But the bid results were not changed, nobody was punished, and nothing happened. In some cases, the journalist who publishes the story is imprisoned, despite the fact that the story is factually correct. This happened in 1993 in a drug case when a justice of the Supreme Court felt he had been offended by a reporter. The conclusion is that the press alone is not strong enough to defeat corruption.

Another conclusion is that, with very few exceptions, newspapers rarely take the lead to denounce corruption. This is due to the fact that the links between state and media ownership in Brazil are still very strong. Radio and television licenses are still being given away as political favors as they have been for decades. Many of these license holders also own newspapers and magazines. State controlled banks have always been much more than generous in the way they deal with loans to media organizations. A recent investigation shows that the largest state-owned bank, Banco do Brasil, was giving privileged treatment to the Bloch group, owner of magazines and a television network, from the 1940s to the 1990s.[17] State-owned telephone companies choose the publishers of their phone directories, one of the most profitable contracts in the publishing sector, according to political reasoning and frequently the contracts are given to companies that belong to groups who also own newspapers, magazines, and television stations.

It is not only media owners who have overly intimate relationships with those in political power. The return to the civilian regime in 1985 had an very unpleasant side effect: many of the people who became ministers had been associated for years with the most influential journalists resistant to the military. Those friendships and ideological affinities became a serious obstacle to the media performing their watchdog role and continues to be an obstacle under the present government. As far as I know, President Cardoso is an honest man and his government cannot be accused of much corruption. But it should be noted how discreet the coverage has been of some dubious affairs including one involving financial institutions that collapsed under fraud allegations and had their debts absorbed by the government, an action that will cost billions of dollars in public money. Agreements between the presidency and Congress avoided public hearings to investigate those affairs. One of those institutions is Banco Nacional, with losses that amount to $5 billion. It happens that that bank belongs to the president's son-in-law's family and the president's daughter is a member of its board of directors. Those connections are barely mentioned by most of the press when covering the case. Were Cardoso not who he is, would the press have behaved in a similar way? Probably not, and that is very worrisome.

Some journalists have been making large sums of money in bribery networks. Two of them recently had their names revealed in documents showing they had received $500,000 and $150,000, respectively, from a congressional representative who was the chair of the Ways and Means committee. One of the journalists was, at the time, the editor-in-chief of the most important daily newspaper in Brasília and present owner of the title of the first Brazilian newspaper, *Correio Brasiliense*. The other one was a former editor-in-chief of the same paper. They lost their jobs and their credibility as journalists, but that was all. As is the case for 95 percent of alleged perpetrators in white-collar crime cases in Brazil, the two journalists did not go to jail. In the case of the Ways and Means committee scandal (bribery paid to the member of the committee in exchange for votes), although dozens of congressional representatives were involved, two were impeached, of whom only one was indicted (one of them, Ibsen Pinheiro, had presided over the committee that was impeaching Collor), and neither of them went to jail or was punished in any way. Like Collor de Mello, several of those who resigned to their mandates to avoid being impeached now prepare their comeback in the 1998 elections.[18]

In another scandal that became public in 1992, two well-known journalists in Brazil, Augusto Nunes (former editor-in-chief of the second largest daily newspapers in the state of São Paulo, *O Estado de S. Paulo*) and Paulo Moreira Leite (editor of the largest weekly newsmagazine in the country, *Veja*), accused an advisor to the then-governor of São Paulo, Luiz Antonio Fleury, of attempted bribery. Despite the public charges, nothing happened to the advisor except that he lost his job in the government.

Many journalists do not get money as payment. As former finance minister Delfim Netto, the czar of the economy during most of the military regime and presently a powerful congressional representative said, every journalist has his or her price: some must be offered money, others must be offered praises, and a third group must be offered information. The worst mistake a politician can make when dealing with journalists, he said, is to offer money to those who are expecting information or vice versa. As already mentioned, a huge number of journalists accept expensive trips overseas, fine gifts, fancy dinners, and other presents from companies or politicians. Most newspapers do not mind. Outside São Paulo and Rio, it is still the rule rather than the exception that journalists work both for a newspaper and as public servants in government, although as long as they write positive things, or at least not negative things, about their government bosses, they need not show up at the office.

Despite these examples, there has been a lot of change in Brazil regarding corruption. For decades a famous statement attributed to a popular three-time governor of São Paulo, Adhemar de Barros, was used to define the dominant public attitude toward corruption: "I am an embezzler, but I am also an accomplisher." Many politicians were elected under the logic of such attitudes. Nowadays it is safe to say that there is a strong reaction against this reasoning. Yet leaders who have their names associated with corruption have still been successful enough to win important jobs. For example, Paulo Maluf was elected mayor of São Paulo in 1992, one month before Collor's resignation. In November 1996, his candidate to succeed him, an unknown and his virtual puppet, was easily elected. Maluf is considered a potential front-runner in the presidential election of

2002. His notoriety for corruption seems to have been either forgotten or forgiven.

The increase in public disgust with corrupt officials and institutions in Brazil seems to be part of an international tide. The World Bank, the International Monetary Fund, the Inter-American Development Bank, and other multilateral organizations seem more and more concerned with the destination given to their loans around the world. In the 1980s and the 1990s many countries, such as Italy, France, Spain, South Korea, India, Colombia, and Venezuela, saw surges of collective indignation against corruption. Some former high-level public officials, including former heads of government, have been sent to jail in some of those countries. The fact that in Brazil the worst that happened to those involved with corruption was the loss of their jobs has helped to disseminate throughout the population the feeling that justice is immune to society's claims no matter their size and intensity.

Despite the advances gained after Collor de Mello's resignation, Brazil is still considered by international standards one of the most corrupt countries in the world. According to Transparency International's Corruption Perceptions Index, 1995 (a poll of polls drawing upon surveys by organizations such as DRI/McGraw Hill Global Risk Service and the Institute for Management Development), the country has the sixteenth worst grade among fifty-four nations researched in terms of the degree of corruption in everyday social activities as seen by the businesspeople who deal with them. (Brazil received a 2.9 grade on a scale of one to ten, with a lower figure indicating a higher degree of corruption; Nigeria is the "champion," with 0.6; followed by Pakistan, with 1.0, and Kenya, with 2.2; the United States received a 7.6 grade; the nations judged least corrupt were New Zealand, with 9.4, Denmark, with 9.3, and Sweden, with 9.0.)[19]

Nevertheless, public cynicism regarding corruption in Brazil is probably at its lowest level in this century. In 1996, no advertising whiz would conceive an ad such as the one created in the 1970s for a brand of cigarette, Vila Rica, in which a famous soccer player, Gerson de Oliveira Nunes, one of the heroes of the 1970 World Championship, advised consumers in a very roguish style: "But you also like to take some advantage in everything you do, right?" That ad was so popular that it became common to talk about "Gerson's law" as a way to refer to the generalization of corruption practices in the country. Nowadays, a decisive majority of public opinion in Brazil refuses the "Gerson's law" and considers it immoral and unacceptable. It would also be considered outrageous today if the federal government decided to finance apartments to correspondents in Brasília as it did, without raising any amazement, in the 1950s.

By publicizing, even with delay, scandals such as the Collorgate, the Ways and Means committees briberies, and many others, the press has been an important agent for such change. But the fact that stories denouncing corruption have become popular among readers seems to have encouraged the press to find corruption even where there is none and to give a lot of print space to even minor misbehavior cases. Several critics have noticed that some readers complain about the "lacerdismo" or "denuncismo" that dominates the press (meaning the trivialization and sensationalization of corruption stories in the news). This exaggeration of corruption and the general feeling that impunity is the rule have had dangerous results among sizable groups of the population, particularly the lower income ones: they doubt whether democracy is a good idea. Because censorship prevented the public from learning about the corruption that occurred during the twenty-one years of military rule, many people associate that period with honesty. A recent public opinion poll showed that support for democracy among the population in Brazil was the lowest in Latin America, and that only 50 percent of the respondents said they prefer to live under a democratic regime, while 24 percent said they would rather live under an authoritarian government, and 21 percent said they do not see a difference between an authoritarian and a democratic regime. The average support for democracy in Latin America was 61 percent (the highest, 80 percent, was scored in Uruguay).[20]

The press must be responsible when it publicizes charges against politicians and others suspected of corruption. The press also has to be tougher with its own behavior and with the behavior of those who practice journalism. Corruption within the press (as well as within any other institution) will persist as long as it is considered an acceptable means of survival, as it presently is in many cases. Finally, the press should be more realistic when assessing how important it has been in the effort to combat corruption in Brazil.

Notes

1. Roberto DaMatta, *Carnival, Rogues, and Heroes* (Notre Dame: University of Notre Dame Press, 1991).
2. Ibid., pp. 218–19.
3. Richard Morse, *O Espelho de Próspero* (São Paulo: Companhia das Letras, 1988).

4. Joseph Page, *The Brazilians* (Reading, Pa.: Addison-Wesley, 1995).

5. Ibid., p. 125.

6. José Marques de Melo, *Sociologia da Imprensa Brasileira* (Petrópolis: Vozes, 1973), pp. 111–41.

7. Nelson Werneck Sodré, *História da Imprensa no Brasil* (Rio: Graal, 1977).

8. Juarez Bahia, *Três Fases da Imprensa Brasileira* (Santos: Presença, 1960), p. 45.

9. Michael Schudson, *Discovering the News: A Social History of American Newspapers* (New York: Basic Books, 1978), pp. 30–31.

10. Ronald Schneider, *Order and Progress: A Political History of Brazil* (Boulder, Colo.: Westview Press, 1991).

11. Sodré, op. cit., p. 419.

12. Márcio Chaer, "A cobertura dos salafrários," *Imprensa* (March 1994).

13. Antonio Carlos Fon, "Toda força à CPI da imprensa," *Imprensa* (March 1994).

14. "Collor quer tentar a Presidência em 98," *Folha de S. Paulo* (October 16, 1996).

15. Argemiro Ferreira, "As regras de um jogo pesado," *Imprensa* (August, 1992).

16. Page, op. cit., p. 121.

17. "Auditoria mostra que banco favoreceu o grupo Bloch," *Folha de S. Paulo* (April 18, 1995).

18. "Anões preparam seu retorno à política," *Folha de S. Paulo* (October 14, 1996).

19. "Brasil perde a olimpíada dos corruptos," *Folha de S. Paulo* (October 16, 1996).

20. "No Brasil, só 50% apóiam democracia," *Folha de S. Paulo* (October 18, 1996).

8

The Complexity of Anticorruption Policies in Latin America

EDMUNDO JARQUIN[1] AND
FERNANDO CARRILLO-FLÓRES[2]

Corruption is an ethical problem worthy of our greatest concern. It is also an economic and political problem affecting the possibility of achieving sustainable and equitable development, and consolidating the democratic political system. Corruption erodes our faith in institutions, undermining the credibility of politicians and politics alike. Its effects are insidious: it changes the ideals of citizenship, destroying the social fabric and blurring the lines that unite and define our citizens, limiting the chances of achieving a common vision and shared goals as a society or nation. In this sense, there is a very real link between corruption and development.

There are economic reasons for ridding ourselves of corruption. Among other things, corruption acts to undercut the efficiency and effectiveness of public policies and programs, distorts incentives for proper allocation of resources, destroys conditions for fair competition, contributes to ever greater concentrations of income, casts doubt on the legitimacy of profit-making and taxation alike, and—in the end—undermines the credibility and efficiency of the market and the state. In short, to borrow a phrase from the president of the Inter-American Development Bank (IDB), Enrique V. Iglesias, corruption "is a tax on society as a whole."[3]

Clearly, corruption is a relevant topic for those interested in economic development and the consolidation of democratic political systems, and multilateral development institutions such as the IDB are justified in providing support for the battle against corruption in the programs and projects they finance within the region's countries.

A. The IDB Approach

Let us now turn to the conceptual framework under which the IDB approaches this topic. In its strategy document for programs to modernize the state and strengthen civil society, the IDB maintains that "there is a direct relationship between economic development and quality of government" and points out that "the success of economic reforms and strategies for poverty reduction require an increase in institutional capacity. It is necessary to consider the lessons of experience, in which the effects of correct economic policies and strategies have been limited by poorly operating public institutions or an adverse political environment."[4]

The above-mentioned strategy document continues: "Thus, in recent years there has been growing consensus on the importance of good governance for promoting a solid policy of development. First, governability implies political stability, which in turn is associated with conditions of internal socioeconomic integration, buttressing of democratic institutions, and participation by citizens in the decision-making process. Second, governance requires conditions of reliability in which legal, economic and political consequences are predictable and there is an adequate framework of laws governing development and protection of property rights without regard to gender, an environment conducive to development of the private sector, efficient allocation of public resources, responsible and honest government, and transparency in the administration of the State."

In practice, as progress has been achieved in economic reforms designed to consolidate the model of sustainable and equitable development, economic operations are increasingly coming up against traditionally structured state institutions, inadequate government policies and management methods, and obsolete laws. Recognition of the importance of institutional, legal, and political environments as a setting for economic activity is what led the board of governors in 1994 to include under the IDB's Eighth Replenishment a call for the institution to adopt a more comprehensive approach to development, one that, in addition to consolidating economic reforms, would promote internal socioeconomic integration, modernization of the state, and the strengthening of democratic institutions and civil society.

The strategy document indicates that if the state is to fulfill its role in this comprehensive development strategy, then programs for its modernization or reform must steer clear of traditional approaches that either restrict their attentions to the executive branch or focus exclusively on technical and administrative reforms. While acknowledging the importance of the so-called institutional or structural reengineering programs, modernization of the public sector must now be conceived of primarily as a process of political reform designed to consolidate the democratic rule of law within a country, which means that it must be comprehensive, including the full institutional and regulatory apparatus that provides a framework for economic, social, and political activity. Hence, government reforms must extend to the judicial and legislative branches, as well as the other public institutions in a democratic government, such as the electoral system and political parties. Moreover, modernization of the state requires a corresponding and mutually reinforcing strengthening of a country's civil society—as the IDB has put it "there is no such thing as an efficient State with a weak civil society."[5] Nor can this strengthening be separated from the process of economic and social reforms.

The point of departure for the IDB's current approach to judicial reform was the creation of the State and Civil Society Unit in 1994. The unit was the consequence of the consensus that the marketplace, our most efficient means of resource allocation, has demonstrated the need for democratic reforms to ensure its vibrancy. The need for significant democratic reform is the reason for the unit's dual purpose of modernizing the state and strengthening civil society. We have been saying for a long time that these two topics—modernization of the state and the strengthening of civil society—are two sides of the same coin; it's impossible to separate one topic from the other.

The complementary nature of these concepts is important because the economic changes that have been taking place in Latin America are the consequence of substantial change in the role of the state coupled with a change in the role of social agents involved in formulating public policy. The result has been more productive interaction among the state, civil society, and the private sector, and their increased involvement in sustainable, equitable development.

B. Modernization of the State and the Fight against Corruption

Since the market economy requires the rule of law and a modern and updated legal framework, the IDB's experience in this field has diverged from previous projects, which had been designed to complement the modernization of the executive branch.

1. A Comprehensive Approach

The role of the state may be dutifully defined and all of the required technical, institutional, and structural elements may be in place for fulfilling this role, and yet the lack of transparency—or the presence of significant levels of corruption—may completely nullify the results. Since corruption undermines the efficiency of markets and states alike, government reforms must have among their most important objectives that of guaranteeing transparency in public administration. And if, as established earlier, modernization of the state is to be conceived of as a process of political reform aimed at consolidating the rule of law, then we must remind ourselves that there are no effective means for safeguarding the rule of law in an environment in which corruption is systemic.

The need for a comprehensive approach to government reforms, as mentioned above, is essential for ensuring transparency since it is not only the executive branch, but also the judicial system and the legislative branch that must function efficiently. And because of the complementary and mutually reinforcing nature of the relationship between the state and civil society, it will also be essential to strengthen the latter.

This comprehensive approach suggests the following state reform activities, which are directly related to the strengthening of transparency and can be supported by IDB programs:

1. Strengthening of government financial administration for the purpose of establishing tax, budgetary, customs, and financial audit systems that are both simpler and more efficient. The design of more efficient and transparent expenditure systems and policies, together with reduction of unproductive costs. This is a field in which the IDB has been providing support for many years, but which—in the context of more comprehensive state reforms—has now taken on greater importance.
2. Establishment of government procurement and contracting systems that are more efficient and ensure greater transparency.
3. Reduction of excessive regulations and the establishment of modern, efficient, simplified, and transparent regulatory systems that—particularly in the context of privatization programs—ensure competition and efficient procurement of goods and services. Under this heading, support will be forthcoming for institutional strengthening of superintendent's and controller's offices.

4. Promotion of transparency in privatization processes through technical assistance in the use of bidding procedures and the negotiation of concessions.
5. Development of a true civil service capable of, on the one hand, guaranteeing the independence of the government from corporate and political interests, and, on the other hand, ensuring more efficient public administration.

2. The New Approach Involving Judicial Reform

The comprehensive approach was the classical development approach to modernization of the state. But beginning in 1993, the IDB began designing its own projects, starting with the judiciary. In fact, at this moment there are fourteen projects already approved by the board of the IDB in which the main purpose is consolidation of a sound legal framework in order to reform and modernize the judicial system.

Now, the IDB seeks to support the countries in establishing a reliable, independent, effective, predictable, flexible, and accessible judicial system by focusing on the following components:

1. modernization of the legal framework and the promotion of basic citizen rights
2. administrative strengthening of the judiciary (which involves the design of public policy)
3. the establishment of alternative conflict resolution methods, which the IDB's Multilateral Investment Fund has already undertaken with some success
4. the implementation of legal aid and legal education programs for the general public
5. human resource development
6. the modernization of physical infrastructure
7. the strengthening of public safety and citizen security.

These judicial reforms must include updating each country's laws to keep pace with new and sophisticated criminal activities. Our focus on the judiciary, in accordance with the steps enumerated above, and complementing our experience with the executive branch, is one of the cornerstones of a program against corruption.

3. Parliamentary and Legislative Reform

The anticorruption strategy is relevant to the legislative assemblies in Central America, the parliaments in the Caribbean, and the congresses in

South America. These legislative bodies suffer from political, institutional, and technical weaknesses, which, in fact, are factors in corruption. To date, through loans and technical assistance, the IDB has helped countries to improve the technical and political capacity of these bodies to perform their legislative oversight and control functions. Components of these legislative reform projects include:

1. training of parliamentary officials in the technical and political areas
2. establishing technical advisory service systems
3. establishing a professional parliamentary organization
4. setting up modern information systems
5. developing channels for dialogue between legislators and citizens
6. promoting citizen political participation and consensus
7. implementing methods to better control the quality of legislation
8. strengthening of legislative bodies to improve their lawmaking capabilities and ensure that they become truly responsive to and representative of their constituencies and that they perform their basic supervisory and oversight duties with efficiency.

C. Some Specific Anticorruption Measures

Focusing on modernization of the executive, judiciary, and legislature is important because a comprehensive strategy vis-à-vis corruption has to include all the branches of power. This is one of the conclusions we have reached at the IDB. When we talk about anticorruption measures, we refer to tools and policies in all of these branches. These measures are usually in different areas.

1. Sociopolitical Changes

The first area is the sociopolitical sphere where the mechanisms of social participation, with which we are all familiar, are in place. For example, public disclosure legislation, where high officials must disclose their assets, has become a typical parliamentary reform in Latin America. And the creation of channels of participation has been among the most important megatrends in the sociopolitical reform process in Latin America. The fourteen processes of constitutional reform taking place over the past five years include such participation-inducing changes as the creation of the offices of ombudsmen, the conducting of referenda on popular initiatives, and the installation of class actions in the legal system. In the political arena, the financing of political parties and political campaigns has been one of the hot issues in Latin America and one of the main factors of corruption.

2. Legal Changes

In the legal and institutional area, many reforms have been made in concert with changes in the legislative branch. In modernizing the judicial system, we have accumulated extensive experience. For instance, the creation of the office of the prosecutor general has been one of the trends in judicial reform in Latin America. The reforms in many countries have been the landmark not only in the fight against corruption, but also in the recovery of credibility and legitimacy for justice. And the cases of Colombia, Honduras, Guatemala, Venezuela, and many other Latin American countries that have been drafting or changing constitutional provisions in this area serve as evidence that the reform of the prosecutorial system from the traditional inquisitory system to the accusatorial one, from the written process to the oral process—all these new conduits for the fight against corruption—has been effective. Specific policies such as the institution of faceless judges, which involves the protection of the identity of judges, victims, and witnesses, and the protection of the evidence from contamination, has been key in the prosecution of drug traffickers.

D. Engagement of Civil Society

Finally, as it was stated at the outset, this process has to be complemented by the power of civil society, engaging organizations like nongovernmental organizations for public integrity as they have become part of the sociopolitical landscape throughout Latin America.

As indicated earlier, from our viewpoint reforming the state and strengthening civil society are complementary and mutually reinforcing processes. From this perspective, certain aspects can be seen as particularly relevant. First, the role of citizens (both individuals and the public as a whole), trade groups, and the various organizations of civil society in carrying out so-called social audits is crucial to the effort to combat corruption. Second, the task of subjecting the media to close scrutiny and responsible criticism—complaining about dishonesty and inefficiency while at the same time acknowledging honest and efficient performance, thereby holding those who commit acts of corruption accountable without undermining the institutions themselves—is an essential instrument that civil society must wield in the fight against corruption. Third, we must recognize that corruption is not restricted to the state, nor is government the only source of dishonest practices. Corruption in the state would be impossible if it had no counterpart in civil society. Therefore, it is up to civil society to develop the ways and means (such as strict codes of ethics for trade associations, professional organizations, and employers' groups) for exposing corruption for the social evil that it is.

E. The Path Ahead

To conclude, it is essential to highlight a few things. First, the role of international cooperation has to be focused not only on the size of the government, but also on institutional development, in terms of the framework of policy analysis, public policy analysis, best practices against corruption, and the use of adequate tools to fight effectively against corruption. The IDB has clearly had a pioneering role in the international effort to incorporate what can broadly be termed the institutional dimension into successful economic development strategies. And we can take satisfaction in the growing consensus in this respect.

An article in a recent issue of *The Economist* notes that economic development theory has rediscovered the fact that institutions matter. The ideological opponents of free markets have tended to forget that for markets to work properly, an economy requires a complex network of effective institutions ranging from basic property rights and well-managed legal systems to effective and incorrupt judiciaries.[6] Countries in which respect for property rights is weak, where a rule of law cannot be taken for granted, and where governments are corrupt tend to grow more slowly. The article therefore demands that "improving institutions should be the top priority," concluding that "the basic ideas behind all this institutional emphasis are that the markets need the rule of law if they are to work properly, and corrupt bureaucracies can do less damage if they have less room for maneuver." It is clear that an efficient operation of a market economy requires a secure rule of law, so that modernization of the state must be comprehensive and should include the full institutional and regulatory apparatus that provides a framework for economic, social, and political activity.

Therefore it is important to work with the three branches of power and the control bodies because, in many Latin American constitutions, control bodies belong to neither the executive, the legislative, nor the judiciary. New actors must be taken into account within the many megatrends in political development in Latin America, like decentralization and local governments, the design of a modern regulatory system, civil service, and the use of technology against corruption.

Institutional reform in general as well as judicial reform in particular has to include at least some of the above-mentioned characteristics. It has to be integrated into the general approach to economic and social development. It requires, of course, political will. It involves complex changes and clash with myriad vested interests without first achieving broad social and political consensus. It must include many disciplines and the assessment of political, economic, and social costs before the design of any strategy. It has to consult all of the unique characteristics of each country. And of course, it has to engage civil society.

For this reason, activities like the publication of this volume draw attention to the problem, raise awareness, promote exchange of experience, and identify and (above all) involve the various sectors of society in the search for solutions that will have a continuing impact well beyond the words written here. These activities are of course intended as a means of marshaling that essential consensus, but they are also (and this is no small accomplishment) a reaffirmation of our faith that human beings and whole societies are capable of bettering themselves.

While we probably don't yet know the precise path to follow in eradicating corruption, we can safely assume that a program that addresses all of the political, economic, and institutional variables laid out above will head us in the right direction. Conclusively, this fight against corruption is not simply a cosmetic procedure, but one of the most important major surgical procedures in the recent history of Latin America.

Notes

1. Chief, State and Civil Society Division, Inter-American Development Bank.
2. Senior Advisor, State and Civil Society Division, Inter-American Development Bank. Former Minister of Justice in Colombia.
3. Address by the president of the IDB at the conference on "Probity and Social Ethics," organized by the OAS in Montevideo, Uruguay, in November 1995.
4. "Frame of reference for the Bank's actions in programs to modernize the state and strengthen civil society," GN-1883-5, March 13, 1996.
5. IDB document GN-1883-5.
6. *The Economist*, March 1, 1997.

Part 3

Views from Three
Major Organizations

9

The Role of the World Bank in Combating Corruption

IBRAHIM F. I. SHIHATA

Scholars and experts from many disciplines have long debated the nature
and impact of corruption. What emerges from the literature is that corruption constitutes a highly complex set of interlocking economic, political, social, moral, and historical phenomena. This suggests that we must
avoid simplistic solutions and the narrow approaches advocated by any
one social discipline; attempts to deal with corruption must, in my view,
commence with analysis of local circumstances and how they affect values
and behavior, and hence the nature and level of corruption in a given
country.

Some theorists have argued, or at least have implied, that corruption
should be accepted as so deeply rooted in social norms as to be ineradica-
ble or, alternatively, as a "second-best" way of getting things done in a
world that is far from perfect. My personal view, informed by years of experience with a number of development institutions, is that corruption in
its varied manifestations is negative on the society as a whole.

Its distributional effects discriminate against the poor and the underprivileged. It increases the cost of development and, on a wide scale, can
retard its pace. It creates a law in practice different from the one in the
books. It allows special interests to prevail over the public interest. And it
disrupts public confidence in government, leading over time to social and
political tension.

Corruption in its broad sense is not confined to the public sector and, in that sector, is not confined to administrative bureaucracies. It is not limited to the payment and receipt of bribes. It takes various forms and is practiced under all forms of government, including well-established democracies. It can be found in the legislative, judicial, and executive branches of government as well as in all forms of private-sector activities. It is not associated with any ethnic, racial, or religious identity. However, its level, scope, and impact greatly vary from one country to another and may also vary, at least for a while, within the same country from one place to another. While corruption of some form or another may inhere in every human grouping, the system of governance has a great impact on its scope. Systems corrupt people perhaps more than people corrupt systems.

Some cultures seem to be more tolerant than others when it comes to certain forms of corruption, particularly favoritism and petty bribes. In some countries, favoritism is so pervasive in human behavior that those who, in the performance of their public functions, decline to favor friends and relatives are generally criticized as being unhelpful or unkind. Petty bribes are also seen in many countries as a charity, an advance incentive or expression of gratitude, or an acceptable substitute for the low pay of public officials—not the extortion it is recognized to be in other countries. Such cultural variations, though real, should not be taken as acceptable excuses for what is basically a corrupt behavior.

Since the end of the cold war, both economic and political liberalization have given rise to conditions that make corruption much less tolerable; hence, we have arrived at an opportune moment in history to make a concerted effort toward its significant reduction. We must realize, however, that corruption is not the monopoly of heavily regulated systems. Loosely regulated systems with weak supervisory institutions also invite corruption and even organized crime. Periods of transition (from command to market economies and from closed to open societies) are particularly conducive to the spread of corruption. The latter thrives on the conflict of values, then turns them to distort them and destroy them.

Both in theory and practice, many ways have been proposed to achieve the reduction of corruption. However, these amount to so many empty gestures unless there is (1) real commitment from national leadership, (2) a broad and sustained campaign by civil society to keep that commitment alive, (3) institutional capacity to implement and enforce, (4) public disclosure and a free flow of information, (5) a social enabling environment of norms and values supportive of anticorruption measures, (6) the adoption by multinational corporations and international agencies of standards and practices that address corruption with a view to fighting it in their work, and (7) international cooperative efforts to deal with transboundary corrupt and fraudulent practices.

The World Bank and Corruption

Is there a rationale for the World Bank's concern with corruption as a general development issue that is beyond the specifics of a project financed by the Bank?

The World Bank is required by its Articles of Agreement to ensure that the proceeds of its loans will be used only for the purposes for which they are granted and to disburse its loans only as expenditures on the projects it finances are actually incurred. It is also required by these articles to finance such expenditures "with due attention to considerations of economy and efficiency, and without regard to political or other noneconomic influences or considerations." The Articles of Agreement do not specifically include "curbing corruption" among the Bank's purposes or functions. They generally prohibit the Bank from taking noneconomic considerations into account in its decisions and from interfering in the political affairs of its members. For this reason, the Bank has traditionally been explicitly active in ensuring that procurement under its own loans is done in a transparent manner and on a competitive basis but has avoided, until very recently, any full-fledged attempt to adopt an anticorruption strategy. Since the early 1990s, however, the Bank has identified corruption as an issue to be taken into account in its work on governance and, in a few cases, began to raise it in the country dialogue. It has also sought to assist its borrowing countries in introducing economic, administrative, legal, and judicial reforms through a series of structural and sectoral-adjustment loans, technical-assistance loans and grants, and sectoral-investment loans. While the Bank was not in this way directly involved in fighting corruption, it was aware that these reforms have a direct positive effect on more than just the growth prospects of the borrowing countries.

The Bank's explicit concern with corruption as a general development issue was highlighted by its president, James D. Wolfensohn, in his first speech before the annual meeting of the board of governors in September 1995. He then asked me to review all proposals and consider initiatives for possible actions by the Bank. Detailed discussion of such proposals and initiatives at the senior-management level led to specific action, which has been approved by the president and, as needed, by the board of executive directors. Such action covers a number of different fronts, all related to measures deemed to be within the Bank's competence. In the meantime, a comprehensive strategy to address corruption, both as an issue of the Bank's own effectiveness and, more generally, as a development policy issue, was prepared for consideration by the Bank's board in early 1997.

The Bank's involvement in addressing corruption issues beyond the projects it finances has not been free from controversy. On the one hand, it has been argued that the World Bank is not a world government for the borrowing countries; its mandate as an international institution for the financing of reconstruction and development is defined by its Articles of Agreement. Being subject to a weighted voting system and limited in its operations to the borrowing countries, the role of the Bank as a world reformer beyond its defined purposes would inevitably carry the marks of rule by the rich countries of the poorer ones. In any event, the Bank should only be concerned, under this argument, with the functions provided for in its Articles of Agreement, among which the main one is to help finance specific projects for productive purposes. It should, in particular, avoid involvement in a subject matter that has obvious domestic political connotations and could otherwise entangle the Bank in complex political considerations, which it is explicitly prohibited from taking into account under its Articles.

It should nonetheless be stated that as the world's major development finance institution and the coordinator of foreign aid to many of its members, the Bank cannot realistically ignore issues that significantly influence the effective flow and appropriate use of external resources in its borrowing countries. It has already been able to deal with a large number of governance and institutional issues that have direct relevance to its development mandate without entanglement in partisan domestic politics. Its concern with public-sector management in its borrowing countries has been an important part of its operational and research work through the years. Any intervention by the Bank would, at any rate, take the form either of a financial agreement to which the country involved would be a contracting party, as a borrower or guarantor, or advice that must be related to the Bank's development mandate. In neither case can the Bank take a coercive stance or impose a particular direction on a borrowing member. It can only play a facilitating role, the effectiveness of which would depend largely on the borrower's full commitment and cooperation.

As a practical matter, the World Bank can hardly insulate itself from major issues of international development policy, of which corruption is one. The prevalence of corruption in a given country increasingly influences decisions at the Bank regarding the flow of public assistance and lending. From a legal viewpoint, what matters is that the Bank's involvement must always be consistent with its Articles of Agreement. The Bank can take many actions to help the fight against corruption without violating these articles. It can conduct research on the causes and effects of this worldwide phenomenon. It can provide assistance, by mutual agreement, in the areas of economic reform, civil service reform, legal and regulatory reform, judicial reform, and other institutional reforms, to enable its borrowing countries to curb corruption. It may take up the issue of the effect of corruption on development as a subject of discussion in the dialogue with its borrowing members. And, if the level of corruption is high according to factual and objective analysis and the government is not taking serious measures to combat it, the Bank can consider this as a factor in its strategy toward the country. The only legal barrier in this respect is that in doing so, the Bank and its staff must be concerned only with the economic causes and effects, and should refrain from intervening in the country's political affairs. While the task may be difficult in borderline cases, its limits have been prescribed in detail in legal opinions endorsed by the Bank's board.

According to one such legal opinion ("Governance Issues and Their Relevance to the Bank's Work" issued in December 1990), the concept of governance in the sense of the overall management of a country's resources cannot be irrelevant to an international financial institution that at present not only finances projects, but is also deeply involved in the process of economic reform carried out by its borrowing members. Clearly the concern here is not with governance in the broad sense of the exercise of state powers in all its aspects, but specifically with the appropriate management of the public sector and the creation of an enabling environment for the private sector. It is a concern for rules that are actually applied and institutions that ensure the appropriate application of these rules, to the extent that such rules and institutions are required for the economic development of the country and in particular for the sound management of its resources.

No doubt, the Bank has to address issues of corruption in this context with great caution, acting on the basis of established facts and only to the extent that the issues clearly affect the economic and social development of the country. It cannot, however, ignore such issues at a time when they have become a major concern, not only to the sources of international financial flows but also to business organizations and indeed to the governments and peoples of most of its member countries.

---

1. The views expressed in this chapter are those of the author and should not be attributed to the institutions with which he is associated.

10

Efforts of the U.S. Agency for International Development

MARK L. SCHNEIDER

In March 1996 the Organization of American States held the Inter-American Convention Against Corruption. The meeting was in Caracas, but through a videoconference, "Problems of Fraud and Corruption in Government," about 4,000 people in twenty-two countries and twenty-six cities in the region participated, as well as the U.S. Agency for International Development, the U.S. Information Agency, and many Latin American nongovernmental organizations (NGOs).

At the various sites, local coordinators distributed a questionnaire to all 4,000 direct participants, and about 1,500 completed and returned the form. The group that completed the form consisted largely of accountants, comptrollers, and government administrators. This was a highly selective group of respondents—mainly individuals who for ethical and/or professional reasons are deeply concerned about the adverse effects of fraud and corruption in government, and it is important to note that from some countries we received very few forms. For these reasons, I think we should be careful about generalizing too much with this information, but also think it's information worth sharing.

Sixty percent or more in half the countries saw their own level of corruption as comparable to others in the region. Only in Argentina and Mexico did more than half of the respondents say the problem in their countries was greater than in others.

There was almost unanimous consensus on the biggest cause for corruption: legal sanctions against corruption are weak. Two other problems were also ranked high: "citizens don't want to get involved" and "corruption is tolerated as part of the cultural tradition."

In almost all the countries surveyed, 50 percent or more of the respondents thought their judges and police were corrupt. El Salvador and Costa Rica have more confidence in the honesty of their police forces than do other countries in the region, but Salvadorans perceive high levels of judicial corruption.

The four highest priorities for combating corruption were: transparent financial management systems, educational programs, mechanisms that allow individuals to report corrupt acts, and prosecution of corrupt civil servants.

Interestingly, we learned from a recent technical assistance mission working with NGOs in Nicaragua that while there is ample awareness by the NGOs of the problems of corruption, there is limited awareness of reform efforts or the effect they will have in combating corruption.

Almost everyone said that international instruments, such as the Inter-American Convention Against Corruption, were vital. The respondents believe that all of us should do everything possible to ensure that every nation in the region ratifies this key convention and that model laws and regulations are developed to enforce compliance.

Finally, we asked people if they would report acts of corruption if they knew about them, and if not, why not. Four-fifths of the participants said they would. Those who said they wouldn't said they were afraid of the consequences. People in some countries also told us that they wouldn't know where to report acts of corruption or that, if they did, it wouldn't make any difference.

Such answers show that much more must be done both to create awareness of the problem of corruption and to implement solutions—concrete actions that each of us can personally take to combat corruption in our countries.

Earlier this year at the Second Inter-American Mayors Conference, La Paz mayor Ronald MacLean emphasized that Latin Americans are no more corrupt or dishonest than North Americans or Europeans. The problem, he said, is an institutional equation still too prevalent in the region that breeds corruption.

His equation is: Monopoly of Power PLUS Wide Discretion MINUS Accountability EQUALS Corruption.

Breaking down that equation for corruption and creating a new equation will generate an environment that not only discourages corruption, but also develops the expectation of good government.

I believe that new equation is: Dispersed Power PLUS Transparency PLUS Accountability EQUALS Good Government.

So, political pluralism must emerge. Power must be fragmented and dispersed from a single central entity to many entities. Power must be transferred from the monopoly control of the leader to shared possession with intermediary groups or civil society. In that way, countervailing centers of political influence check the ruler's power. In a pluralistic democratic society citizens can openly demand accountability and in that way expose and curb corruption.

Competition must develop; there is no more effective antidote to corruption. On the one hand, an uncompetitive political process masks corruption; on the other hand, public vigilance and the threat of losing a subsequent election motivates elected officials to mind the law. Choice within the political sphere helps to ensure accountable official behavior.

Legal standards must be set and followed so that the rule of law transcends absolute discretion. Once a legal framework places responsibilities and obligations upon the regime, holding leaders accountable for their actions becomes a tangible and realistic goal.

Accountability in all of its forms— political, financial, and legal—must be increased. This creates a lethal weapon in the war against corruption.

Democratic societies should strengthen incentives to expose secrets, cover-ups, and questionable deals and demand from their leaders full, accurate, timely, and honest reporting to the citizens they represent.

Officials must also be held accountable under the law. Criminal and corrupt acts that betray the public trust must be proscribed by law, and offenders of the law must be subject to the full weight of the law, regardless of the prestige, power, privilege, or influence of the corrupt official.

How do we establish the new formula for good government of dispersed power, transparency, and accountability?

First, support governmental efforts to forge and implement international instruments and mechanisms to combat corruption.

Second, push for decentralized power structures, including a vigorous, honest, and independent media, and an active NGO community focused on fighting corruption.

Third, support judicial reform, particularly efforts that would eliminate impunity for certain crimes and criminals. Such activities might include judicial career laws, ethics and disciplinary procedures for judges, and oral trials.

Fourth, work with other donors and governments to promote the adoption and implementation of transparent financial management systems. Decisionmakers need accurate financial information quickly to make sound decisions, and citizens need to know what decisionmakers are doing with public resources and be able to weigh in on decisions. I can't stress donor coordination enough in this area. Financial management reform is a complicated, long-term process at both national and municipal levels. USAID provides funds for an executive secretariat to coordinate a Donor Working Group on Financial Management; I hope that at some point in the not-too-distant future, a group will be set up to coordinate anticorruption efforts.

Fifth, push for reforms that make it easier for citizens to expose acts of corruption, such as sunshine laws and hot lines, and finally, sponsor non-formal educational programs and help integrate ethics into education sector curricula.

In closing, let me offer this strong assertion from Robert F. Kennedy, "Laws can embody standards; governments can enforce laws—but the final task is not a task for government. It is a task for each and every one of us. Every time we turn our heads the other way when we see the law flouted—when we tolerate what we know to be wrong—when we close our eyes and ears to the corrupt because we are too busy, or too frightened—when we fail to speak up and speak out—we strike a blow against freedom and decency and justice."

11

Inter-American Development Bank Initiatives against Corruption

STEPHEN QUICK

The issue of corruption is receiving increasing attention from the countries of Latin America and from the international institutions responsible for dealing with it.

One of the strongest declarations to this effect was the inclusion in the Summit of the Americas meeting in Miami of the following statement: "Effective democracy requires a comprehensive attack on corruption."

In the work of the Inter-American Development Bank (IDB), we are increasingly coming to the view that corruption and the rapid and successful development of market economies are late; that corruption is an enemy not only to democracy, but also to the full and effective functioning of the market economies.

In a speech by the president of the IDB, Enrique Iglesias, given in November 1995 in Montevideo at a conference on probity and civic ethics sponsored by the IDB and the Organization of American States, President Iglesias made two points that I think are worth repeating and have been repeated elsewhere in the region. His first observation was that corruption is one of the greatest evils plaguing the consolidation of democracy in Latin America. It's not just a minor problem. It is central to the issue of the consolidation of democracy because corruption has the capacity to undermine not only the performance of the government, but also the confidence of the citizens that the government is capable of acting in pursuit of public objectives.

That undermining of confidence of the citizens in the ability of the government to perform its task as an arbiter of conflict and as a carrier of public interest is the most serious threat to democracy. It used to be fashionable to talk in economic circles about the problem of Latin America and development being the problem of inflation. It was infrequently referred to as attacks on the poor because the poor disproportionately suffered when prices rose and their incomes did not.

President Iglesias made the point that corruption is the use of public office to extract private gain rather than effectively discharge public office, and that, as a tax on the whole of society, corruption exacts economic costs by diverting resources needed for development, producing popular disaffection to democratic regimes, and rending the social fabric of society.

The president in that speech announced that the IDB had made what he called an unequivocal commitment to working with member governments to address the problem of corruption. The issue for us as an institution is how do we do that, how do we use the resources that we have, and how do we work effectively with member governments to deal with the problem of corruption.

We have been working in this area in a number of different ways. We have been sponsoring research, we have been holding conferences, and we have been doing our own work in procurement. I hope this book will contribute further to our understanding about what more can we do other than what has been done.

In order to frame the discussion of what we have been doing, I would like to start with a few general principles derived from work done for the IDB by a consultant, Robert Leiken.

As we approach this issue, we should make five general points. The first is that there is no silver bullet to the problem of corruption. There is no magic fix. We don't possess a recipe for dealing with the problem in a stroke.

The second point is that the nature of the problem is different from one country to the next. There are institutional differences. There are regulatory differences. There are systemic differences. No one single approach will be equally effective in all cases. We need to tailor local response to local problems.

A third general observation, and this is one that I think has a profound implication for us, is you can't do everything all at once, it's not possible, even if you were mounting a successful broad attack on the issue of corruption, to do everything at the same time.

The fourth general point is that in a democracy, corruption must become a public issue. A population must be engaged. The institutions of popular opinion need to be engaged before effective action can be taken.

Finally, in addition to involving the public, changes will ultimately need to be made both in law and in institutions in order to deal with the problem of corruption.

In terms of setting the broad agenda, I also have the Caracas Declaration that the OAS took the lead in creating, and it describes twelve preventative measures that the heads of the convening governments agreed were important for addressing the subject of corruption.

I will summarize quickly the twelve points because they provide a sort of panorama for the discussion.

For the purposes set forth in this convention, the state parties agree to consider the following: establishing standards of conduct for honorable and proper fulfillment of public functions; creating a mechanism to enforce these standards of conduct; educating and instructing government personnel to understand the rules; creating systems for registering the income, assets, and liabilities of persons who perform public functions; establishing systems of government, hiring, and procurement of goods and services that ensure the openness, equity, and efficiency of such systems; establishing government regulator control systems that deter corruption; creating laws that deny favorable tax treatment to any individual or corporation for expenditures made in violation of the laws; creating systems for protecting public service and private citizens who in good faith report acts of corruption; creating oversight bodies with a view to implementing modern mechanisms for preventing, detecting, punishing, and eradicating corrupt acts; creating a mechanism to ensure that publicly held companies can be audited by objective third parties; creating mechanisms to encourage the participation by civil society and nongovernmental organizations in efforts to prevent corruption; and finally, studying additional measures to take into account the relationship between equitable compensation of public servants and probity of public service.

That is a pretty ambitious agenda. It describes broadly the areas of activity. The IDB, as an institution, is trying to find its way to work within those general areas. Until fairly recently, our principal activity in the area of corruption had focused on two areas, the fifth and sixth points mentioned above, the first of which is establishing government procurement systems that ensured transparent, open, and fair decision making. That, in a sense, has been the historic function with which governments have sought assistance from the IDB.

In many of the countries, we are not simply a lending institution. We provide capital, but we also provide an institutional structure within which the capital is invested in an open, transparent system in which opportunities for corruption are minimized. That service has been sought many times by government. The IDB has a requirement for all of its policies that any contract be subject to open, competitive bidding. It requires that there be a mechanism for protest by any aggrieved party in the bidding process and that protest be heard and resolved by an independent arbitration panel. That function has been extremely useful, and we are getting increasing demands from governments to extend the system of procurement that we have been using for our own contracts to other kinds of contracting operations in the government as they work with their own systems of procurement, in order to improve the transparency and accountability.

The second area in which we have worked has been the creation of mechanisms for fiscal control. One of the major opportunities created for corruption is the historical tendency in much of the region to use public office as a way of compensating the office holder because the state revenue system does not collect revenues fairly and adequately from the rest of the population.

There is a broad interest in all of the regions in improving the systems of fiscal control, revenue collection, accounting, and auditing of tax systems and we have provided extensive assistance in this area.

We are now interested in pursuing new areas to work with governments on the problems of corruption. One of the new areas is the work in the legal environment because it is clear to us that creating open and competitive economic systems requires the transparent execution of individual contracts and individual negotiations. That is something that cannot be effectively controlled by a central government institution. What needs to be in place is a legal system capable of granting to private parties the opportunity to bring grievances and contracts into the court system and have them resolved in a fair, transparent, and equitable manner.

That has required, in many of the countries of the region, an extensive strengthening of the judicial system and improvement of the functioning of judicial case management, and in some instances, new systems of case management. It has also required additional resources into the judicial system in order to improve the functioning of the judicial system so that private parties may use it to increase the transparency of the system.

Finally, we are interested in pursuing new mechanisms for public oversight of public transactions. We have been working recently in response to demands from governments for strengthening the legislatures so that legislative bodies acquire an effective oversight function (which has historically been one of the major roles of legislatures in other countries in dealing with corruption), and the legislature becomes a place in which the decisions of public officials are effectively reviewed in order to ensure their transparency and accountability.

We are also interested in working with the creation of public inspection panels. As many of you know, the multilateral banks have recently adopted internal mechanisms of inspectors general and oversight mechanisms for overseeing the work within each institution, both to review the quality of our decisions and to ensure that officials in each institution maintain the highest standards of conduct.

There are in Latin America a number of such institutions that have been extraordinarily successful. Chile's controller general's office is the one example that comes most frequently to mind. Institutional development of institutions for public inspection creates opportunities for us to work more closely.

There is a final important area in which the Bank is interested in working but has not yet figured out how. That area is the mobilization of civil society, as the OAS declaration suggests, in the issues of exposing, monitoring, and engaging the public in the issues of corruption and government. This involves the print media, radio, and television, and also the creation of citizen institutions that are capable of dealing with this issue.

I am sure many of you are aware of the work of Transparency International, one of the major nongovernmental organizations that work in this area. As an institution, we have been seeking ways of cooperating with the local chapters of that institution in Latin America to deal with the problems of corruption and recognize that this is not something that can be solved by technocratic reforms of the state alone.

From that brief panorama, it's clear that we view the problem of corruption as a systemic problem relating to history, institutions, and practices in the economy that create patterns of behavior that need to change and will change slowly.

The question for us as an institution is not whether it is desirable to move in the direction of effective control of corruption and openness and transparency of government, but how do we attack these systemic problems most efficiently using the resources that we have at our disposal and working with the governments that are members of our institutions in order to accomplish these goals effectively.

Our commitment is to work aggressively in the area of the struggle against corruption. We are in the market for ideas about how to do that and are seeking out partnerships not only with governments, but also with private-sector organizations in order to try to combat this disease, which our president has called one of the greatest obstacles to the consolidation of democracy and successful market economies in the region.

Contributors

Susan Rose Ackerman is the Henry R. Luce Professor of Jurisprudence at the Yale Law School in New Haven, Connecticut.

Alberto Ades is an economist and senior analyst at Goldman Sachs, Inc., in New York.

Fernando Carrillo-Flores is senior adviser at the State and Civil Society Division of the Inter-American Development Bank (IADB) in Washington, D.C.

Rafael Di Tella is assistant professor at the Harvard Business School and worked formerly for the Argentine Ministry of Economics.

Ralph H. Espach is a former program associate of the Latin American Program of the Woodrow Wilson International Center for Scholars.

Eduardo Jarquin is the director of the State and Civil Society Division of the Inter-American Development Bank (IADB) in Washington, D.C.

Luigi Manzetti is professor of political science at Southern Methodist University.

Luca Meldolesi is professor of economics at the University of Naples in Italy.

Luis Moreno Ocampo is the co-founder of the civil society organization Fundación Poder Ciudadano, in Buenos Aires, Argentina, and the president of Transparency International-Latin America and the Caribbean.

Stephen Quick is manager of the Department of Strategic Planning and Operations at the Inter-American Development Bank (IADB) in Washington, D.C.

Carlos Eduardo Lins da Silva is a journalist based in Brasilia, Brazil, and the former Washington correspondent for *Folha de São Paulo*.

Mark L. Schneider is the director of the United States Peace Corps. Schneider was formerly the assistant administrator of the Bureau for Latin America and the Caribbean of the United States Agency for International Development (USAID).

Ibrahim F. I. Shihata is Senior Vice President and General Counsel of the World Bank and Secretary General of the International Centre for Settlement of Investment Disputes.

Joseph S. Tulchin is director of the Latin American Program of the Woodrow Wilson International Center for Scholars.

Laurence Whitehead is official fellow in politics at Nuffield College, Oxford University, in England.

Index